"*Watching the Door* brings it all back: the sounds and the smells. In this bittersweet madeleine of a book, Kevin Myers recreates the moral and political slum that was Belfast, and dispels political illusions with irony and caustic wit. What a way to lose your youth." —Christopher Hitchens

"Autobiography doesn't come more vivid than this . . . Fired up with testosterone and the adrenalin of war, he is rapidly absorbed into the heaving local community . . . With suicidal recklessness Myers fraternises with Protestant and Catholic paramilitaries, trying to figure out the bewildering allegiances of loyalist gangs, Provos, paratroopers, squaddies, Northern Irish police and the general conflict-crazy population . . .

One night he beds the wife of a senior IRA man who returns unexpectedly, crashing drunkenly down onto the divan beneath which a naked Myers is trembling, his face squashed against the floor boards. Raw, passionate, dirty, this is the best book ever written about the most murderous calamity to befall Northern Ireland, it will make you flinch, weep, laugh and gasp at the sheer lunacy and rampant wickedness that pervades a community caught up in civil war."
     —Val Hennessey, *Daily Mail* Best Book of 2008

"His narrative, searingly sharp and honest, macabre in its black humour, does not hide his moral and spiritual deterioration as he becomes numb to the everyday atrocities he witnesses. Myers is lucky to have escaped with his life; we are lucky he has decided to tell his story."
     —Freya McClelland, *Sunday Times*

"*Watching the Door* will become an essential part of the history of the troubles in Northern Ireland. It is the most astonishing memoir of its kind that I have read in years, and must be read by anyone interested in the happenings of those terrible years."
 —Jack Higgins, author of *The Killing Ground*, and *The Eagle Has Landed*

"This is memoir as exorcism, and it's a beautiful, brutal piece of work."
     —Jessa Crispin, Best Books of 2008

"Searingly honest and beautifully written." —*Mail on Sunday*

"[A] sparky and pungent narrative." —*Independent*

"This is a book so remarkable that after finishing it you will find yourself casting the film that will surely get made." —*Spectator*

"Raw and memorable . . . sharp and laconic . . . A book that will be read after many others about that horrible turbulence are forgotten."
—*Times Literary Supplement*

"An illuminating social document . . . Here is a man without illusions, and mankind has always had a need of such free spirits."
—Michael Henderson, *Telegraph*

"*Watching the Door* is an unflinching historical memoir, but it is also a blackly humorous confessional, with plenty of sexual encounters to temper the scenes of violence and bloodshed."
—Simmy Richman, *Financial Times magazine*

"An engaging and energetic description of a strange and dangerous time."
—Jean Hannah Edelstein, *New Statesman*

"A rollicking good read about tribal violence in Seventies Belfast? Surprisingly, yes . . . As well as historical analyses of the conditions and personalities of the Troubles, this is a personal coming of age story, full of drink and lust." —Genevieve Bates, *London Lite*

"This is a lyrical, savage, richly comic account of one man's experience of the Troubles. It was written to give the reader 'a slightly sharper moral eyesight about the wickedness and folly of political violence on this island.' It fulfills its purpose perfectly." —Melanie McDonagh, *Telegraph*

"Dark, witty, grim, caustic, despairing, wise, searingly honest and beautifully written, this may well prove to be the best-informed and most exciting personal account of the Troubles ever published. It is also a fine memorial to the many innocent people who were killed for the most fatuous of reasons." —James Delingpole, *Mail on Sunday*

"This is the best book you will ever read about Belfast in the 1970s. It is by turns ghastly, hilarious, black with humour, black with death and cruelty, and lucid with humanity . . . It is not just about Belfast during the Troubles, but about a young man learning that though the world is a tragic and painful place, all the tragedy and pain is not without the redemption of laughter and love . . . This is a wonderful book: autobiography, memoir, reportage, sociology and, not least, a beautifully written and often dolly self-deprecating story of the yearnings and loneliness of a young man as he grows up." —Mary Kenny, *Literary Review*

Watching the Door

Drinking Up, Getting Down, and Cheating Death in 1970s Belfast

Kevin Myers

Soft Skull Press
Brooklyn

First published by The Lilliput Press, Ireland.

Library of Congress Cataloging-in-Publication Data is
available.

ISBN (13) 978-1-59376-235-3

Cover design by Adrian Kinloch
Printed in the United States of America

Soft Skull Press
An Imprint of Counterpoint LLC
2117 Fourth Street
Suite D
Berkeley, CA 94710

www.softskull.com
www.counterpointpress.com

Distributed by Publishers Group West

10 9 8 7 6 5 4 3 2 1

To my friend the great David McKittrick,
who told us almost all.

Preface

WHY WRITE about events that occurred so long ago, at such a terrible time in our country's history and in a place few outsiders even now really want to visit? The answer is simple. This was a defining period of my life, and the secrets that it disclosed have been locked within me ever since. I saw murder face to face, and heard the keen of bereaved and broken hearts. I witnessed the bloody chaos that results when the tribe is exalted over the individual, and when personal morality is abandoned to the autonomous ethos of some imagined community, independent of God and law. Moreover, the publication, in 1999, of David McKittrick's majestic *Lost Lives** provided me with both the moral compulsion and the documentary material to set my fingers to the keyboard.

The resort to violence in Irish life is still celebrated by people who call themselves constitutional politicians. It is my hope that those who read through these pages will understand something of the reality of what violence does. This is why I have related

---

* David McKittrick, Seamus Kelters, Brian Feeney, and Chris Thornton. *Lost Lives* (Mainstream Publishing; Edinburgh 1999).

the names of so many victims. Their deaths were the result of the failure of politics, but more crucially for me, each death formed a tiny brick in the edifice that was my earlier life. Their tragedy was my income. That is how I made my living, the beetle in the sarcophagus.

My sarcophagus had initially been the Protestant state for a Protestant people, which mirrored the Catholic state for a Catholic people that was the Irish Republic. However, such simplifications mislead. Senior judges and police officers in both Northern Ireland and the Republic were of the minority faiths. Contrary to subsequent fable, Catholics enjoyed the same voting rights as Protestants, but gerrymandered constituencies diluted their voting power. Most of all, Northern Ireland oozed a smug Unionist sense of dominance, and it was that which most riled Catholics. However, nothing about that state, or the conditions of its minority, justified the murderous calamity that befell its inhabitants during the years I write about, and the many more that followed.

This book is also about a naive young man in pursuit of the adrenaline of war and that cocktail of hormones accompanying love and sex. During the 1970s I behaved like young men have always wanted to, and always will. I have been as frank about this as possible. The truth does not, as the battle hymn of another republic declares, make us free, but at least it enables us to see where evil lies a little more clearly. If anyone finishes this narrative with a slightly sharper moral eyesight about the wickedness and folly of political violence on this island, then what follows will not have been wholly in vain.

I owe a unpayable debt to the many people who feature in this account of my life in Belfast. But for the purposes of this book, I want to thank my editor at The Lilliput Press, Mary Cummins, and of course Rachel, my wife, my rock and my love at all times.

Prologue
July 1972

DRIVING SLOWLY up Shaw's Road, Belfast, on a rare and lovely summer's day: the sun radiant, the sky a Corsican blue. To the left, in the distance, an army foot patrol coming downhill towards me, threading its way in incongruous olive-fatigues past an urban-jungle barricade of ancient, burnt-out cars, dodging the bottles and bricks from clusters of shrieking children. Much closer and to the right, behind a block of flats, and invisible to the soldiers, an excited group of feral teenage males seethed like primates. Farther to the right, a bucketing car skidded to a halt, the din of its arrival concealed by the noise of the riot.

I stopped, put on the handbrake, and watched. The soldiers continued to advance in a single green faltering line. The car-driver leapt out and opened the boot, a triumphant Santa Claus at the back of his summer sleigh, to reveal his presents – a Garand semi-automatic rifle, a couple of M1 carbines, some handguns. They were distributed, in no apparent order, and the teenage gang instantly and intuitively dispersed to their various firing positions.

I had chanced upon an IRA ambush. Slowly, I drove off right, within the lee of the flats, from where I could still see most of the soldiers. They were stumbling forward, sweating, confused and clearly reluctant – outsiders from England, barely out of their teens and in a strange and hostile place. Stones whistled past their ears as capering children taunted them.

Directly in front of me was a bone-thin lad with an M1 carbine and his back to the wall. He was wearing a blue plaid shirt and blue jeans cut off above the ankles, and his dank, unwashed hair hung in curls. He stuck his nose around the corner, so he could peer right, towards the soldiers who still remained within sight. His head came back, and he waited, his back rigid against the wall. His lips moved, as if he were counting. I opened my car door and stole sidewards, and kneeling, turned on my tape recorder.

The foot patrol drew closer, through shimmering heatwaves rising from tarmac thinly puckered with the acne scars of recent vehicle fires. The air reeked – the rancid smell of burnt rubber and seared steel now as ubiquitous in Belfast as coal dust in a mining town. From nearby hills came the rattle of pebbles in a drum, echoes of gunfire from odd skirmishes around the city. The IRA ceasefire had ended a couple of days before, and bloodshed had vigorously resumed, as if making up for lost time. In nearby Ballymurphy, paratroopers had gunned down half a dozen people, one by one, each casualty a lure for the next vain-helper, who in turn had been shot, the icing on their cake a priest they finished off as he administered the last rites to their penultimate victim.

There was no mercy on the streets that hot July day. The boy in front of me peered around the corner again, and drew back. The soldiers were still not quite close enough. He was good. He looked around, checking his rear, seeing but certainly not registering me as an enemy, then he cocked his weapon and swiftly turned, stepping sharply leftwards to give himself a clear field of fire from his right shoulder.

His carbine barked – *bang! bang! bang! bang!* – prompting supporting fire from the other, now invisible youngsters. The lead soldier collapsed in the middle of the road, falling vertically, his bones turned to water, and the rest of the patrol vanished behind cremated cars, rubble, lamp posts, anything. In front of me, the gunman had returned to cover, his back to the wall. From not far away, children whooped at the sight of the motionless heap in the middle of the road. The wounded man's fellow soldiers did not return fire. They had no visible targets, other than the infants mocking their fallen comrade.

A second soldier began to crawl from cover towards the body, triggering a fresh though undisciplined fusillade from my boy and half a dozen other positions, bullets striking in little puffs all around the soldier. His leg jerked, an arterial leap of blood from his thigh a moment later confirming the hit.

Two squaddies down; yet still no return fire from the rest of the foot patrol, apparently paralysed where they lay huddled under cover. The first soldier was hit several more times: with each strike, his body appeared to be plucked, as if by a large invisible bird, while the children exulted. This had the makings of a real massacre. Now even the gunmen were cheering, the lad in front of me almost out of hiding, brandishing his carbine like an Arapaho at his war dance.

Suddenly, a large Humber armoured car, a 'Pig', came lumbering down the hill, its 120 horse-power Rolls-Royce engine roaring angry defiance, a mother elephant charging towards her endangered calves. My boy-gunman instantly withdrew from the edge of the wall, shouting an order that mysteriously carried some kind of authority over the ambush's backing track of childish yells. The shooting stopped as soldiers deployed around the Pig.

The ambush party was already throwing its weapons into the car boot, before dispersing, civilians once again. Simultaneously, squaddies took the two casualties by feet and shoulders and unceremoniously chucked them into the back of the Pig, the bodies landing like sides of warm beef. The rest of the patrol crammed in after them, the Pig bellowed, its exhaust belched a puff of smoke and fire, and roared up the road.

On the ground, sitting in a pool of blood, lay a soldier's

helmet. Children rushed over to examine it. One boy of about twelve scooped it up with a long stick, whirling it above his head as he pranced in the blood. Then, like an Orange band-leader, he yanked the stick upwards, sending the helmet even higher.

It fell vertically and he caught it expertly on his head, as if he's been practising for this moment all his young life, still dancing in the blood of the stranger from England. This other stranger watched for a while, turned the tape recorder off, got into his vehicle and drove away, with almost no emotion at what he had seen.

From home I filed a report for Australian radio, for whom I freelanced, but did not make one for RTÉ, my employer. How could I have explained my entirely accidental presence at the ambush? Or my failure to have prevented it? To have intervened or warned the soldiers of the ambush, would have been to have taken sides – and probably cost me my life.

I care about this now. I didn't then. After just over a year in Belfast, I thought I was the hard man. In those fifteen months, I had seen enough death and, like so many Belfast people, thought I was inured to it.

How in the name of God had I come to this?

Watching the Door

One

IT IS NEVER the ambition of a wise person, who knows
anything about the place, to live and work in Belfast and I was
no exception. My family history had sniffed at the city, and had
positively fled from it. During the Second World War my father,
an out-of-work GP in Dublin, had been offered a share in a practice on the Antrim Road, which reaches from Carlisle Circus to
the north of the city, beneath the shadow of the Cave Hill. He
went up for an interview with a Jewish doctor called Glasgow,
but that short trip alone was enough to convince him that Belfast was too bitter and divided a place in which to raise a young
family. Instead he opted to work in wartime England, where he
lived alone for some months before being joined by my mother,
and the first instalment of the Myers family. On the Liverpool
ferry they were given U-boat drill: then my mother and the three
children with all their luggage plus one dog travelled endlessly,
almost the length of England, from Merseyside to Exmouth in
Devon, through night and day, in a series of blacked-out, slow-
trains full of troops, pausing in sidings from one dusk to the next,
before trundling off into the dark again towards distant Devon.

Three years after the war the second half of the Myers family arrived in England, this time by childbirth, and in Leicester, where my father had found a practice. I was the first-born of this group, named after my uncle, Captain Kevin Teevan, RAMC, attached West African Field Force, a volunteer in the fight against fascism, who had died on active service in Africa.

Families defy stereotyping. The Teevans, for example, were not inclined to wear the uniform of the Crown, being constitutionally republican, and Kevin's older brother Tom within a few years became the Irish Attorney General. My father – though I did not know it until long after his death, and nor indeed did my mother until I told her – had in his very distant youth, between 1919–21, been in the IRA. In the adulthood that I remember, he was an ardent Tory with a Dublin accent who even cheered when RAF Vickers Valiant bombers attacked Port Said in Egypt in 1956. The only references that I remember him making to the IRA were ones of utter loathing: as I later discovered, he truly knew the beast of which he spoke. Moreover, he spent the last years of his life a weeping melancholic: was he simply the victim of some hereditary chemical imbalance in the brain – or was he haunted by some terrible deed he had performed in the service of an organization that now, all these decades later, remained faithful to its remorseless agenda?

Far from being raised a republican, I had not even been raised in any real sense as Irish, just Catholic, although Ireland remained a constant drumbeat to my heart from over the horizon, not least because I so adored my aunts and uncles in Dublin. One Christmas, when I was fifteen, I found a corner of our dining-room where my transistor could get RTÉ's Athlone signal. I triumphantly told my father, who cast his eyes distantly, as he often did to conceal his impatience. 'A fat lot of good that will do you.'

He was, as I say, a troubled man, and I was an adolescent boy. On the last day of my school holiday we had a disagreement, over what I cannot say. He knocked me down, and then kicked me as I lay on the floor. His foot was slippered, he did not kick me hard, and most of all, I inwardly knew that something unwonted and terrible was happening in his heart. I loved my father then and he loved me – I love him still – and this was a ghastly, troubled aberration by a good and kindly man. However, at the time, it was not an easily forgiven aberration, and that afternoon my mother drove me to my boarding school with a studious absence of goodbyes between father and son.

A couple of weeks later, asleep in the fifth-form dormitory, a hand upon my shoulder wakes me. A priest, Father Moss, is whispering. I blink, and try to make sense of what he saying to me in tones of low urgency: 'Kevin? Can you hear me? Get up and get dressed. Your father's unwell.'

Actually, he wasn't: by this time he was dead. A heart attack, our farewells now and forever an unfinished business. Thus was I introduced to the elaborate rituals of death and grief and guilt in that bitter winter of 1963: '*Dies Irea dies illa*' chanted the choir in the church in front of the coffin, while I stoically performed the duties of altar boy, witless with shock. Then to the cemetery: that vicious winter, the entire world seemed an ice field, a small rectangular corner of which had been opened up to admit my father's body. The marl lay in frozen mounds, from which with our fingernails we scraped our small, icy burial-tokens, and cast them onto the coffin below.

My father's death threw my teenage life into chaos; I was broken with grief, and what had been a promising academic career at Ratcliffe came to nothing. I studied fresh A levels at a technical college in Leicester, but I did poorly again: my results came through that summer when I was earning £10 a week wielding a broom for Leicester Corporation Cleansing Department. There wasn't a college in the land – even one offering diplomas in street sweeping – which would have accepted me. At my mother's suggestion I enquired of University College Dublin if it had any places for such wretches as me. By an extraordinary stroke of luck, at a time when the demand for university places was the highest ever, the quota for foreign students – which I technically was – at UCD remained mysteriously unfilled: so possessing the bare minimum of requirements, I squeaked in to read Social Studies – in which I was as interested as I was in Mandarin.

I did not feel I was coming home when I arrived in Dublin. I was very English in accent and manner, and I knew how that seemed when my taxi driver overcharged taking me to my digs. I challenged him and he was unable to explain the fare. He apologized, and I then tipped him. Why? Very simply: I wanted to be accepted.

I was an outsider, and remained one, made more so by my aloofness in manner, my supercilious speech, and my utter lone-liness within. That first year in Dublin, my few friends were non-Irish, and my personality did not invite affection from the general student body. I did not choose to be arrogant; but that was how I appeared.

After my first year, I changed courses to pure History. I found I loved medieval Irish history but utterly loathed seventeenth-century history, and wrote only one paper on it over the next two years. This century was the very antithesis of the optimism I sought: its darkness, its cruelties, its conclusions for the peoples of Europe were quite unspeakable. But it was to the preserved version of the seventeenth century, pickled in the drumlins of Ulster, that I was destined to return.

Before, that, however, I had a personality-transforming visit to the USA. Working one summer with poor children from the ghettoes of Philadelphia knocked a lot of the edges off me. Then I hitch-hiked across the States, meeting people whose opinions about the war, then at its height in Vietnam, I despised, but who were good and honest. I learnt then that what you think or say does not make you a better person, only how you behave. Two dozen states or more felt the fall of my foot, as for weeks on end I tramped across North America, my nightly resting place being my sleeping bag in ditches. In my nomadic solitude I knew great hap-piness, in my daily adventures I found courage and inspiration.

I returned to Ireland a changed young man, and in a time of great change, as across the world young people were being radicalized. I was emphatically of that generation, accepting almost *in toto* the emerging dogmas of the New Left. We believed capitalism caused racism, sectarianism, class barriers, hunger and Third-World poverty, and we rapidly created the theological texts to justify the tenets of the new global religion, drawing on the existing gospels of Marx, Engels and the Russian revolutionaries, with the new epistles coming from the USA and France.

We accepted the Marxist fantasy that the historic dynamic came from the organized working class: we believed the patronizing myth that the proletariat embodied the holy grail of a better society, and all that was required was for the working class to see in themselves the truth that was so evident to us. In essence, this meant that working class movements were of themselves necessarily good things.

The summer of 1969 was warm and as usual I was full of lust, and avoiding studying for my finals in September with an unremitting distraction in girls, of whose company and bodies I could not get enough. But far greater forces at work in the North were to interrupt my endocrinal safaris. For nearly a year, there had been regular civil rights marches demanding an end to discrimination against the minority population of Catholics – who are also in this account known as 'nationalists', a roughly synonymous term – by the all-Protestant unionist government there. These had often ended in riots, which seemed serious enough at the time: a few hours of stone-throwing and car-burning.

But in August 1969 serious communal violence between nationalists and the police, the RUC, flared in Derry in the westernmost part of Northern Ireland: and the usual two-hour skirmish turned into a full-scale battle without apparent end: finally, after two days of petrol bombs and baton charges, it seemed the revolution was coming to Ireland! It was too good a chance to miss. A friend and I – bidden as much by a desire to experience the heady drama of rioting and lawlessness as by any political principle – decided to go north to 'help' the nationalists.

We hitched to Newry. Beyond it, lining the hill on the Banbridge Road outside the town that August evening, stood a silent army of B Specials, the all-Protestant police reserve that was so detested and despised by Catholics. Black hats, black tunics, black coats, black trousers: black, black, black. We passed them, half expecting to be stopped, hauled off into a ditch, beaten, shot. Those genuinely were our thoughts, however absurd, as we walked that silent gauntlet, hearing the odd clink of an invisible Lee Enfield rifle or a Sterling sub-machine gun. In truth, they were probably frightened country-boys, as fearful of Newry as we and Newry were of them.

We got a lift to the Falls Road in Belfast, where – two ridiculous figures – we began to look for some headquarters to report to, even as people with closed, set faces hurried homewards, the air electric with terror. So we offered our services to strangers: 'Good evening sir. My friend and I have just hied from Dublin post haste to proffer some assistance. Would you be so good as to tell us – where do we go for riot-duty?'

'Where do youse go? Home, is where youse go, the pair of youse! Get ye back to Dublin. Get out of here. The guns are coming out the night and there's nothing youse can do, unless you've got some guns. Have youse uns got some fuckin' guns, aye? Of course youse fuckin' haven't. Youse are childer, wee childer. Get you on out of here while youse still fuckin' can. Belfast isn't fuckin' Derry. We do it with guns here, so we do.'

Next we saw a young man wearing a Connolly Youth badge, which identified him as a young republican activist. Naturally, we gallantly offered him our services in the forthcoming street disorders. Had he any preferences? Instead he began to snarl.

'There'll be no rioting here the night. See them peelers? See them come up this road? They'll not be fuckin' met with fuckin' stones, I'm telling ye.'

The subsequent nationalist dogma is that the IRA resorted to guns only in a surprised response to a violent and wholly unexpected police invasion of the Falls. Well, I would not argue with a conviction now clung to with a religious vehemence: the forecast of imminent gunbattles was so convincing that we decided to forgo riot-duties in Belfast and instead take our finely honed guerrilla skills west across the province to Derry, where the embattled nationalists would without doubt joyfully fall on their knees in gratitude at our arrival.

But then we found that all trains to Derry had been cancelled, and the last remaining train out of the city before the station closed down for war was to Ballymena. Now we showed our encyclopaedic knowledge of the Troubles in which we were so keen to participate: was that, we asked the ticket seller, on the way to Derry?

She didn't want to let us go anywhere, but a vibrant sense of calamity was descending on the city, she really wanted to get home, and after a will-I-won't-I-pause, we got tickets for the train to Ballymena. Once there, guided by a signpost near the station that said 'Londond'y', we started down a deserted country road, giddy with ignorance and terror, while B Specials' Shorland tenders rumbled through the night.

After we'd walked several miles in the pitch dark, a baker's van stopped and the driver greeted us.

'Boys a boys, such a night to be out,' he carolled. 'Where are youse going the night, boys?'

'Londonderry,' I said in my English accent.

'Londonderry? Hop in boys, hop in.'

It was midnight, the North was falling apart, and this cheery, fat, bald, middle-aged unionist baker was giving lifts to complete strangers determined to add to his province's woes. There were Specials' roadblocks a couple of miles ahead, he added, with warnings to look for strangers: best we should hide amid his buns and baps in the back.

'And boys, help yisselves,' he chortled merrily. 'Lads like you is always hungry.'

Famished, we obeyed him as he prattled through the window behind him about his business, twice a week over to the Mull of Kintyre to sell his bread. His economic community was Dalriada, that ancient kingdom defined by the shores of Antrim in Ireland, the western seaboard of Argyll and Bute in Scotland, and the scattered archipelago in between: this was a world of which I knew nothing, yet here I was, anxious to turn it upside down. We arrived at the roadblock. Would he turn us in?

'Ach, what about you, Mervyn, Wilbur, Cecil?' he bellowed with hearty Protestant cheer. In the back, would-be Fenians paused, mid-bun, waiting for betrayal. None came, and finally the van rumbled on.

He dropped us off, and we continued our journey through the darkest night I had ever known. Now the silence seemed infinite, and when we spoke our voices seemed to boom to the heavens, across which shooting stars raced. Finally, after much wandering, houselights and a statue of the Virgin Mary in a window told us we were in nationalist territory. There were voices within. We tapped on the door. It was three in the morning, yet after we had explained our mission, more pathological hospitality awaited us.

'Agh come in boys, come in! Faith, youse must be starving. Will ham sangwidges do ye? Have ye heard? Wild bad it is in Belfast, wild bad, a dozen dead. Armagh the same. Specials everywhere. Towns and villages burning all over the place. More tea? Have another sangwidge, agh go on ...'

Finally, a couple of hours' sleep, sort of, on the carpet, before hitching on to Derry, where the British army had deployed overnight, and the RUC was gone. Baffled Yorkshiremen stood in a strange city about a strange duty and were the heroes of the hour to the Bogsiders. Tea at street corners, officers with street-maps scratching their heads, coils of barbed wire everywhere.

So, we had missed the fighting in Derry. The Troubles were

over now. We caught the bus back to Dublin, where a few days later I sat my finals. I was then called in for an interview – I presumed to assess whether I should be allowed a pass degree rather than a failure. Instead, I had got a first.

I left University College Dublin without interest in anything very much, except sex and socialism. Ireland's first current affairs magazine, *Nusight*, had just opened. I knocked on the door. And though I knew nothing about journalism, had no shorthand and couldn't even type, I was offered a job.

Nothing that I ever did with the magazine had any merit, but it did reintroduce me to Northern Ireland. On assignment in Belfast, I stayed in a hotel called The Elsinore on the Antrim Road, not far from Carlisle Circus. It was a vile hotel; apart from the Holiday Inn in Sarajevo whose joys I experienced over twenty years later, it remains the worst I have ever stayed in. Another guest was a veteran of the Great War, a Protestant who had returned to his native city from Canada, and who still wheezed from the gas poisoning he had suffered in 1917. Intuitively, he was utterly despondent about Belfast's future.

'This is my last visit,' he gasped sadly in Canadian-Ulster. 'This place is doomed. Spent my life's savings on this trip. I'd have never come back had I known.' He was talking rubbish, of course, I thought. A couple of days later I stood on Granaghan Hill on the foothills of the Sperrins, not far from the market town of Maghera with a country solicitor and nationalist called Kevin Agnew. He gestured grandly all around him, over much of Northern Ireland, visible from that point. 'We're in for a twenty-year war, and when it's over this will all be a wasteland,' he said with bloodthirsty gusto. 'But at least it'll be *our* wasteland.'

I returned happily Dublinward. *Nusight* folded shortly afterwards, and my article on the North never appeared. But at least my visit had taught me one thing: never to go near Belfast. So I mooched around with no money, but that didn't matter initially. Dublin was a delightful city for the young of my stratum, for we were free and quite sexually active. But even to the easily contented, which I was, poverty over time is a burden. The freelance writing I dabbled in as I claimed the dole of £3.10 shillings a week was not enough to live on. I was dossing in some friends' flat, my life without shape or future. Something had to change.

A friend in RTÉ told me that the newsroom was advertising for a news-reporter in Belfast. Well, I couldn't possibly get the job, and certainly didn't want it – having seen enough of Belfast – but I applied, almost purely as preparation for some future job application. And though possessing not a single journalistic skill, or experience of broadcasting, or the least morsel of knowledge which would have qualified me in any way for the job – rather in the serendipitous manner in which I had become a student in UCD – to my astonishment I was appointed as junior reporter in the Belfast bureau of RTÉ News.

TWO
Dublin, Saturday morning, 28 February 1971

I AWOKE on the settee in Dublin's Pembroke Road. On the radio, the Edwin Starr song, 'War', reverberated through the flat. 'War, what is it good for. Absolutely *nothing*. Say it again …'

The news came on, with the familiar voice of RTÉ's Northern correspondent Liam Hourican. 'Belfast this morning is a city of fear,' he declaimed: but he could get away with both the cliché and the faux-solemnity, for his gravelly gravitas conveyed extraordinary power.

Two RUC detectives had been shot dead during rioting in Ardoyne in north Belfast the previous night. Not long before, the first British soldiers had been killed in Northern Ireland. The campaign for civil rights within the state had been elbowed aside by the emergence of atavistic tribal forces aiming to overthrow that state. In other words, as in every decade since 1916, yet another IRA military campaign to achieve a united Ireland by force of arms was under way, and in the spirit of, *it'll be all over by Christmas*, I was now desperate to get up to the North before the Troubles ended.

This was the impatience of youth, not the judgment of a young man with a first class honours in History. From that I should have learnt that there is in Irish republicanism an energy and a sense of time that are unlike anything normal organizations can conceive of. Republicanism is an almost autonomous state with an internal folklore that embraces and indoctrinates those admitted to its mysteries. Suffering, either inflicted or endured, is a keynote to its ethos.

So that day, after two months' semi-training, I impatiently and ignorantly went North with a camera crew as an RTÉ journalist to report on the opening stages of yet another campaign to expel the British from Ireland. And, apart from the prescient Kevin Agnew, no one had the least idea of the decades of sorrow that lay ahead.

Ulster is the runt of the Ice Age. Ireland, like Britain, was once part of the Eurasian land mass, and our common destiny was initially shaped by simple glaciation. First of all, the weight of ice upon the original mountain mass which covered this part of the world pressed the once towering peaks into plains.

Then, the ice withdrew towards the Arctic, retaining a last glacial redoubt in the northern part of Ireland. A generous central plain came into existence in what we now call the province of Leinster, just south of the ice ramparts: but an unyielding ice field lay across most of what is Ulster, for thousands of years.

The world was warming, the ice melting, the seas rising. Britain and Ireland became separate from Europe, the two islands like twins conjoined at nose and toe, enclosing a vast freshwater lake. The twins danced their insular gavotte together before the Atlantic finally broke in and turned the lake into a separating sea. The days of the ice colony in Ireland were coming to an end: the deep frozen garrison in the north was obliged to withdraw from its border ramparts. It did so reluctantly, doing the glaciate equivalent of an army salting the land it is surrendering to the enemy, its bergs gouging deep trenches along across the frontier it had defended against the assaults of the new warmth for so long.

The result was the creation of a line of hillocks that run across the northern third of the island. They are called drumlins, *droim*, Irish for ridge and lin from the English *ling* 'being like'. This etymologically appropriate word, mixing Irish and English, in essence describes where English rule ended and Irish rule began, or vice versa. From that division rose the boundary between northern and southern Ireland.

It is hard for outsiders to exert their authority over such a terrain and its disparate peoples. The Normans had tried and failed. Foreign armies can be endlessly harassed in the clefts running between the myriad array of hills: every high point conquered reveals another half a dozen ahead requiring similar conquest. Each conquered peak requires a garrison; each garrison requires supplies; each supply route is vulnerable to ambush. Moreover, the land is poor. So what outsider would freely choose to try to govern such largely unproductive acres from afar?

My first job in Belfast that Saturday afternoon was to go to RUC headquarters to introduce myself and to collect the photographs of the two dead officers. My taxi driver was a cheerful, saturnine man, with a peculiarly Belfast complexion, as if coal dust ran in his veins: his skin was white, but a sub-cutaneous dark resided under it. His name was Tommy McIlroy, and he was the first example of the strange truth-drug relationship that I was to have with so many Belfast people: uninhibitedly, he told me things.

He was overjoyed at the previous night's killings: overjoyed. He repeatedly addressed me by name.

'The war's coming, and it's going to be serious, Kevin. Very fucking serious, you better believe it,' he declared happily. 'The Provies have got fresh gear coming from America, Kevin, and they're making claymore mines. Claymore mines! Brilliant! Kevin, listen here, there'll be people dying in this town who've never fucking died before.' His eyes shone at the thought.

As we approached RUC headquarters, he rearranged his facial features into a facsimile of an undertaker's: grave, expressionless, but touched with a light dusting of grief as if, even in his hard-bitten professional capacity, he found this a deeply saddening occasion.

A round-faced police officer met me in the lobby with photographs of Cecil Patterson and Robert Buckley. His expression was genuinely grave, but his eyes were friendly. His name was Harry McCormack. He shook my hand. It was nice to meet me: any help he could give me, he would. What a friendly city Belfast was turning out to be!

Tommy's mournful mien was unbroken until we got a reasonable distance from the police headquarters. 'Give me that there,' he said, once we were stopped at traffic lights. His eyes once again sparkling, he took the pictures of the two dead officers and gazed at them avidly, almost as if they were a particularly tasty item of pornography. 'Brilliant,' he breathed. 'Fucking brilliant. And just think. There's loads more where that there come from, so there is. You know who done that? I'd say Martin Meehan done that. Or Paddy McAdorey. Two of the best fucking men in Ardoyne.'

Neither name meant anything to me. But in the course of a single taxi journey, I had learnt a great deal. And so it continued to be throughout my time in Belfast. People kept on telling me things. They even appeared to like me and trust me.

How very strange.

I stayed in the Wellington Park Hotel for a couple of nights, before moving into Miss Cuthbertson's bed and breakfast nearby. At that time I didn't drink or smoke and she liked that, but Mabel Cuthbertson liked my English accent even more, as – I was to discover – unionists often would. She twittered and purred as she served me breakfast. She favoured pastel colours and a purple eyeshadow throughout the week. But on Sunday mornings, however, she became an essay in Calvinist beige and Knoxian brown, topped with one of those strange Ulster Protestant felt hats, which sported a small, startled bird on her scalp and a little fencing mask over her face. She would then depart for a couple of hours of dire ecstasy and jubilant terror in a fundamentalist mission hall, before returning, her eyes glowing, her lips slightly parted.

One day I had to do a story about housing conditions in Ballymurphy, in west Belfast, a candidate for the much-coveted Le Corbusier Trophy for Vilest Housing Estate in Europe & Possibly the Entire World. Tommy McIlroy drove me through its streets; it was mesmerizingly dreadful.

Ballymurphy was built just after the war and was a miracle of forward thinking. Intended to be a slum from its first day, it had instantly realized this heroic ambition. Although it was outside the city on the side of the Black Mountain, upon whose broad flanks space was almost boundless, it imitated in meanness and misery the conditions in the horrific Victorian slums its new residents had come from: tiny streets, shoe-box rooms, damp walls, wet-rot, scurvy, rickets and impetigo, all as standard Corporation-issue.

That evening, having eaten in the Presbyterian Total Temperance Restaurant – its menu and wine-list a model of brevity – I returned to my bed and breakfast. Mabel Cuthbertson asked me how my day had been, and I wandered off into a rant about the horrors of Ballymurphy, and the sins of the unionist government in building it, and the numerous imperfections of the Northern Ireland state. As an exercise in youthful arrogance, it was utter perfection.

'It's all very well for outsiders like you to complain,' she finally said, a long spine of ice connecting her words, 'but the people up there really don't want to work. They want to live off the state, have babies and drink. Do you know they chopped up their doors for firewood when they first moved in? And kept coal in their baths?'

I replied initially with a meaningful silence before raising a supercilious eyebrow of disdain. 'Opinions such as those', I murmured finally, 'are precisely the reason why this wretched place is the way it is.'

She did not bid me good night: she could have been forgiven for drawing her sword and running me through. Next day I began a serious search for a flat.

My broadcasting career was not meteoric. On neither radio nor television did I possess much presence. What I had, however, was an amazing nose for danger. Or maybe, it had for me. Either way, we became firm friends in the coming years, starting soon after my arrival in the city, when Tommy or another driver, Bob Moon, the only Protestant in the taxi company RTÉ used, would leave me off on the Falls Road for the evening's entertainment of minor rioting.

That's what I did, night after night: I would watch the riots, which invariably erupted around the junction of the Falls Road and Leeson Street. On one such night, in the full glow of a burning car, a figure materialized right beside me. He nodded agreeably. 'What about ye,' he said, smiling, then shoulder to shoulder with me, drew a Browning pistol and opened fire on a group of soldiers thirty yards away. Ten rounds rapid: *bang! bang! bang! bang! bang! bang! bang! bang! bang! bang!*

Oh here, this was not on. Probably as astounded as I was, the soldiers didn't begin to return fire until the final *click!* announced – to me anyway – that this first phase in the proceedings was over, to be followed immediately by the next act – the soldiers' furious fusillade in reply. By which time I had taken the short route to New Zealand.

The gunman didn't drop down, or crawl for cover, but – amazingly – he actually ran away into the dark, as if in a cartoon: exit, pursued by bullets. If he wanted to stay alive, this street-fighter was definitely going to have to improve his departure strategies.

The war that was emerging from the red bricks of this city

had already taken a terrible turn. Ten days after the Buckley and Patterson murders, three off-duty Scottish soldiers, two teenage brothers and their friend, had been lured from a Belfast pub and shot dead as they urinated along a country lane.

These killings, breathtakingly evil even by the standards of all that followed, caused much quiet satisfaction amongst republicans. Scottish soldiers were presumed to be Protestant and Glasgow Rangers' supporters. British soldiers simply had what was coming to them, and if it was delivered by foul means, so be it. War was foul. For a real war was already taking shape in people's minds – most especially in the greater Falls Road area, which had experienced catastrophic evictions of Catholics by rampaging loyalist, Protestant mobs two years before, the night I had prudently fled Belfast.

The houses of west Belfast were squalid. Tiny, lightless kennels, they reeked of coal smoke, sour milk and the rancid liquids of reproduction. They had no bathrooms, merely outside privies, and their inhabitants washed in hip-baths in their kitchens. Perhaps the most striking and heroic feature of the people here was that, amid such chronic deprivation, how clean they actually managed to be.

One of the minders of the Holy Flame of Republicanism was Proinsias Mac Airt, who lived in Clonard just off the Falls. His real name was Frankie Cards, which he had gaelicized into the present confection, apparently unaware of its preposterousness: for that vital sense of the ludicrous, which provides an intellectual and aesthetic censor in other societies, had been genetically excised in the creation of Northern Ireland society.

His home was a minuscule brick hovel, with barely more than eyeholes for windows, and he was sitting before a couple of coals glumly glowing in the fireplace when I met him. He was a bachelor and daily communicant; his rosary-beads lay coiled at his hand. He was, unquestionably, a virgin and even in his rampant teens had probably drowned his lusts in prayer. Indeed, in his unworldly simplicity, he was almost saintly – aside, that is, from the small matter of adoration of violence. The only way Ireland would be free, he told me, with ghastly if genuine sanctimony, was by the gun and human sacrifice.

The Protestants didn't seem to want that, I suggested. He sadly addressed the ashes with a thoughtful silence before turning to me: 'Ah well, these poor Protestants must learn the error of their ways, through the twin forces available to the men of the Republic – the moral force of our noble republican sacrifices and holy force of the gun. There's no other way.'

He sighed, and then readdressed the fireplace with his unspoken thoughts.

When Proinsias referred to the Republic, he was speaking of that fleeting entity declared in the 1916 Rising in Dublin. That Republic remained as real and as vital as it had been at the moment of its declaration. It lived within him, awaiting incarnation beyond his flesh: a reverse of the Catholic sacrament of communion. Listening to him talking about the Republic, which had been momentarily seized before being lost, it was as if his Ireland had died on the cross, and we were waiting for its return on a somewhat delayed third day.

In a sane society this lunatic muttering morbidly into a few cooling cinders would not have been taken as anything other than a candidate for special care: in the asylum of Northern Ireland he was being hailed as a prophet. People welcomed the message that there was a cure to all their woes: a united Ireland, achieved by the purifying flame of war. That's what he believed; and after the shocking trauma of the summer of 1969 – and the enduring humiliations of the previous fifty years – so too did many Northern Irish nationalists.

But though the Provisional IRA seriously wanted war, it didn't know what the coming war would consist of. Nor did anyone. The British army certainly didn't. I got to know some of its press officers. They were decent young men of the kind I had gone to school with, and they laughingly dismissed any notion of the IRA ever mastering the technology of Tommy's claymore mines. They were usually without nuance or subtlety: their favourite word for the street-rioters was yobs, as if that somehow reduced the problem they faced to one of youthful delinquency and public disorder.

Brigadier Frank Kitson, one of the most important military thinkers of the time, had already identified the gravity of the insurgency threat that could be posed by terrorists within common-law jurisdictions and reported by a free media, but one bright mind cannot alter the habits and instincts of an organization the size of the British army.

Moreover, its sure public-relations touch was exemplified by its new crowd-control device, a large armoured vehicle with huge horizontal barriers built across the nose. It was officially called a 'Paddy-Pusher'. The road to war is paved with many materials, but surely one of the most important is stupidity.

I found somewhere to live, sharing an unkempt ground-floor flat with a university lecturer called Peter Doherty, whose real income came from gambling. With a home of my own, I was able to move all my belongings from my friend's flat in Dublin. So great were the divisions between the two parts of the island that all incoming luggage was impounded by customs and carefully searched: from the appearance of my bags, they had been systematically ransacked, and some items broken. Meanwhile, in the reverse direction, baggage going into the Republic was carefully sifted by customs for condoms and copies of *Playboy*, which were immediately confiscated. Two states, two civilizations, two sets of intolerance, together bound for a common destiny of war.

The house was on Eglantine Avenue, in the university area, where the Victorians had built whopping great copies of the tiny lightless hovels their ambitious owners had originally escaped from. These buildings had large rooms, but opened almost directly onto the street: in the back were not gardens but tiny yards, almost perfect imitations of the dank spaces that had once housed the slum-privies of their first inhabitants' childhoods. It was as if they and their city could never quite distance themselves from their roots.

My early work for RTÉ was undemanding. I covered the near-daily rioting and did some broadcasting, but for the most part compiled reports to be read by newsreaders. So with time to spare, some six weeks after I arrived, I began to study *The Belfast Telegraph* for titbits, trying to discern a pattern in the bric-a-brac of violence.

One Friday afternoon I noticed a single paragraph story, a filler: the previous night a military police mobile patrol had been halted by a line of youngsters in the Markets area, who had pelted their vehicle with stones.

This sounded wrong. Riots were things I knew about. Rioters didn't stand in lines: soldiers did. The stone-throwers were clearly an organized come-on for soldiers. Behind them, I guessed, gunmen lay in wait. That evening I sat in the RTÉ office in the centre of the city, monitoring army radio traffic on VHF, as one could in those days. A military police patrol reported that it had been again attacked by a line of stone-throwers in the Markets, and asked for a regular unit to investigate. The bait again.

I called an RTÉ taxi, and by chance one arrived almost instantly. I just told the driver to go to the Markets. We cruised down Cromac Street, now totally unlit – as much of Belfast was rapidly becoming – then, suddenly, a volley of shots, screams, more shooting: in the dark – we didn't know where. The driver, in panic, turned right, then left, down the narrow Victorian streets, hovels crowding round us in his darting headlights. He turned left again, more shooting; and then we were in Cromac Square, and directly beneath the only street light still working stood an army Land-Rover, perfectly exposed in the otherwise blacked-out square.

'Jesus,' said my driver. 'I'm getting the fuck out of here.'

'No,' I said. 'There's a man down.'

The army vehicle's passenger door was open, and a soldier lay slumped on the ground. Nervously, my driver drew alongside him. The soldier had radio headphones on his ears, which had been disconnected from the radio, thereby disabling it. The vehicle was out of contact with base. Feet away, I could see the soldier had been hit in the groin. He said nothing but looked at me directly, and by the light of the lamp above, he died.

'Christ mate, get us a fucking ambulance,' screamed a soldier hiding behind the vehicle. 'For fuck's sake!' A soldier lying at the back of the jeep fired half a dozen shots into the surrounding dark, and began to cry.

I wanted to get out and help the wounded soldier, but I knew that was futile. He was doomed and even if he wasn't, how could I treat a gunshot wound?

The taxi driver now declared: 'Fuck this, *I'm* getting the fuck out of here.' The car moved away, leaving the soldiers in the dark. I said, 'Radio for an ambulance.'

'I'm radioing for fucking nothing. That there's none of my fucking business, and I'm not interfering.'

We went directly to his taxi depot in the city centre, where I asked the girl on the switch to send an ambulance to the square. She refused. 'If you don't, I fucking will,' I said.

'It's all right, the lads'll be away by now,' said a waiting driver calmly. 'I'll make the call.'

I took a cigarette from a driver – an untipped Gallagher's Green – inhaled deeply, and it fell from my trembling lips. Some time later, I returned to the flat I was sharing with Pete. It was Friday. A card school, playing for unbelievable stakes – deeds for houses often changed hands – was as usual underway in the sitting room. I told the players about the killing. Not an eye flickered from their cards. I went to my bedroom, and after a while shaking, I wept.

The dead soldier's name was Robert Bankier, of the Royal Green Jackets. He was my age, twenty-four, from Ipswich, and was married with two children. I have since seen a fair number of people die in my life, but I remember him most faithfully. I remember his face, I remember his eyes, I remember the stricken cry of his mates.

I remember that I had had an intuition about what was going to happen, and did nothing to prevent it.

There was and is no resolution to my moral dilemma: should I have told the army about my suspicions, when their intelligence officers were being paid to make the prediction I had privately made? If I *had* done, might I not have thereby enabled the army to launch a counter-ambush, possibly killing the IRA men? And anyway, it was an amateur hunch. Yet, that does not ease the guilt I still feel about his death, about poor young Mrs Bankier being woken with the news in the army base in Germany where she lived, as I had been once been woken eight years before, and about those two fatherless Bankier children, in whose lifelong fatherlessness I was and shall remain forever passively complicit.

Yet I have to accept: the shooting of Robert Bankier provided a break from the ennui that filled my young life. In the early 1970s nothing opened – shops, pubs, cinemas, supermarkets, even chip shops – on Sundays in Belfast. In the morning people hurried to their churches and their chapels. In Catholic churches priests would patter irreverently through the Mass. Protestants were more measured and demotic. As I later discovered during my one visit to Martyrs' Memorial church, Ian Paisley would endlessly proclaim upon the virtues of the circumcised, pronouncing each syllable with a measured and sibilant relish, *shircumshished,* while his women worshippers shuddered beneath their hats and silently groaned at his repeated references to the male organ.

But all good things must come to an end, and by noon the churches had emptied, the really brilliant part of the day now over as an unutterable boredom set in. I would stand in RTÉ's bureau eleven storeys up in the centre of a lifeless city, watching nothing happen, for hour after hour after hour, smoking the cigarettes which in desperation I had taken up. Because the truth is that, for the most part, nothing did happen in Belfast.

I was friendless in the city, alone amid the mists of its brooding memory, its vapours of hatred. I had no one to speak to about Robert Bankier, and so I started to write to an American woman with whom I'd had a brief affair in Dublin. Audrey was unlike any Irishwoman I'd met. She would chucklingly describe how, after I had scrambled out of her bed and off to a training course in RTÉ, she would lie there thinking over the sex we'd hurriedly seized before my departure, pleasuring herself for much of the morning. That, she once told me as she sat in the bath and I washed her hair, was in a funny way as good as sex with me: I became her fantasy, she said, and with that fantasy she could do anything. *Anything, Kevin*, she said, sinking into the bath, *anything*.

Audrey was a lighthouse on the promontory of that fair land of sanity I had left behind. She was a symbol of sex, wisdom and sense. So I would write to her in the USA, telling her about the darkness of the city where I now dwelt, and how some of that darkness was seeping into my soul. I knew I could tell her of the troubles inexorably growing within me. I was, and remain, close to my brothers and sisters, and could allude to some but not all of what was going on inside me, for sibling introspection can be a burdensome thing.

Moreover, I think it was the torpor that oozed through the city's granite slabs that helped drive me to my own strange nocturnal sojourns. The natives and I agreed: Irish Catholics do not lie easy amid Calvin's austere stones, which was perhaps why they nightly gathered, and why I nightly went to watch them. For riots often became gunfights, and then, finally, Belfast really became interesting.

There was, I think, another reason why I so often cruised the streets at night. Just about every first-time visitor to Belfast receives the same impressions: drabness encased in hills. Red-brick mission halls, mean houses, tiny streets, endless rain. A strange melancholy oozes from the pores of the buildings in the city centre. By 1971 the Victorian grandeur of one of the great industrial cities of the world had faded into the drab and unconvincing pretence of a minor vaudeville star living in a damp and grubby boarding house.

For Belfast is a lie. It is unreal. The consensual agreement that shapes and cements other urban communities is absent from this city. At best, people agree not to disagree, matter and anti-matter mingling and yet declining to eliminate one another; at worst, they agree to disagree, with all the predictably deplorable consequences you do not need to come to these pages to learn about. But they do not define themselves or their city in a common language, with common feelings and common meanings.

A visitor to Belfast might judge that it was just another city on that rusting shipyard meridian that passes through those founders of nineteenth-century industrialism: Glasgow, Gdańsk and Kaliningrad. What do they have in common? Short winter days, unending diets of grease and starch, and weather that is cold and grey. But in reality, the natives of Belfast live lives of enormous colour in their parades and their imagination, and within the walls of their ghettoes.

While in the commercial heart of the city, they administered a sedative to their facial muscles; yet these pursed lips, these unseeing eyes, came truly alive within the tiny, warring sanctuaries where they lived, and where they alone felt truly free. Here, their faces could be liberated from the tyranny of city-centre tolerance; here they could exult in the triumphs of their tribe; and here they could freely indulge in Belfast's most powerful indigenous art form, the sculpting of ancient grievance into a dynamic life-force.

When I saw riots, I saw one of the most honest and defining features of the city, kept secret from most visitors but not from me.

Three

9 August 1971

BY THIS TIME, the summer of 1971, my gambler flatmate had long fled Belfast, and I'd found a small bedsitter with a little kitchen and bathroom. My landlord was an engaging Catholic magistrate called William Staunton, who collected rents on the last Friday of every month. Over tea, we usually discussed our various tastes in literature – which included a common enthusiasm for Damon Runyon, and which in his case embraced an excited knowledge of the single occasion when Runyon had departed from the present tense. He told me he wouldn't tell me where it was, just insisted I find it for myself. When I had – presumably, unsuccessfully – gone through the stories again, he'd let me know.

He was a true gentleman, who seemed reluctant to take my money from me, always worrying whether I had enough to get through to the next month. I had of course, for I was working all the hours that God sent me, and more: I wasn't earning much, but then again neither was I spending much.

I was in Dublin staying with friends the first Saturday in August when the IRA opened fire on the oft-attacked Springfield Road barracks. Soldiers returned fire, and killed an innocent lorry driver. Belfast erupted in transports of wrath, out of all scale to the provocation, and I was ordered back to the front line. Wearily, I caught the train back, and went to Ardoyne, where the worst of the street fighting occurred that evening, with more the next day.

That Sunday night, the rioting worsened. It was wild stuff: automatic gunfire, nail bombs, petrol bombs. There was no way of knowing where was safe and where was not. In the half-light of that late summer night, as I lay in cover, I saw a British army foot patrol running diagonally across the Crumlin Road, its overweight radio operator, burdened with a huge, old-fashioned wireless set on his back, waddling along in the rear. A burst of machine-gun fire, and he stumbled and fell. He was dragged away, but I suspect poor Private Malcolm Hatton, aged nineteen and married only a few weeks, was already dead.

As I know now, he had presciently told his wife he would not return from Belfast. That woman, childless and alone, still lives in the house she inhabited when she received the telegram breaking the news that she was a widow.

But back then, no sense of future or grief informed my responses. I was a war journalist, and that was that. After hours of lying in cover, the fighting died down sufficiently for me to be able to leave. I had to walk the several miles back to my flat, where I fell onto my bed at around four, shattered, and rose again at 6.30. Haggard, hallucinating with fatigue, my mouth as foul as a sewer, I walked the mile to work in the bright dawn light, columns of smoke rising across the horizon, the brisk sound of gunbattles crackling distantly through the summer air. During my couple of hours' sleep, internment without trial had been introduced. Across the province hundreds of suspected IRA men and political activists had been dragged from their beds and taken into military custody. In response, barricades had been hurriedly conjured from unpopular neighbours' cars, milk floats, buses and lorries: smoke now spiralled everywhere. Rioting and gunbattles stretched from centre to suburb, from slum to drumlin. Northern Ireland had dropped down a mineshaft.

After working for the early bulletins, I was on the road, with Bob Moon as my driver. We headed up beyond Carlisle Circus to the tiny area that I'd left only hours before, and which, more than any other, typified the architectural and geographical horror of the city. Old Ardoyne was barely two hundred yards by two hundred yards. It was composed of a huddled jumble of houses made for proletarian elves who had once toiled in Flax Street Mill, which was now an army base. These dwellings were so small that modern man, with his arms extended, could just about touch the opposite walls of a living-room with his fingertips. They were certainly smaller than the coalhouse in my childhood home.

Violence seemed to emanate from the damp, brown bricks of Ardoyne like the spores of an ancient and virulent fungus. Ardoyne republicans had murdered two RUC policemen the night before I arrived. Ardoyne republicans had shot the first soldier killed in these Troubles. Ardoyne republicans had murdered the three Scottish soldiers: Ardoyne men – aye, and women too – seemed capable of almost anything.

From dawn there had been gunbattles between soldiers, the IRA and loyalist gunmen on the fringes of Ardoyne. In one such clash a leading IRA man, Paddy McAdorey, whom Tommy McIlroy had mentioned to me on my first day, and who – I'm told – hours before had shot Private Hatton dead, had himself been killed. Now he was laid out in Butler Street Hall, a bandage masking the hole in his head, while locals filed by, blessing themselves and kissing their beads as they recited the rosary. The ceremonies of death were ferocious and exultant: it was as if the people of Ardoyne were rolling up their sleeves to establish once and for all who they really were.

Bob drove me to the far side of the city where he went to his home in the Protestant Village area for a cup of tea. Instead of joining him, I walked up the Broadway, which linked the Village with the Catholic Falls. Ahead of me, some soldiers. I paused in a front garden to watch. Suddenly, from behind a bush, a familiar figure appeared beside me, turned, and nodded. 'What about ye,' he said affably. Then, once again, shoulder to shoulder with me, he emptied his entire Browning 9mm at the military.

I hit the ground, leading with my teeth as once again my Browning man successfully scampered away from the pursuing fire, this time in broad daylight, as bullet-shredded privet leaves scattered over my back. After about half an hour, I slunk down the road, and found Bob.

To Lenadoon, a new estate on the south-western tip of the city. Paratroopers had dealt with stone-throwers there simply by shooting them. A long-limbed young man lay dead in the road, spread-eagled, the flowing golden locks of his hair framing his head. It was a hot day, and flies were buzzing. As ambulance men collected the body, a group of laughing paratroopers were standing in a front garden being given tea, presumably by a Protestant couple. Did the latter consider for a moment what their future in this community would be after their beloved paratroopers had gone?

But then how much thought went into any deed in this place? Was it an abiding characteristic that the iron law of consequence was not in the least understood, so that people were endlessly conforming to Einstein's definition of stupidity by doing deeds with entirely predictable consequences which always surprised them? And was I now also pretending that this very same law did not apply to me?

Next, we went to Ballymurphy. The British army's base in Henry Taggart Hall overlooked the estate; it was by this time – the Mekong Delta excluded – perhaps the most shot-at army base in the world. So, leaving Bob sitting in his car out of line of any fire, I walked along the Springfield Road, which lay between the Hall and Ballymurphy, but which sat even lower, in a recess beneath the road. This gave attackers from Ballymurphy a protective lip from which to fire at the sentry in his sangar in the Hall. I walked the length of this lip, at one point twenty yards from the watching soldier, my hands clear of my body, in shirt sleeves, so that anyone could see I was not armed.

Why was I doing this? Why did I take the chance that the soldier was not jumpy, or that a sniper would not open up on him? And entirely predictably, a lad approached me from below the lip, and not uttering even the mildest word of warning, he lit a nail bomb and tossed it neatly over my head. I had dived down, beneath the lip, before it exploded.

'What happened?' Bob asked when I got into his car, and he saw my exposed and bleeding knee.

'I fell.'

'You want to go home, get changed?'

'No. Let's go back to Ardoyne.'

It was a society in free-fall. The Protestants of the area, claiming intimidation, were leaving, and had called forth vehicles to remove their belongings. Such a departure was proof in Catholic eyes that they were feigning victimhood, and this was an outrage: how dare Protestants – *how dare they!* – lay claim to something that was a Catholic monopoly?

So Catholics were attacking Protestants because Protestants were falsely – the fiends! – alleging that Catholics were attacking them; and Protestants were attacking Catholics because ... oh, because they just were. The weapons were out; people tottered out of their homes bearing furniture while gunfire swept the streets. Departing Protestants, determined that Catholics should not benefit from their absence, then set fire to their own homes. By mid-afternoon hundreds of houses were ablaze, and murderous chaos ruled.

A man ran out of his house. 'Son,' he said, plucking at my sleeve, and presumably taking me for an IRA-man, 'there's a blu-enose gunman in the houses round the back.'

An intelligent person would have taken this as a clear warning not to do what I proceeded to do next. I entered the man's house and went up the stairs. 'Don't you go into the back bedroom son, or he'll blow your fucking head off,' came the shouted warning from below.

So naturally, I went into the back bedroom and looked out the bedroom window at the back bedroom windows of a line of identical houses opposite and only about twenty feet away. Beneath me, the two sets of tiny gardens backing onto one another were separated by a narrow alley. I looked down: his supposed 'gunman' was in reality a single wary soldier looking nervously around the alley.

I looked up, and saw a man in the opposite bedroom looking round, just like me. Our eyes met, and we nodded, as people do, and as my Browning-man habitually did. That was this other man's first, individual and human instinct: his second, and tribal instinct was to raise a gun and fire directly at me. For a spur of the moment shot it wasn't bad: the bullet passed just above my right ear. The next shot would probably have got me, for I was frozen still with shock, but below me the soldier turned and fired at my attacker.

Freed from my trance, I plummeted downstairs. On the street a group of children were lobbing stones at the end of the terrace, through the gap between the final house and the high brick wall of a warehouse. 'Watch out, lads, there's a sniper in there,' I cried.

'I'm not scared of no fucking bluenose sniper,' scoffed one of the boys, an impish little urchin who looked about ten. He gave me a scornful what-do-you know look that children reserve for their more stupid elders: then he winked forgivingly at me, wiped his nose, turned and threw another stone at some unseen Protestants. A moment later, a single shot, and he collapsed; beside him two other boys stood shrieking, wounded.

We know now what happened. The soldier who had saved my life had seen yet another gunman in a garden, had fired, but missed. The bullet had hit the warehouse wall, where it shattered and ricocheted sideways. A fragment had, like a can-opener, sheered off a piece of skull from the back of one boy's head. Another had hit the hand of a second boy, slicing off two fingers. A third had hit the boy who had been cheerfully mocking me.

He now lay silent on the ground. I reached out and touched him. Leo McGuigan, aged sixteen, but looking so much younger, was lifeless beneath my fingers. A tiny red hole sat on his cheek, but of blood there was none, for he had been killed in a microsecond; there was no exit wound, the shard expending all its energies in destroying the youngster's brain. I helped put his mutinously lolling corpse into a car. A soldier's two shots; the first had saved a life, the second had taken one.

Gunfire was now raking the streets of Ardoyne, the sense of murderous anarchy being intensified by roof tiles exploding like rifle shots. I made my way out of the Catholic area, and crawled into a street still held by Protestants, and which was now being evacuated. I found a Protestant man on the ground, a bullet wound through his abdomen. I contemplated giving him first aid, but hadn't a clue what to do. So instead, I held his hand and murmured a few positive though prudent words of encouragement, avoiding any of those native popish sentiments which, all things considered, might have gone down rather badly.

'Them Fenian bastards, they'll fucking pay for this,' snarled a bystander.

'They already are,' I replied. 'I just put a dead Catholic boy in a car.'

'You mean we got one? Fucking brilliant! You hear, that, lads? We got a wee Fenian around the corner.'

There were general noises of acclaim and celebration. 'Aye, and he'll not be the fucking last,' said a man with some relish. Which was true.

I managed to find a phone in almost phoneless Ardoyne, and telephoned in the very first news of what was going on there, giving RTÉ an exclusive – as I was the only journalist there at that stage. Then I was pinned down by fire for at least an hour before I was able to make good my escape. I went to the office, where Liam Hourican roundly upbraided me for not staying constantly in touch. There I filed updated reports, and then Bob and I left, once again for Ballymurphy, to check on rumours of a heavy gunbattle there.

By this time Liam's cliché had become true; Belfast really was a city of fear. Bob drove me up the Springfield Road, which was as black as space before stars were born. As we approached our destination, we came across a stationary British army armoured personnel carrier. Bob turned off his lights. I got out and called out that I was a journalist. No reply. With my hands held high I approached it. There was no one in it. No one. It had been left untended in this darkest of nights, as if its crew were confident that this was a now-unpeopled city, and the streets were all theirs to command.

From the utter pitch darkness of Springhill to my right, a sudden skull-shattering sound of gunfire. A single heart-spasm: bowels tightened within a fist of steel; then, surrounded by that strange, submarine silence that usually follows gunshots at midnight, I slowly backed towards Bob's invisible car – me calling 'Where are you?' – he guiding me back, 'Here, here!' completely invisible, but scared to turn on his lights lest he – we – become a target. So, like bats, we found one another, and once I'd groped my way into the car, Bob did a U-turn based purely on memory, only turning on his sidelights when clear of that armoured *Marie Celeste*. Behind us lurking unseen on the hill, was the residue of a massacre that had occurred minutes before our arrival. Paratroopers had shot eight residents dead, including a Catholic priest as he administered to to the dead and dying. How many of them had me in their sights as I wandered around their empty vehicle?

I got back to the office to find the written instruction that I was to stay on duty till about four. How kind.

In the days after internment Belfast was paralysed. All shops were closed, and the destruction of so many lorries and tankers meant that the city was running out of food and fuel. A perpetual pall of smoke hung in the city's skies, its acrid vapours accosting everyone who stepped out of doors. Few did, as gunbattles raged between soldiers and civilians, and civilians and civilians, in that most improbable of suburbs.

More than anything else, it was an anarchy over which ignorance reigned. One thing that *was* known was that the British government had permitted the wretched government of Northern Ireland to implement a criminally one-sided security policy, ignoring active loyalist terrorists even as it scooped up hundreds of republican opponents of the Stormont government, some on purely political grounds. The anger in the nationalist community, which dearly nourished a grievance anyway, was both volcanic and justified: moreover, the conduct of the British army, especially the Parachute Regiment, ensured that the volcano would not soon be sealed.

I remember August 9th with abysmal clarity, but few events from the succeeding days remain: merely sensations of hunger, fear, isolation and astonishing fatigue. I visited the Catholic ghetto of Ballymurphy each day. It was a sinister hell of sporadic and unpredictable gunfire, in the midst of which the adult residents attempted to survive and live and feed their families.

One afternoon I watched children throwing stones at soldiers, as they did at the same time every afternoon. The squaddies were patiently shoulder-to-shoulder with their riot-shields, next to a side street, from where a young man emerged with a sub-machine gun, and fired a burst of rounds at the line of soldiers, missing them all. Thirty yards away, a young army captain promptly unholstered his pistol and returned fire, missing his target as consummately as his adversary, who then directed his fire towards the officer. There they stood, unmoving, firing at one another until they both ran out of ammunition, at which point the IRA man promptly vanished: two men, each desperately trying to kill the other, and failing hopelessly.

A couple of days after, Bob Moon and I were doing one of our nightly magical mystery tours. We passed through an army checkpoint on the Crumlin Road, and as we eased away, and turned left into Ardoyne Road, another car came behind us. A single shot rang out from a soldier, hitting the car. It immediately stopped.

Bob and I got out and went back. The other vehicle contained three terrified men. A fourth occupant, William Ferris, was either dead or dying. A mix-up of signals at the roadblock, the driver thinking he had been waved on when the soldier had called on him to stop. A soldier, perhaps exhausted after days without proper sleep, had fired. No one really trying to kill anyone, and this time a man was dead.

So, why were Bob and I – or sometimes Tommy McIlroy and I – cruising the streets as we were? What infatuation was this? Me, we know about. Bob, the only Protestant in the taxi firm, loved driving. It was his identity, his world. He liked to say that when asked on a census form his religion, he wrote down: 'Taxi driver.' Driving was what he did. It defined him. But Tommy was married with three children. Why did he take such risks?

Strangely enough, because he loved his car. He didn't drink or smoke, and I think that he was only truly happy when he was in it. Unlike other taxis of Belfast at that time – mostly run-down, black Morris Oxfords or Austin Cambridges – his was a powder-blue Mercedes 220, impeccably maintained. Bob apart, his workmates had a typically Catholic disregard for neatness: in Belfast parlance, 'Protestant-looking' was synonymous with pristine order. So, uniquely amongst the Catholic drivers, and rather like Bob, Tommy was always polishing his car's bodywork, and wiping its dashboard with a cloth he kept in the glove compartment.

The Mercedes – new – would have cost more than four times the price of any other taxi in the firm. But Tommy had bought it as scrap from an insurance company that had written it off after its driver had been killed in a crash. He had carefully rebuilt it, and then reregistered it. Not only was it the finest taxi in the company, it was probably the finest in Belfast, with cream kid-leather seats and a wondrous sense of space and luxury. The only complaint he had about his beloved car was that it was hard on batteries: he was forever changing them.

I always welcomed a lift from Tommy, because he was so informed about the IRA. He told me of a shipment of US rifles with strange names that had arrived in town and were being distributed to IRA units. Something-light, they were called.

Light machine gun, I suggested. No, he said, smiling at me – he always smiled – he would have remembered that. No, this was a new word he'd never heard. Recruitment was going through the roof: gelignite was being stolen in vast quantities in the Republic, and no one was trying to stop it. Training camps were springing up everywhere across the Border, which was wide-open for IRA infiltration. Better still, the war would soon inevitably spread to rural areas, once the British army heeded Unionist demands for greater presence along the Border. 'Our boys are waiting there to give them a welcome they won't remember, Kevin,' he said, his eyes crinkling happily.

His strange complexion always mottled with pleasure as he talked about the coming war. The British – I don't think the term 'the Brits' had been coined at this stage – wouldn't know what hit them, he declared with relish.

Why didn't he join the IRA, I asked. 'Who's to say I haven't,' he replied, grinning darkly. But I don't think he was in the IRA, not least because he had his hands full feeding his family. Moreover, it soon became clear that in the part of Ligoniel where he lived, well north of Carlisle Circus, life was getting distinctly uncomfortable for Catholics, with loyalists regularly petrol bombing their homes.

One day he told me proudly that he had found a house where loyalists absolutely couldn't petrol bomb him. Really? Where was that? Opposite Henry Taggart Hall, he replied.

Opposite Henry Taggart Hall? Was he out of his fucking

mind? That was the most shot-at place in Belfast, the world. All right, maybe living beneath a sentry post might protect him from attacks by loyalist terrorists, just like living in a tent on a motorway means you are in little danger of being killed by a meteor, but that's only because a lorry will certainly get you first. For not only did people shoot at the soldiers in the area, but soldiers often fired back – and sometimes without waiting to be shot at first, as many bereaved families could testify.

Tommy shook his head knowingly. He'd be fine. So would Susan and the kids. 'I know what I'm doing,' he said. 'See me, Kevin? I'm no mug.' The little eyes crinkled, and the coal dust beneath his skin changed hue, rather like a chameleon.

Four

MY FIRST FEW months in Belfast were relatively women-free. I had actually gone several months – since Audrey – without having sex, which nearly killed me. Indeed, this partly explains those long journeys through the lengthening Belfast nights. Later there were occasional one night stands: an artist, a woman the week before she got married – a final fling – and a married woman for whom I was her first extra-marital affair.

There was also a night with an avowed lesbian lady who had decided to confer upon me the dubious privilege of taking her heterosexual virginity. It was a measure of my desperation that I agreed. Before actually deflowering this maiden, I digitally laboured long and hard, possibly even inducing the sort of minor pelvic disturbance that might loosely be called an orgasm. It could equally have been indigestion. I cannot be sure. Then penetration, which in my case was possible and sustained only through a heroic act of imagination; after which, we both – with relief – sought the refuge of slumber. She stayed lesbian; and believe me, I quite understand. Any more such encounters and I would have eagerly opted for the monkishness of which my life was usually composed.

Then one night in the Wellington Park Hotel, in the aftermath of the mass arrests of the internment operation of August 9th and all the violence that followed, I saw the most beautiful woman I had ever seen in my entire life. She was blonde and had a figure that would have made even Mother Teresa snarl with lust. Unhesitatingly I approached her and made a small joke. She laughed, and said, 'Very funny. I charge a tax on men who make me laugh.'

'What's the tax?'

'You buy me a drink.'

'Do I have to buy you a drink every time you laugh?'

'Not if I make you laugh.'

I laughed uproariously.

'That's cheating,' she said, smiling. 'I charge a tax on men who cheat.'

'What's that?'

She kissed her finger and laid it on my cheek. I trapped it there for a moment before letting it go.

She fixed me with her eyes, interest glowing there.

I said: 'You're Swedish.'

'And you're Sherlock Holmes.'

I laughed again. 'Now you *really* owe me a drink.'

'It wasn't that funny. You're a journalist, I presume,' she said. 'I'm in the same line myself.'

'The same line? What does that mean?'

'Oh you know, this and that.'

We had a couple of drinks, all bought by me. Naturally. I didn't mind. She looked like Britt Ekland's infinitely better-looking sister. It was warm in the hotel, and I suggested we get some fresh air.

'A good idea,' she said, taking my hand and leading me into the car park, where she manoeuvred me against a van. We were unseen, and she kissed me, holding her body against mine. She was not wearing a bra. She took my hand and placed it under her cotton jumper onto her breast. It was perfectly wonderful – large and firm, and you could have hung your hat on her nipple. Her own hand dropped onto my groin.

She stopped kissing me, and looked at me, a little smile on her exquisite Nordic face as she massaged me. I have seldom been seized by such rampant lust, and I almost laughed with joy that finally, *finally*, I was going to have sex again. It was too good to be true.

'Twenty pounds,' she whispered.

'What?'

'I charge twenty pounds for a fuck; or, fifty pounds a night. What's it to be?'

Ah, yes: it was too good to be true.

'Neither,' I said. 'I don't pay for sex.'

'In that case, you're going to buy me a drink. That's my little tax on men who waste my time.'

She trilled a little laugh. I didn't trill anything, but dolefully followed her back to the bar, and with unpardonable weakness bought her yet another drink. 'Excuse me,' she said when the drink arrived, and rising, took it over to join a three-man French camera crew. She spoke to one of the Frenchmen. He said something, and she laughed out loud. I heard her say: 'Very funny. I charge a tax on men who make me laugh.'

Which is how I learnt that 'Excuse me' is whorish for 'goodbye forever'. She was to spend the next week servicing the three Frenchmen whenever and however they wanted. No doubt, she gave discount on bulk purchases. However, I never heard her laugh again, before she was expelled for 'immoral behaviour': yes, that was possible in those days.

Her presence in the hotel showed that Belfast had finally qualified as an international trouble spot. She made her living going to war zones where large numbers of male journalists from all over the world would gather, and where she could usually find creatures who were prepared to pay all her various taxes.

I found I actually liked very few of the foreign journalists covering the Troubles. Hotel life, and a perpetual exposure to high drama, or the need to create it where it didn't exist, seemed to have created a vapid, insincere species. Jack Laurence and Bob Fisher from CBS seemed to be exceptions, as was Ulf Gudmundson of Swedish television. But otherwise, I found that I didn't really get on with my fellow news hounds. Some visiting BBC journalists were graduates *cum laude* of the University of Hauteur.

I had developed a low opinion of RTÉ personnel during my training period in Dublin, as no doubt – with some justification – they later had of me. Company culture was infected by the most diseased kind of trade unionism; too many employees knew only of workers' rights, and nothing of workers' duties, and took a wilful pride in being able to obstruct projects rather than to assist in them – and none more so than then the camera crews.

The most 'eminent' cameraman was Gay O'Brien who had taken the 'famous' news film of the first Derry Riots on Craigavon Bridge in 1968. (Well, it was famous in Ireland.) It's true he happened to have *been* there: the film wasn't all that technically sensational, but you would have thought he had filmed *The Bridge Over the River Kwai* from the airs and graces he had acquired. He was an elderly, prissy, pompous and obstructive know-all, and not fit for the sort of action now common in Belfast. Cameramen needed to take risks, and he was too querulously self-important to do that.

At least, though, he could point a camera in the right direction. Some couldn't even manage this. Of course the levels of ineptitude that were commonplace and tolerated in the station helped explain how it was that I had been given a job in the first place, but still ...

A handful of people stood out: Liam Hourican, who for all his bullying, overbearing management style was a superb broadcaster, with a silky, scholarly delivery; John Slye, the Belfast-based cameraman, brave and unwaveringly sharp; John McAleese, my colleague, a superb reporter and a delightful, loyal colleague; and the incredibly tall Deasey brothers, Brendan and Seamus, who came up from Dublin regularly, and who were all you could ask of a camera crew: technically superb and quite fearless in action.

However, Mike Burns and Sean Duignan were the most terrifying colleagues of all. They presented the radio programme *News at One Thirty*, a straight copy of the BBC's *World At One*, and were legendary for their broadcasting skills. When up from Dublin for special occasions, after finishing their programme, they would return to the Wellington Park for a few whiskeys before lunch with wine, and then they would retire to the bar, where they would stay, downing milk pails of whiskey until, perfectly sober, they would go to bed at around about 3 or 4 am.

They would rise at eight, eat a hearty breakfast in which every single thing was fried, including the grapefruit and the cornflakes, and looking as healthy as a couple of postulant, spinach-eating nuns who run a couple of miles every morning before matins, they would turn up at RTÉ's Belfast headquarters, yodelling with joy.

Two fifteen, and the pattern of the previous day would repeat itself. Drinking with them, I felt how those French generals in 1940 must have felt when the Panzers waltzed right past them and on to the Paris and the Channel ports. Three hours in their company and I was a babbling lunatic, four and I was driving the porcelain bus. And I have never been able to face but one breakfast, even after a teetotal night before, with the carnivorous relish with which they joyfully welcomed theirs, morning after morning.

There were other, perhaps even more lethal perils in Belfast than their company, so RTÉ supplied us with flak jackets. One night in McDonald Street, off the Falls Road, I was creeping forward in the oily, impenetrable dark that I later learnt in Beirut and Sarajevo is a characteristic of any city at war, and carrying my trusty tape recorder: such intelligent conduct, especially since the hand-held mike so resembled a gun. In the dark ahead the din of rioting – bricks against army steel, rubber-bullet guns in reply: suddenly, a stentorian English voice barked, 'Nail bomb incoming'! A line of sparks trailed upwards in the dark sky, but missed the armoured personnel carrier, and, hitting the ground, came slithering towards my half-crouching body, instantly exploding. My flak jacket caught the blast, and though I was sent flying, I suffered no injury apart from to my ears which rather sang the *Hallelujah Chorus* – the lo-fi tinnitus version – for about two days. My poor Sony, however, was shattered. An RTÉ engineer was able to extract the tape from the broken machine, and next day, it made a sad little radio item entitled: 'The Death of a Tape Recorder.'

However, far more important for me was the immediate aftermath of the bomb blast. This time, I was elated. War without death: an incredible sensation, closely related to the joys of splendid sex with lovely Audrey, but with nuances and depths that lingered far longer than the remembered (if now only vaguely) pleasures of intercourse. Boy stuff.

Gradually, a picture was beginning to emerge of the thuggery, abuse and torture that accompanied and followed internment. The question we asked then, the question we still ask now is this: how did anyone, from the prime ministers of Great Britain and Northern Ireland, down to the intelligence operatives conducting these experiments, ever think this could go undiscovered?

It was as if the ruthless methods, which had probably seemed to make sense in Aden and Kenya, could by the suspension of the laws of consequence be applied without legal or political repercussions in this lawless corner of Her Majesty's United Kingdom. How wrong they were.

Some disclosures were beyond parody. One blind, yes blind, sexagenerian with a weak heart was, after a few days' detention, released from Girdwood Barracks at two in the morning, shoeless and sockless, and told to walk home. As one republican mordantly pointed out, at that hour the poor cunt couldn't even use his bus pass. It was during these days that famous graffiti on the Whiterock Road asked: 'Is there a life before death?'

The British army's astounding Brigadier Marston Tickell told journalists that the army had shot fifty terrorists in the first two days' fighting, killing thirty. (In fact, just one IRA man, Paddy McAdorey, had been killed, and not necessarily by British soldiers.) The initial 'cache' of IRA captured was well up to expectations, he declared, and subsequent operations had virtually defeated what remained of the IRA. The month was August, the year 1971. Another twenty-five years would elapse before a long-term IRA ceasefire seriously began.

No one foresaw the long dark Calvary that lay ahead for the peoples of Ireland and Britain. I certainly didn't. Moreover, no government can sit back and watch its soldiers being killed as I had seen Robert Bankier die, and no army can stomach such attrition without reply. It is easy to say what should not have been done. It is more difficult to say what should have been done to counter the rising threat of a determined, dynamic IRA, considering the technical ineptitude and deplorable intelligence of the security forces, never mind the unbridgeable divisions between the political leaders of both islands, and nationalists and unionists within Ireland itself. The truth is that the only people who really knew what they wanted were the leaders of the insurgency: one of the singular characteristics of almost any terrorist war.

Not that I was engaged in any such useful speculation. Unsuspectingly, I had passed a moral and psychological Rubicon. War had become a natural condition of my life now, as the city closed in on itself, tribal village by tribal village, each withdrawing to its clearly defined boundaries; and when they were not clearly defined, they were redefined by ruthless expulsions and intimidation.

It was if the entire population of Northern Ireland had been steeped in an electrolytic bath in which synapses sparked and ganglions were galvanized with wholly novel currents. New realities and duties were being created in people's minds, and real ones abolished. Only tribal identity survived – and indeed prospered from – these ionized hallucinations.

Life in Belfast was now defined by murder, indignation, accusation and counter-accusation. Historical forces were at work here, and like flotsam in a raging sea, people found themselves being hurled against the implacable rocks of fatal injustice.

One night, I was crouching beside an army major, near a military armoured personnel carrier on the Springfield Road. An unusual kind of gunfire opened up in our direction.

'Fuck me,' he whispered. 'I don't fucking believe it.'

'What is it?'

He paused, and there were more shots. 'Armalites,' he said, appalled. 'They've fucking got Armalites.'

He had been trained to recognize .223 rounds, and now the new weapon firing it had arrived, just as Tommy had promised it would, except his '-light' should have been '-lite'. With the arrival of this version of the US M-16 army rifle, the war was taking on fresh dimensions, as, briefly, did my life.

In the emotional heat of the time, a long-term platonic friend-ship from UCD times had, during R&R trips to Dublin, trans-muted into a sexual one. Such alterations can be extremely pleasant – in fact one of the most delightful relationships of all is sexualized friendship, but it should not be mistaken for its parallel emotional force, sexual love, for the two generally meet in infinity. But mistake one for the other is precisely what we did, and we even got engaged to be married, formally, complete with newspaper announcements. After we had made love one afternoon, Dympna lay on the bed, staring at the ceiling and mused: 'You know, having a fuck with you is just like having a very big shite.'

With that delightful endorsement of my sexual prowess ring-ing in my ears, I went alone to Spain that October, to a small hotel in a village called Castel de Ferro. My heart and my soul were wracked with the pain of the summer, and with the death and the suffering I had seen. What was going on? Whose side was I on in this conflict? The IRA was working class and therefore – by my insane reckoning – 'progressive': but I still carried a British passport, even if only out of laziness, and the killing of Robert Bankier continued to haunt my conscience. On the other hand, the internment operation had been an exercise in massive state criminality. What was right any more? What was wrong?

I spent each day alone, gazing at the seashore littered with the skeletons of the fish that had been filleted by the local fishermen, smelling their smell and wondering about the purpose of my young life. Each night I would withdraw to my room with two litres of red wine, my hosts mystified and exchanging baffled looks, and I would drink until I passed out.

Then I visited my mother in Leicester. I was unable to tell her about my personal life, as largely I was the rest of my family. I have five brothers and sisters, and I could and did often discuss the political realities of Northern Ireland with them. But I did not usually talk about my emotional response to what I had gone through. To have done so would in part have seemed vainglorious, but more relevantly, I had the sense they couldn't possibly have understood what I was talking about. Most people who have been in conflict feel this, and many shape their future identities around a denial of what they have been through.

What I remember most about that trip is that I went alone to see *Death in Venice*. Perhaps only those who have been touched with the bitter wand of utter isolation know the extraordinary truth about loneliness contained in that film. Watching it, I realized for the first time in my life that isolation is my natural condition. I do not easily attract or keep friendship.

I returned to Ireland. In Dublin, Dympna and I agreed to end our formal 'engagement'. Then I was back to Belfast, and its many delights, one of them however entirely genuine. This was the night when eight IRA internees detained in a prison-hulk, the *Maidstone,* in Belfast Lough, cut their way through a port hole, eased their way into the water, and swam ashore, where they hijacked a bus. People in the nationalist Markets area alongside the river Lagan gave them fresh clothes, and they were long gone by the time I arrived there, tipped off by a local girl.

She was about seventeen, as was her male companion, and I met them in a pub in the Markets, just as the area was being sealed off by paratroopers. Some other journalists soon gathered there, where we learnt that the intention of the two youngsters was to give the impression that the escapees were still present.

The boy had an ancient, pitted Thompson sub-machine gun, the girl a huge .45 Webley revolver in her tiny hands. They knew that in the area were paratroopers who would drop them in a second, which is what paras invariably did to anyone merely in the region of gunfire, never mind actually using guns. So they would sit beside the pub door, exchanging glances, terrified, before nodding to one another, rising, and walking outside. Each would then fire in opposite directions into the night, one the laboured staccato of the Thompson, the other the slow, trigger-wrenching bark of the revolver.

Then they would scramble back into the pub, white with terror. Once their hands were steady enough, they would reload, but fumblingly, their common ammunition scattering on the floor. A few minutes breathing, they would exchange glances, and repeat their actions. This was courage of a high order. There were a couple of journalists of unionist background in the pub, and they too were impressed. The escapees made it across the Border – to my delight, and I imagine that of many others. Those were strangely innocent days, and what the British, Irish unionists, Irish nationalists, and Irish lefties like me had in common, was a total ignorance of the world we were now inhabiting.

We were all far more anxious to find out what was going on in Long Kesh internment camp. A couple of months after it had opened, an excited civil rights activist contacted me: an internee called Barney Cahill had been allowed out to attend a funeral. Would I be interested in interviewing him?

I certainly would. This would the first time an internee could give a first-hand account of conditions in the camp. I rang Jim McGuinness, head of news in Dublin, and told him we had a major scoop. Being a hard-nosed newsman, he was keen to get a story about British brutality in the North. We would do a radio interview first, then television. Jim would sit in the control suite in Dublin, which would record my interview down the line.

Barney arrived at the offices. He was very pale and had that vacant stare which – I'd read – was caused by deep trauma. His footsteps were faltering, his manner hesitant.

I ushered this broken figure into the studio in Belfast: in Dublin, the head of news, news editor, and various luminaries gathered to hear the interview that would finally gain me serious respect: why, this interview might be sold on throughout the world!

I sat Barney down and I told him not to worry: if the interview went badly at any point, we could stop and start again. Did he understand? He stared at me with those unforgettably haunted eyes and nodded.

'Count to ten for a sound check, please,' I told him. He mumbled some digits: the man was clearly broken by the brutal treatment he'd endured, and was now in an unbearable torment.

I began the interview. 'Barney Cahill, you are the first internee to have been released from the now infamous Long Kesh camp. Tell us about the conditions there.'

Barney blinked at me, slowly and sadly, his eyes little pools of agony: clearly he was yearning to speak, but he nonetheless stayed silent – the classic diffidence of the torture victim.

'Barney,' I urged softly, 'I think we all have an idea of what you've been going through. Just take it easy, and tell us what it's been like.'

Barney shook his head, clearly beside himself with distress.

49

'We need to know what it was like in that place,' I murmured, spiritually reaching out to him.

He lifted his sorrowful gaze from the studio desk, looked at me, then suddenly smirked, put his tongue between his lips and made a large, wet farting noise. Next, with a vast idiotic grin written all over his features, he turned and, with perfect equanimity, vomited a handsome gallon of stout onto the studio floor.

A drunken Barney was led out of the studio back to the confinement which I now felt he richly deserved – indeed, if it was to be criticized at all, it was for its scandalous leniency. Meanwhile, the executive gathering in Dublin silently dispersed, with my reputation even further enhanced.

Five

THROUGHOUT MY TIME in Belfast, I had had no reason to drive because RTÉ always supplied taxis, but equally because I couldn't. The ability to drive a car had not seemed a necessity to me. I walked to work and assignments were arranged by RTÉ. Finally, I started taking driving lessons, and the instructor – a kindly Protestant man – used to direct me to north Belfast, beyond Carlisle Circus. Sometimes, to show off my confidence in my ability to cruise through nationalist areas, I would drive up the strongly republican New Lodge Road. He would get very nervous, but I assured him: I knew about the IRA, and what made it tick – he was in no danger while he was with me.

We were doing some reversing practice in some small streets off the Cavehill Road which all bore the name Ben Madigan. 'Who was Ben Madigan?' I asked my instructor.

'I thought you knew all about this city,' he replied, his voice a mixture of incredulity and disdain. 'And here's me, letting you drive us up the New Lodge.' He laughed. 'Aye, that's a good one right enough. Who was Ben Madigan.'

The week before Christmas 1971 we received a report of a bomb alert in a pub, nearby on the Lisburn Road. John Slye and

I immediately headed off, arriving soon after the bomb had exploded. Dust was shimmering downwards like dry ice as we got out of the car, and on the street, barmen were reeling and gibbering, grey-faced with shock, But the explosion hadn't been inside the pub: it was outside.

We stared around. There were tiny fragments of pink on the ground, mere smears, but hundreds of them, a confetti of human flesh. A weeping barman stood reciting an account of events, to himself and to all. The IRA had left the bomb and shouted a warning to leave, which the staff had heeded. But then the owner, Jack Lavery, chose to remove it, and thereby save his beloved pub.

Which is what, in part, he did. He had just got outside, a large grin of triumph on his face, when the bomb exploded, spattering the area with droplets of tissue. John had started filming the shattered facade of the pub when a woman drove up and got out of her car.

'Where's Jack?'

We instantly knew that here was a widow, freshly minted. John stopped filming. I whispered to him to turn on his camera. I wanted to capture this moment, unique in the history of television news, when a woman would learn on film that her husband was dead, and yes, ladies and gentlemen, those are the fragments of his corpse all round her.

John refused to move. I whispered to him again, but to no avail. Mrs Lavery looked at the barmen, at their faces, their horror-stricken eyes, and then looked around her, and seeing what we all saw, and suddenly knowing what we all knew, she unleashed a wail of grief that rings down the years and fills my heart with shame at how I wanted the world to witness this moment, not just because it should learn of the evil amongst us, but because part of that evil had already infected my soul.

But I was not alone. The infection was everywhere. Fifteen Catholics had been killed in a terrible bombing of McGurk's pub in Belfast, not far from Carlisle Circus, by the UVF two weeks before. A couple of days later, IRA men from Ardoyne detonated a no-warning bomb in the middle of Saturday shoppers on the Protestant Shankill Road, killing four people, including two Protestant infants, Tracey Munn and Colin Nicholl.

So now this war was truly following the usual twentieth-century pattern: most of its victims were innocent, blameless and uninvolved, sometimes killed by heedless, frightened or inept soldiery, but, far more often, by terrorists who were either uncaring, or were far worse: they cared so passionately that it mattered little to them who they killed. The IRA's immediate political foe was the all-Protestant Northern Ireland government at Stormont, which was notionally subordinate to London. But in a bizarre reversal of authority, security policies in the province, with the British army at the forefront, were decided by the dimwits of Stormont, who would have had trouble managing a garden tap.

With the might of the British army being governed by fools, and the IRA being directed by maniacs, we all knew terrible trouble was coming. The estuarial gates were opening, the river was mounting, and at source surged a vast and impatient cataract. We all sensed it: it is not hindsight to say we knew calamity was coming, for we were all certain of it then. It took cretinous arrogance to bring the maniacs and the fools to the one place in our history.

John Hume, the leader of the nationalist community in the largely nationalist city of Derry, knew full well of the mighty perils that lay ahead: he lived in the increasingly militant Bogside area, could sense its turbulence – and knew also from personal experience that elements of the British military were apparently growing impatient. Some senior commanders clearly believed that there was a military solution to the crisis, one that involved the use of the Parachute Regiment. In late January, there had been an anti-internment march to a newly opened prison camp up the Derry coast at Magilligan Strand. Paratroopers had beaten the marchers into the dunes, causing fist fights between them and other soldiers: 'We're supposed to be stopping them, not killing them,' bawled a soldier from the Green Jackets regiment.

John Hume wisely refused to have anything to do with the next anti-internment march planned for the following weekend in Derry on 30 January 1972, and which had been banned by the increasingly desperate Stormont government. A lethal danger was in the air, and almost all of us could foretell its imminent arrival with the absolute certainty with which a child senses the onset of Christmas. The march meant blood on the streets as assuredly as 25 December means presents under the tree. Few doubted that – and for the organizers to have gone ahead with such a demonstration when no single person or group could prevent or even contain the violent consequences was foolhardiness pushed to its limits.

The entire island held its breath as the evil day approached. Despite the danger in the air, other civilians, who were out of touch with the volatility that was building, went ahead with plans for the Derry march. One was Ivan Cooper, a nationalist of Protestant background who little understood the dark angers and lethal passions that were emerging in the city of Derry, of which he was not a native. Another was Eamon McCann, a former student activist in the city who departed to Dublin, where as a journalist, with a number of other émigré Northerners, he was at the forefront of a great deal of agitation about the North.

The Sunday evening of the march Harry McCormack, the RUC press officer I had met on my first day in Belfast, rang me at home. Had I heard what was happening in Derry? No, I hadn't. It looked like a fair old massacre was taking place, he said. Three or four dead, but many wounded too.

By this time I knew that Harry was unusual. We occasionally met for drinks, over which (before passing out beneath the juggernaut of his thirst) I had over time learnt that he was a Protestant Irish nationalist unionist republican Ulster British policeman.

He was a unionist, because he was a policeman and he was obliged to protect the institutions that most people wanted. He was a nationalist, because he personally favoured a united Ireland. He was also a passionate supporter of the Gaelic Athletics Association, going down to All-Ireland matches, especially if they featured Down, his native County, whenever he could.

On this dark January evening he was spitting with rage: he clearly knew some terrible calamity was upon us, and he was angry because he was a good man, the kind of policeman, it must be said, the IRA detested most of all.

Later he rang again and declared emotionally: 'Those murdering para bastards have killed nine people.' Maybe he was drunk, but drunk or otherwise, he was right, sort of. The final total was to be fourteen.

Snow was falling that night in Belfast as Tommy McIlroy drove me up to the strongly republican estate of Andersonstown. I wanted to judge the mood there. It was incredible. Far from the anger and gunfire I had expected, civilians were talking to soldiers. I joined one group: the soldier stood there listening as the locals in quiet, earnest tones told him of the horrors that lay ahead.

'I know,' he said, 'fuckin' terrible, ain't it. It's going to be pure fucking 'ell from now on. I know this, mate and there's fuck all us poor fuckin' soldiers can do about it.' We all knew he was right. We went our separate ways: Tommy driving, fat snowflakes as large as thumbprints melting on his windscreen, and my heart full of foreboding.

Tommy, however, remained exuberantly upbeat about the future. From this point it was simple. Bloody Sunday was a tragedy, but everything was now changed. The UN would not tolerate this kind of conduct. The British would be compelled to leave Northern Ireland and the unionists would finally realize that their true interests lay with those of the nationalists: a united Irish paradise was but a moment away.

He dropped me off at my flat, his small dark eyes shining

in that cold January night. The moment of victory is near, he assured me, as I was about to get out: and once the Protestants realize the error of their pro-British ways, our problems are over. Or, on the other hand, they could always go home to Britain. He smiled again. 'Dead simple, so it is. Never you worry Kevin. It'll be all right, so it will.'

The Republic declared a day of national mourning after Bloody Sunday, and RTÉ went into overdrive. I was seriously tempted to resign in protest at the extravagance of the RTÉ response to the massacre. The dead of Bloody Sunday were given, in broadcasting terms, a state funeral, but Bloody Sunday was not at that point the worst atrocity of the Troubles: after all, fifteen Catholics had been murdered by loyalist terrorists in the McGurk's pub bombing barely a month before. However, they had not been murdered by British soldiers, which of course made them less worthy victims than those killed by the paras. So more ancient, atavistic emotions were being evoked with high ceremony, and low farce, by the state broadcaster.

At Stormont, unionist speaker after unionist speaker, even 'moderates' in an assembly that nationalists had long since boycotted, proclaimed the glories of the union. Their minds ionized, none – not one – expressed regret for the deaths publicly, nor offered sympathy to the bereaved. In Westminster, the odious Home Secretary Reginald Maudling offered no regrets or condolences, and the British press was more indignant at the entirely justified physical attack on him on the floor of the Commons by Bernadette Devlin than it had been by Bloody Sunday. The poison of the drumlins was spreading everywhere.

A strike was called across nationalist areas in Northern Ireland for 2 February. All commercial activity – such as it was amongst the Catholic population anyway – was to cease, and no nationalist was to report for work. Across Catholic Belfast, all corner shops and pubs were shut. Taxis were not running. The few surviving unburnt buses huddled gratefully in their garages.

On this day of grieving days, peace of a fitful, desultory kind had settled on the cold city streets.

That evening we learnt there had been a shooting in Ballymurphy. The RUC press office merely confirmed that fact. Who had been shot? With what result? The RUC didn't know. We made telephone enquiries: no one could tell us anything, but happily we had our own more reliable source. As Tommy McIlroy had no phone, John McAleese drove me up there so he could tell us who had been shot.

As it happened, he couldn't. Unable to drive that day, he had been working on his taxi. He had removed one tiresome battery, and was just installing its replacement, when a nearby IRA gunman open fire on Henry Taggart Hall. The sentry returned fire at the only moving object he could see, a 'gunman' apparently peering above a car with a weapon in his hand, and shot him neatly through the head.

By the time we got there, Tommy's body was gone: but on the road next to his beloved Mercedes lay his brains, and beside them, the guilty battery.

Contrary to what the Scriptures command and the good believe, grief does not soften but hardens: bereavement begets bereavement. For all those who declare that they don't want others to suffer as they have done, there are many more for whom death merely steels the human soul. Violence is a virus that colonizes the human heart, and transmutes all emotions into a steady, focussed hate.

One of Tommy's mates, as he bore the coffin through the vile streets of Ballymurphy, kept tapping on the side and intoning Tommy's call sign, in a kind of controlled dementia: 'Come in, Number Seven, I can't hear you. Come in Number Seven …' Soon after he would leave Belfast, never to return.

But another driver – who had earlier in the Troubles been

seriously wounded by Protestants – glared at Bob Moon at the graveside, and afterwards in the pub told me it was time that a Protestant like him joined a taxi firm of his own kind: there was no place for Catholics and Protestants to be together any more.

Bob was determined to stay with the company, but the fissures within society were growing deeper and more violent by the day. He had, I think, few friends: twenty years younger than him, I was one of them. Sometimes he and I would sit in the Wellington Park Hotel, he drinking vodka and coke, me whiskey and ginger, him smoking his roll-your-own in brown, liquorice-flavoured paper, me my tipped cigarettes, which delivered slightly less poison into my system. Or sometimes he would come to my flat, and I would play Irish music, which was entirely new to him. He particularly loved Seán Ó Riada's 'Mise Éire'.

'It's like the sun, rising,' he said intuitively, not knowing that it was a lyrical paean to the 1916 Easter Rising, which in those days I think I rather regarded as a good thing. Bob was a profoundly decent and equally unhappy man. He'd had a good job in England, a nice home, no trouble; but his wife Lill had insisted that they return home to Belfast. She had then been drawn into the emotional and financial control of Oliver Cromwell White-side, the leader of one of Belfast's innumerable Protestant sects, and who could only exist in a society from which all sense of the preposterous had been excised. Bob had often dreamt of escape, but none now was possible: he was stuck in Belfast, a city he loathed, doing a dangerous job in a company where many of the workforce hated him.

There is an essential truth about Northern Ireland; there are not just two tribes, but Bob Moons galore who belong to no tribes at all. And there are numerous variations within those tribes. Within Belfast, Ardoyne Catholics were quite different from Andersonstown Catholics: for the former were more quick-tempered, prone to violence, rasher and generally less competent. Within the Protestant communities, there were numerous subdivisions between different religions, and there were geographical divisions also.

Fermanagh, for example, was colonized during the seventeenth-century plantations by immigrants from the marches between England and Scotland. These colonists – for the most border reivers – had been driven from their lands by James I, who being the first king of both Scotland and England, was the first monarch to have the authority to assert his will over the turbulent borderlands of the two countries.

Where did he send these stalwarts, with sturdy marchernames like Elliott, Armstrong and Saunderson? To guard the south-west area of conquered Ulster. They had been Anglo-Scottish Catholics when evicted from their homeplace, but were soon convinced of the wisdom of embracing the new official Protestant, Episcopalian faith in Ireland. In return for their new lands, they unquestioningly accepted the authority of the king, and buckled down to farming and to loyalty. Over three centuries later, the law-abiding quality of Fermanagh Protestants remained visible throughout the Troubles. Though goaded by ferocious terrorism emanating from the southern side of the drumlins, in Fermanagh there was little Protestant paramilitary activity in reply.

The drumlins shaped south Armagh also, but in a different direction. Few planters had been interested in moving there; and those who did either became meekly compliant with or sternly belligerent towards the natives. My maternal grandfather's medical dispensary was at the southern tip of the south Armagh salient that sticks into the Republic. When I finally took my mother to the old house where the dispensary had been – years after the period discussed here – I looked north. As far as the eye could see, across an entire quadrant, hillocks rose like the backs of swimming serpents. She stood there and memories came flooding back to her of being woken up as a little girl, night after night, by Black and Tans or IRA men, wanting her father to treat their wounds from gunbattles in those drumlins.

War was truly known here. The wars of conquest of Ulster by English and later the Anglo-Scots armies were amongst the most terrible of the sixteenth and seventeenth centuries. An early plantation by the English ended with the leader being killed by his Irish servants, who boiled his body before feeding it to their dogs. Sir Thomas Norris dealt with the problem of Rathlin Island, off Ulster's north coast, by murdering all 600 men, women and children there: more to the point, someone was counting.

The Nine Years' War of 1591–1600 was one of murder, genocide and famine, and concluded with the English General Mountjoy at the head of 14,000 soldiers laying waste to an entire landscape, slaughtering civilians, burning woodlands and destroying crops. But even then, the drumlins still had their way. The tail-ends of English patrols were regularly ambushed around the Gap of the North, the pass through the drumlins along the flank of south Armagh, and the beheaded bodies of soldiers were tied to their horses' tails and allowed return to the garrison.

The only way that the English could impose their will was by eviction and plantation, both then, and half a century later in the Cromwellian conquests. Certainly, you could steal the land, but no force on earth could wipe the memory of its theft from the minds of the natives, who withdrew to the gravel of the upper peaks of south Armagh, there to nourish their grievances for a few centuries or so.

So there was hardly a better place for protesters to gather to denounce the Bloody Sunday shootings than Newry, the once-elegant and now bomb-battered market town that provides the gateway to south Armagh. I went down there the night before to report on the prelude to the demonstration, which was expected to attract perhaps hundreds of thousands of people. I stayed in the local hotel, where the march organizers, including Bernadette Devlin, were staying. She was a strangely attractive women and though plain-featured she exuded an incredible sexual energy and an extraordinary room-filling presence, which she reinforced with a wickedly witty tongue. That night she held court in the bar, and journalists and protesters alike gathered around her in a semi-circle of courtiers, as we carpet-bombed ourselves with alcohol.

There was a shortage of rooms, and around four in the morning, I drunkenly but chastely offered to share my bed with my lesbian bedmate of the year before, and her current squeeze. The three of us fell asleep, and I woke up only to find myself having sex with the girlfriend, while my earlier chum snored vastly beside us, her mouth agape. We other two grappled clumsily towards a fairly peremptory and forgettable sexual conclusion before falling asleep again.

The next morning as I joined the demonstration, I felt my bowels had been transformed into a soup kitchen, eager to dispense large quantities of boiling hot broth all around me. Thus unable to walk alongside the marchers, I remained stationary, drooping miserably, and passed my time by counting the average number of protesters passing me per minute. In a miracle of multi-tasking, I even managed to time the march as it went by. The mathematics produced a figure of 25,000 marchers. This done, I tottered over to a council house – if walking with your knees tightly glued together can be called tottering – and weeping only slightly, I asked to use the lavatory, which I reached just in time. My cacophony shook the house: such looks I got as I left.

Later, the march and demonstration over, I met my fellow journalists, who were swapping figures. How many protesters were there? They scoffed that the police were saying 25,000, and that was clearly wrong, ho ho ho, bloody RUC liars. But I had done the sums: there were only 25,000. However, the journalistic consensus was emphatically hardening around a baseline of 100,000. I tentatively proffered the suggestion that maybe the police figure was right, to be met by the general ridicule with which social consensus is usually enforced. With my will weakened by a still-simmering colon – or perhaps just cowardice – I backed down. Either way, that evening I reported on RTÉ radio and television news that over 100,000 people had marched, which was simply a figure that had been agreed between journalists in the press centre. And this sometimes is how the media's attempt at 'truth' is arrived at.

Nights were long in Belfast, and sometimes it seemed as if it could rain incessantly for days on end. In the evening, their faces grey and shuttered, people would hurry out of their city centre workplaces, to their ghettoes or suburban homes. By nightfall the centre would be deserted. The IRA bombing campaign had closed it down; security gates limited access, and it was impossible to run a pub or a restaurant there.

Some evenings, before night and total closure finally fell, I would go to Kelly's Cellars, an eighteenth-century pub where it was said the United Irishmen had plotted their rebellion of 1798. It was still a republican meeting place, though many of its customers were now behind bars, or on the run. One evening there after work I met a young physiotherapist. Her name was Laura, and she was very beautiful. She was describing some incident on the Falls Road, and laughing loudly, declared: 'I was that scared, I near shit myself.' I found such frankness attractive. Middle-class women of my acquaintance in Dublin seldom admitted ownership of bowels – unless they wished to discuss my talents as a lover – never mind an inability to control them. We had a drink, and as we were leaving, we unexpectedly kissed. Two days later we slept together. Now I had a girlfriend, and living in west Belfast as she did, she was able to introduce me to that hitherto largely closed world.

It was, unintentionally, a vital connection. I was no longer just a journalist, but soon became a trusted boyfriend of a local girl. It was good that I had the stabilizing presence of an extremely attractive woman around, for now killings came daily, some individually, some in clusters: I grew used to seeing a scattering of bodies around the site of a bomb blast. A wand had been waved somewhere in the minds of the IRA leadership which exonerated its individuals for sending their young volunteers out to kill, and often to die in the process. It had happened before in Irish history, and the IRA had been subsequently validated by historians and politicians; and so, quite reasonably, the present generation of leaders must have thought they'd try for their own place in the history books.

Why would they not? The vilest murders in the past had been blessed with a retrospective absolution. Countess Markiewicz, the revolutionary – her name came from her unfortunate Polish husband, who soon fled her neurotic badness for the serenity of war on the eastern front – murdered an unarmed and helpless police officer, a working-class Irishman named Constable Lahiffe, in St Stephen's Green during the Easter Rising in Dublin in 1916. There is now a statue to her there – but as for poor Lahiffe, he is simply forgotten.

Such fictionalization of Irish history was a staple of Irish republicanism. IRA men had murdered scores of Protestants and Irish ex-servicemen – most of them Catholic – in the period 1919–22, and all these atrocities had been forgotten, not just by republicans, but by conventional historians also. So why should republican mythology not continue to govern a freshly emerging narrative, as it had so effortlessly mastered the official histories to date? Myth enabled; myth empowered; myth permitted, myth forgave, and, most of all, myth forgot. Is not any sin possible in such circumstances?

Naturally, new mythologies flourished. It was in the interest of the IRA that they did. Whenever an IRA bomb killed civilians, republican apologists invariably spoke of a white Ford Cortina – almost certainly a loyalist or British army undercover vehicle – behaving mysteriously before the explosion: it must therefore have been responsible. And so the white Cortina became the malignant *deus ex machina* to explain away any republican mishap. It was ubiquitous and spectral, cruising through Belfast streets like a headless horseman in a gothic horror story, and all that was ever mysterious or inconvenient could be attributed to it.

Armed loyalists and plain-clothes British soldiers were now travelling through nationalist areas in civilian cars. There were mystery shootings, night after night. Nobody knew who anybody was anymore, and though terror grew by day, when darkness fell it was almost total, and who in their right mind would freely and regularly drive round the city at such times?

Without seeking Bob Moon's advice I had bought a banger, a Renault 9, for £400, which was about £390 more than it was worth. The salesman was wheezing with laughter, on his knees and bawling helplessly for oxygen, as I drove out of the car showroom. It was only a week later when I got a flat tyre that I discovered I hadn't even been given a spare. Shortly afterwards, the paintwork blossomed in scores of little rusty waterblisters, like spots on a particularly accursed adolescent. I was so embarrassed at my foolishness in buying such a heap of ferrous crap that I didn't dare take it back.

Moreover, it was flatulent. Sometimes when I put my foot on the accelerator, the engine would go silent, almost thoughtful, as the car slowed down on the point of stalling. Then it would emit a vast explosive fart, before surging off with a great, satisfied grin on its wretched, empty gallic bonnet. The engine, as heavy as an anvil, and with as much power as a butterfly, was in the back, all the better for flipping the car round in the opposite direction to the one intended.

The occasional friend would come up from Dublin, to gaze in awe and horror at the sight of a city spiralling into a pagan savagery, and I would usually give each of them a guided tour, before they fled, never to return. One winter's night I took a college friend on the old circuit. Why? Oh the usual reasons, but most of all, because I was now addicted to the terrors of the unknown in Belfast: its dark was an allure, a terrible mystery, a source of evil that I could only match by encountering and defeating it at every opportunity.

That night I took my friend on the city tour, a bleak down-pour lashing the streets. In the unlit streets sodden soldiers in dripping capes halted cars, looked purposelessly within, and waved them on. Waters washed in gutters made weary with their flow. Belfast was dreary and cold, a seventeenth-century religious conflict bottled in a late twentieth-century industrial decline, a bleak new experiment in purposeless war.

We drove through the control-zones between Catholic areas and Protestant areas, where no one but the security forces ever travelled at night – no one, that is, apart from me. Finally, I drove once again down towards Henry Taggart Hall, turning off my headlights on my approach, as one always did. With only the sidelights on, the Renault eased over the speed ramps outside the sangar containing the sentry, and then right on cue it backfired – *crack!* – before stalling, stone dead. Jesus.

Backfires had often attracted fatal gunfire in Belfast, and here was I perched on a speed ramp beside the most fired-at sentry post in Ireland. Grinning through inanely clenched teeth, I turned on the engine. Nothing happened. I tried again, press-ing the accelerator hard; and the engine burst into life with a series of short, sharp explosive bangs that sounded precisely like the Browning 9mm my old shoulder-to-shoulder friend used to favour me with. Yards away, invisible, a British soldier was calmly making a decision about my life.

The car moved forward, then backfired loudly, and stalled again. Jesus. What was I to do? I was nearly paralysed with ter-ror, and outside it was dark dark dark, not just here, but across Belfast, and vertically upwards, a deep black to the very edge of the universe. And now in this fathomless vault, lit only by the sidelights on my car, with the frayed rubbers of my wipers forlornly trying to wipe the Niagara from my screen, I had to decide how I should manage this crisis. If I got out of the car, how would the sentry respond? In his shoes, what would I have done? In his shoes, I would already be dead behind the wheel.

I had no choice but to start the engine again. My companion sat rigid as a corpse beside me, whispering in terror, his pallor dimly luminous in the utter dark. I turned the ignition, and the engine burst into life. Then I drove slowly away, sending a single sharp bang in farewell. Behind me stood a young working-class British soldier on sentry-go whose name I will never know, who was sitting in the most fired-on place in western Europe, and who had stoically and unflinchingly endured the gunfire-like sounds from a stationary car at point-blank range, without firing once. By such men is civilization made.

Meanwhile it was being unmade by others. I had been on the scene of multiple deaths before, but nothing so far quite matched that in March 1972, the week before my twenty-fifth birthday. Once again, my alert antenna had caused me to ring the RUC press office at just the right moment: 'We have just heard reports of a bomb scare in the Donegall Street area', said the man on duty – 'no way of knowing whether it's genuine'.

RTÉ's offices were five minutes walk away, and where danger waited, I duly went: the bomb went off as I drew near. The strange thing about most accounts of war is that they contain so few references to the smell of death: but it was an odour that most powerfully assailed my senses now as I walked through the billowing clouds of brick-dust and across the carpet of broken glass.

In biology class at school, just a handful of years before, I had regularly dissected recently killed rabbits. The stench from their still-warm abdomens was terrible: sweet, sickly and cloyingly pervasive. And it was the smell of rabbit entrails that now filled Donegall Street, in part vanilla, in part raw steak, in part anus-fresh excrement: the lingering aromatic remains of what had been human beings moments before, and now were scarlet pebbledash. The smell persisted in my nostrils all day: sometimes, when I think about Donegall Street, even now.

Seven men – a van driver, two RUC policemen, three street sweepers and an octogenarian French polisher, Henry Miller – were killed in this IRA explosion. My horror was mixed with indignation as I wondered: if the RUC press office had mentioned Donegall Street as a location for the bombing, why was Donegall Street not cleared? Had the RUC deliberately permitted the bomb to go off in a crowded area?

Conspiracy theories are the most seductive of all explanations, because they require no intellectual input, and they satisfy pre-existing emotional needs. I was a socialist: my instinctive sympathies were with working-class organizations that declared that they were on the side of the working class. The IRA called itself socialist: the RUC most certainly was not socialist. So part of me wanted to believe that the IRA could not have intended this: surely, the RUC must share some of the blame?

The human brain can believe anything it wants to, regardless of the evidence. Two brave RUC men – one of them a Catholic – had actually been killed trying to clear Donegall Street when the bomb went off, which finally satisfied me that the police shared no blame. But shamefully, for a while I had actually believed it possible they did. More importantly, common sense didn't stop the IRA blaming the RUC for the massacre, and worse, being believed. This became the accompanying mantra to every IRA atrocity henceforth: its enemies were responsible for the consequences of its deeds. Not even Clausewitz in all his melancholy adumbrations about war had predicted such perversity becoming a consistent strategy. Needless to say, these dreadful killings by the IRA did not trigger the outpouring of grief that Bloody Sunday had.

Being young and vaguely intellectual, I instinctively sought refuge in modish left views about 'progressive' working-class movements – such as the IRA. Though I knew it was wildly wrong-headed in tactics, I somehow or other thought that its motives were honourable, and that it was politically preferable to 'reactionary' and 'fascist' working-class movements – namely loyalist paramilitaries. The confusion was compounded by the way they expressed themselves; loyalists discussed their activities through uneducated grunts, but republicans articulated themselves with verbal splendour and intellectual ersatz-Marxism. Morally, each spoke the common heathen Esperanto of Cain.

Six

BY LATE MARCH 1972 the British government had grown tired of the grotesque effrontery of the Northern Ireland government at Stormont directing policy (and the British army) in the Province, and abolished it. Unionists were perplexed, astounded, indignant: they had grown used to this absurd dependency status, wherein for fifty years they had been given capital grants by the British government, and had even been lent the British army, but nonetheless expected the British to have little or no say in the conduct of policy. What had once been a favour had over time become a right, and you do not easily remove a perceived right from a Calvinistic Covenanter – well, not without using large earth-moving machinery, and much blood, sweat and tears.

The night that Stormont was suspended, I walked up that heartland of Protestant sensitivity, the Shankill Road, to test the mood. I had expected maddened crowds, as there usually were when loyalist power had gone down another notch, but this night there weren't. Instead groups of men stood at street corners, glaring angrily. Had any of them discovered a reporter from Dublin wandering all alone, I would probably have been torn limb from limb as a spy.

I walked into the Eagle chip shop, which was beneath the headquarters of the Ulster Volunteer Force, the illegal paramilitary organization whose existence was now effectively tolerated in an utterly one-sided security policy. The Eagle, justifiably, was believed to be one of the best chip shops in Belfast.

In my strange accent I chatted away about how quiet the road was, before sauntering past the groups of leather-jacketed young men simmering with ire, back to my car, parked in a side street at the bottom of the Shankill Road. I was, deliberately, testing my nerve: that is, going just a little mad.

The Protestant fuse, however, was burning. Two days later thousands of loyalists marched to protest against the ending of their parliament. They halted outside a small nationalist area of Short Strand and began to chant, in raucous unison: 'Fuck the Virgin Mary, Fuck the Virgin Mary'.

A line of RUC officers stood between the marchers and the Catholic enclave. Behind the policemen stood some soldiers, whose officer went over and spoke to the senior RUC officer to protest at this obscenity. I was able to hear him demanding that the RUC officer deploy his men to move the loyalist crowds on, and to make arrests if they refused.

The RUC officer declined, as the baying increased. 'Very well,' said the British officer, 'I will get my men to move these bastards myself.'

'You will not', replied the RUC man. 'I have operational command here, and this crowd is not to be interfered with.' As I witnessed the confrontation, I actually thought the officer, a young major, was close to hitting the RUC man or even unholstering his sidearm.

'This is a fucking scandal,' he said finally. 'I did NOT join this fucking army to see bigoted mobs rule our streets. This is a disgrace and you are a fucking disgrace, and by God if things were just a bit different I would shoot you for what you're doing here today.' With that he returned to his men, chalk-white with anger; and almost as if the mob had sensed what was going on, the chanting got worse and more obscene, while the besieged nationalists huddled in their houses.

And then a door burst open, and an antic, drunken figure appeared, shouting: 'Up the IRA!' That figure was Joseph Downey, and for his single act of verbal defiance to the Orange mob, he was promptly arrested and taken away by the RUC, despite the strong protests of the army officer, who now seemed close to murder.

No doubt the RUC officer might have been right not to interfere with the Orange crowd, which was a hair-trigger away from being a mob. But it was inexcusable to have charged Joseph Downey, who later appeared in Belfast Magistrates Court. Medical evidence was given which established that he had the mental age of a seven-year-old. He was, nonetheless, sentenced to six months' imprisonment.

Two weeks later John McErlean and his friends were turned into a jumble of tissue and bones in the tiny nationalist estate of Bawnmore, in north Belfast. Steam and smoke were still rising from their bodies when I arrived at the scene. The remains looked less human than like badly dismembered cattle blown apart by lightning, and from them came once again that terrible odour of entrails. This time it was accompanied by a smell that I had encountered only once before, in childhood, when my father had accidentally pressed a red-hot car cigarette-lighter onto his thumb, burning it terribly. Scorched human flesh has a particular fragrance all of its own.

David McKittrick's *Lost Lives* records the reasons for and the consequences of this tragedy. John McErlean's family was non-political. His father Jack had served in the RAF during the Second World War, as had many uncles, and one – a company sergeant major – had been killed in action in Italy. Jack had then served in the British Territorial Army and, when it was formed – and as Catholic leaders had urged – the Ulster Defence Regiment.

Three days after Bloody Sunday, his son and the boy's two best friends, all as thick as thieves, joined the IRA. It behaved with its customary care towards the young, the foolish, the naive, and promptly ordered them to move weeping gelignite. Thus their end.

The ex-serviceman Jack McErlean was asked by the police to identify the possible remains of his son.

'Under the first sheet was the top half of one of the lads, just the upper torso, all covered in cement dust. Under the next sheet there was nothing recognizable, just a heap of flesh and an evil smell. The next one was the same, a big steel tray. The only identifiable piece of a human being was a human tongue sitting on top of it all.'

I have no way of knowing whether Jack McErlean's appalling account of this monstrous police insensitivity is accurate, but it could well have been. All here were humans, all with ionized consciences and perceptions, morally spiralling downwards in judgment, deed and decision in our common pool of insanity, and the spiral continued long after John McErlean's fragmentary remains – and those of his companions' – were lowered into their graves.

The IRA tried to make its usual necrophiliac bonanza of the funerals, but was told to fuck off. But this made no difference: the terminal damage, reaching back to Bloody Sunday and beyond was now done, and a larger Bawnmore tragedy was only now beginning. Firstly, the father of one of the dead boys went into deep depression and, as is often the way of bereavement, soon afterwards died.

Bawnmore, a tiny, passive Catholic community in a sea of Protestants, had not been involved in the Troubles, but was now wrongly labelled as an active IRA area. Loyalist paramilitaries were invariably drawn to soft Catholic targets, like jackals to the wounded fawn, and Bawnmore was the easiest, safest target in the world.

In late 1972 Joe McCrystal, the 28-year-old brother of one of the Bawnmore three was shot dead by loyalists when walking from home. Some time later, loyalists ambushed a two-door car carrying five young people from Bawnmore. The two in the front rolled out, but the three sitting in the back were trapped as machine-gun fire ripped into them. One of the two killed was Thomas Donaghy, aged sixteen. And the other was Margaret McErlean, just eighteen, daughter of Jack, sister of John.

The third person in the back seat was a teenage girl whose brother had been killed in the Bawnmore IRA explosion. She was shot twelve times, but miraculously she survived, and in time got married and had a child. Eleven years later, in 1983 her husband David Nocher was shot dead by loyalists while he cleaned a shop-window.

All this I know now, but didn't even vaguely grasp those parts that were knowable at the time. For in our various newsrooms we were being overwhelmed by a blizzard of facts and atrocities, lies and propaganda, from all sides, and it was simply impossible to tell truth from fantasy, fact from fiction, patterns from chaos and all too often, life from death, as the Ford Cortina and the headless horseman careened through our lives.

The day after the Bawnmore explosion I met the hero of the Official IRA, Big Joe McCann. He had entered nationalist folklore after leading his unit into Inglis's bakery in the Markets area close to the city centre on the night of internment, and challenging the British army to evict him. The affair was encapsulated by a picture of him kneeling beside the traditional Irish socialist flag, the starry plough, with an M1 carbine in his hand, illuminated by a burning car. The picture crossed the world, and the banana-shape of the magazine on the M1 made it look vaguely like an AK 47, one of the revolutionary-chic logos of the time.

The Official IRA was at that time the more glamorous of the two IRAs: it spoke a dialect of Marxism with reasonable fluency, and had contacts with revolutionary groups across Europe. So Joe McCann, its hero, was the embodiment of revolutionary glamour.

I had got to know Brenda, a sister of his wife Ann, while reporting on troubles in the Markets area. She took me to meet Joe during one of his rare trips from his current base somewhere near the Border. We went to his home in Turf Lodge, where he was nonchalantly picking dirt from between his toes, and rolling it into little balls, which he flicked into the fireplace. We didn't shake hands.

He was dressed like a student, even wearing a college scarf. He had dyed his hair flaxen, and was wearing steel-rimmed spectacles, which he only needed as disguise. He was incredibly handsome, and equally charismatic: his presence, like his feet, filled the room.

He looked me directly in the eye when we talked, which few working-class Catholics ever did. His manner was almost academic, studied, shrewd. He was the same age as me, but seemed to possess an innate wisdom, a gravitas greatly beyond our common years. Far from resenting this intrusion by a complete stranger on one of the few occasions when he could get home, he was warm and welcoming.

He told me of the narrow escape he'd had that morning. He was walking towards the Markets when he ran into Harry Taylor, the legendary RUC Special Branchman. They instantly recognized one another. Joe McCann drew a small .22 pistol, but Harry Taylor, who had a notorious aversion to violence, was unarmed. Joe told the officer not to move, or he'd shoot.

Joe hijacked a bus, complete with passengers, and suggested a few small changes in itinerary to the driver, which took him to the Falls Road taxis and so home.

Hold on a second, I chimed in. If Harry Taylor knows you're back in Belfast, won't the police come looking for wherever you might be? Namely, here?

He bathed me in the glow of a warm smile of congratulation. Exactly, said the smile. He began to put on his socks and then stood up. 'Which is why we're going out for a wee drink.'

Ann shook her head philosophically. She had a child or two to mind. Joe had made the effort to see her. Now he must go. Joe, Brenda and I got into my car.

I asked: 'Where are we going?'

Joe replied: 'Where they're sure I'm not. The Markets.'

I turned on the ignition, and the car backfired like an SLR rifle. 'Jesus fucking Christ,' Joe laughed, 'and here's me, thinking I was that fucking wise getting a lift off a reporter. How the fuck are you still alive driving around Belfast in this here one-man gunbattle?'

We drove to the Markets, to an illegal drinking club, where I was treated with the reverence due the equerry of a prince. Joe had a curiously ironic and knowing sense of humour, rather like a very cleverly subversive undergraduate. He began to sing the American country and western patriotic anthem. 'Okie from Muskogee.' 'They don't burn Old Glory in Muskogee,' he warbled, a big broad and ironic grin on his face as he finished. In his world – and in a way mine at the time too – to fight for your country if it was the USA was wrong: to fight for anything that was Irish was, of course, right.

As we later drank a pint or twelve, he cast his strangely gentle eyes on me: 'You ever see any action?'

'Some,' I admitted. And, always hesitant to hesitate, I added, 'like the soldier being shot in Cromac Square.'

'Bankier,' he said, 'Robert Bankier. What did you see of it?'

'Nothing of the actual shooting itself. I arrived in a taxi just after he was hit.'

'Ah. So that was you, aye?'

I bowed my head. This was trust indeed, concerning the most terrible deed I had seen in my entire life. Yet charmed by Joe's charisma, in his presence I was almost agnostic about its morality, as if the death of a young man – and one I happened to know about more than almost anyone else in the world – was an ethically negotiable event.

Joe paused: 'Did he suffer much?'

'No,' I said – I think truthfully, 'I don't think he suffered at all.'

'That's good. I was hoping he didn't suffer.'

'But he had a wife and children …'

'He had, aye, and so have I.'

I had neither, and was certainly not willing to moralize with Joe McCann. No indeed: here was a man I liked and intended to cultivate and even befriend. He was one of the most fascinating men I had ever met, and moreover, he was yet another working-class Belfast-man who seemed to like me. I have no memory of how we agreed to meet again at the end of that Saturday night, but I know we did so with fond assurances of mutual affection.

The following Saturday, stupidly repeating the very same route he had taken towards the Markets on the day that I had met him, Joe McCann, this time unarmed, walked into a waiting ambush by paratroopers, who, not being the gentlemanly Harry Taylor, simply shot him dead. Or, you could say, murdered him.

The circumstances of his death were beyond doubt, but certainly not reproach, which nationalist Belfast proceeded to administer in its own particular way. The violence that followed centred on an area of Lower Falls commanded by Divis Flats, a vile assembly of tower blocks with long lines of open balconies overlooking the street below. The previous night the departing regiment, the Glosters, had indulged the usual last-night ritual of smashing a few republican flats, and giving a hammering to any youths rash enough to fall into their hands.

Joe McCann's death ignited the tinderbox bequeathed by the Glosters' farewell. Rioters took control over Divis Street, hijacking and burning buses, and erecting barricades. Fresh troops were arriving just as I did. I climbed up the stairs onto one of the balconies, where I beheld a vision of hell: fifteen-year-old boys with sub-machine guns and semi-automatic rifles. They were gathered beside one of the now disused lift shafts, and were receiving orders from some infant-Rommel, whom I later learnt was called Gerard Steenson.

With a roar, and barely able to carry their heavy Garand rifles, they suddenly rushed to the balcony on which I was standing, and opened fire, some firing from the shoulder, some from the hip, at targets over a hundred yards away, which was silly enough. But worse still was the fact that some were trying to fire unaimed shots from the hip through the gaps in the concrete balustrades along the balcony, while standing several feet back, and generally speaking they were hitting the concrete bits, and not the spaces in between.

Bullets were ricocheting everywhere, as these demented children emptied magazine after magazine into anything and everything, yet amazingly not themselves, while I pioneered a brand-new commando-skidaddle along the balcony floor. Once I'd put some distance between the gunboys and myself, I peered over the balcony. There were no soldiers left in view, just a single Humber Pig APC lumbering towards the flats. Hideous volleys of bullets from a dozen infant-held guns slammed against its side and nose, and indeed over half the street as well. It stopped, paused for about half a minute, and then reversed.

On the balcony, the children cheered, waving their huge rifles: inside the APC, 2nd Lieutenant Nicholas Hull lay dying. Incredibly, a chance round had passed through an observation slit and fatally injured him. He had been commissioned into the regiment the day before, and this was his very first posting. He had arrived from Britain at Belfast docks with his new unit only minutes earlier, had immediately got into an armoured personnel carrier, and had gone directly into action, to be shot the very moment he arrived. No subaltern in the Great War could have had such a tragically short military career. Needless to say, according to all the predictive rules of dramatic tragedy, his mother was a widow who now had but one son left to cherish, a soldier in the same regiment.

Not long afterwards, a British army press officer told me that they were very worried about this IRA super-sniper who could put bullets through such tiny apertures at such huge ranges. I told him of the mobs of maddened youngsters with guns, firing suicidally from the balconies, which of course he could not have known about. 'Oh, really,' he said, 'that's a bit of a relief.'

No one, least of all me, could have seen or understood what those youngsters – and one in particular – portended: that the virus of evil had leapt a generation, and that new leaders, unskilled, brutal and inured to violence, were now emerging. None of us saw the future; we had trouble keeping up with the present.

The air that night around Divis Flats was filled with a vast volume of noise as murderously inept people shot unsuccessfully at one another. I retired, and with a couple of friends up from Dublin, went to a Sinn Féin drinking club in the tiny national-ist ghetto of Short Strand. I found myself talking to a gaunt and deeply stupid nineteen-year-old. He drank a particular brand of Scotch whisky – highly unusual amongst Catholics who normally drank Irish whiskey – with a steady and undeviating devotion, accompanied by an equally unbroken devotion to Park Drive ciga-rettes. This boy was a nervous wreck. His hands shook throughout the evening. 'You've got expensive tastes,' I told him.

'You got to live,' he said unsmilingly. Funnily enough, even in those days people smiled. But he never did. His name, he told me between puffs of smoke, and long draughts of Scotch, was Martin Engelen.

That Saturday, we three fools from Dublin finished the night in a working-class club by regaling an uncomprehending audi-ence with 'The Internationale'.

The following Monday, British paratroopers shot two unarmed, student teachers as they emerged from a school near Divis Flats for their lunch break, killing one, twenty year old Patrick Magee. That same lunchtime, other paratroopers killed a one-eyed 86-year-old bachelor, Patrick Donaghy, in his flat in Divis.

At the old man's inquest all the soldiers – remarkably – testified that they had seen gunsmoke at the window and all – remarkably – had fired at it. The coroner – remarkably – concluded, without any further evidence whatsoever, that gunmen had taken over the flat, had fired at the soldiers, who had returned fire, and had hit Patrick who therefore must have been – remarkably – (and rather gallantly, to my mind) standing alongside the gunmen, no doubt directing them with his one good octogenarian eye.

Let us pause in this litany of killings for some reflection, and the first point is, that what is quite clearly obvious now was not so obvious then. Belfast had become clinically insane, and no documentary details can convey the spirit of the times. Those simple bonds of faith and trust of broader communities – attenuated enough in Belfast – were now finally severed. It was possible to believe almost anything of the other side, wherever that other side lay. Any fantasy could drive policy, any paranoia could shape doctrine.

Thus at the most primitive forensic level, in the coroner's court, the pursuit of truth was transformed into a grisly charade whose sole function was to cover up for the men who had coldly slaughtered a half-blind old man in his home, and it had done so with the most fanciful confection of lies. Yet I don't doubt the coroner genuinely believed he was doing his duty towards finding that truth.

It is more than just a matter of ionized brains. There is also policy. When the state surrenders its submission to the rule of law so blatantly as it did in the McCann, Magee and Donaghy killings in rapid succession, it is quite clear that either no central will is imposing authority, or the central will is going the opposite direction, and is deliberately embracing state terrorism. Back then I would have said it was a state conspiracy, because I was a lefty, and lefties prefer to believe in conspiracies, because they're neat, and most of all, they need no compelling evidence *because all evidence has been removed by the conspirators.*

I know now that the opposite was the truth. There was no conspiracy, though there was an outrageous, inexcusable inattention to what the Parachute Regiment was doing almost as a matter of policy. But inattention defined British army doctrine of the time. At the most basic military level, there was almost no continuity between units. The Anglians, who replaced the Glosters on the Falls Road, would have inherited a few intelligence files, but few suggestions about personal conduct, patrolling patterns, or managing local relations. Thus wisdom was not accumulated but dissipated, with the cyclical movement of battalions.

It is not good enough to find fault with the British only. In the week or so around the three state killings cited here, the IRA murdered four young British soldiers on duty. Worse yet, a fifth, a 36-year-old Protestant father of three, James Elliott, an off-duty, part-time soldier in the locally recruited Ulster Defence Regiment, was kidnapped by the IRA as he delivered drinks in south Armagh and was held for two days, enduring untold, unimaginable horrors. Finally, he was butchered, and his body was then booby-trapped and surrounded with claymore mines – the devices the British army was sure the IRA would never have. This was evil incarnate, yet then – and probably even now – would not have been recognized as such by the republican community.

The kill ratio in terms of real players over this period (including Lieutenant Hull) stood 6 – 1 in the IRA's favour, and those few days in April 1972 provided the template for much of the Troubles. Because in addition to these killings, two young men were shot by loyalists in Belfast for the crime of being Catholic; a 65-year-old Protestant woman in Ballymoney was burnt alive for the crime of being in her flat when the IRA left a bomb outside it; a schoolboy was fatally injured by a rubber bullet in the course of rioting in Belfast, and the IRA murdered an alleged informer.

I went to Derry with a camera crew for a few days, because it was quiet there, and RTÉ thought I needed a break. It is a small city, properly renowned for the friendliness of its people. By this time, the nationalist areas were controlled by the IRA, beyond the rule of British law or the British army, which watched from its distant vantage points on the city's high seventeenth-century walls.

I spent one evening in the Bogside Inn, drinking with members of the Official IRA, who I found to be bright and intelligent people, and good company. As I was leaving, all was quiet: then suddenly a single shot rang from the city walls. A British soldier had fired down into the Bogside from the city walls, hitting a fifteen-year-old boy, Manus Deery right in the head a few feet away from me. He had no gun, just a bag of chips for his family, which now lay scattered beside his body. Now his skull was broken open like a coconut in a shy, blood pouring out of both ears and his mouth: some brave man tried to breathe life through the bubbling red torrents, but in vain.

Two nights later I was back in the same pub, again talking to the same group of men. One told me proudly about a booby trap of his that had killed two soldiers, and word had spread through the Bogside about who was responsible; wherever he went, people shook his hand and slapped his back – a good job well done. Murder was now acclaimed, its authors gaining status, with hatred the vital bond that held smaller communities together.

Soon after I left them that night, mere minutes, those same men got their hands on a local teenager serving with the British army, William Best, home on leave from the Royal Irish Rangers, which had no security duties in Northern Ireland. But he was a British soldier, and hadn't a British soldier killed Manus Deery? And so they killed him.

Regardless of all calls from 'slobbering moderates', one of those fine fellows declared the next day, 'While British gunmen operate on the streets of the Six Counties, the IRA will take action against them.'

The murder of William Best caused an outcry in Creggan, which just shows how hard a poor terrorist's life can be; because not long before, the same gentlemen from the Official IRA had captured an English soldier visiting his pregnant Irish wife in the Bogside, and had decided to release him on compassionate grounds. And there was outcry about that too, the Provisional IRA denouncing the act as 'despicable'.

As it happened, some years later, the Provisionals murdered a twenty-year-old British soldier named Christopher Watson who was visiting his wife, a local girl from the Bogside, to comfort her following a stillbirth, but without the popular indignation which followed the Best killing. Presumably – according to local mores, whatever they are – it was wholly acceptable to widow a local woman who had just lost a child, but unacceptable to murder a local young male. No doubt there is consistency of a sort there, and one that many of the Bogsiders fully appreciated, because there wasn't a peep of protest over the murder of young Chris Watson or the pain and heartbreak caused to his already grief-stricken widow.

I was back in Belfast from Derry just in time for a spectacular IRA catastrophe. Eight people were killed when a bomb being prepared in the heart of the Short Strand exploded prematurely. Four of the dead were IRA men, and one of those was Martin Engelen, the youngster with the compulsively shaking hands. His death notice declared he was a lieutenant in the IRA, as indeed were the other three. This officer-only army had no qualms about commissioning a twitching simpleton like poor Martin Engelen, and then, of all things, putting him to work in the bomb-making business.

Naturally the IRA blamed loyalists for the massacre, declaring a suspicious car had been seen in the area shortly beforehand. It was, of course, a white Cortina. For now the gyre had widened. The falcon could not hear the falconer. People believed in their own mad myths and now each tribe had its own historical and contemporary injustices to avenge.

Seven

THE PRELUDE to serious war, as so often is the case, was an attempt to find peace. In the summer of 1972, the British government entered into secret talks with the IRA, and probably knowing as much about Irish history as it did about Pluto's moons, thought the outcome would be a negotiated settlement on God alone knows what terms – knighthoods for a handful of IRA leaders, invitations to the Buckingham Palace Garden Party, and season tickets at Lords for the South Armagh brigade, perhaps?

To the IRA, talks meant only one thing: agreement on a timetable for British disengagement, to be negotiated in 1972 for Northern Ireland as it had been for the Free State half a century before. For just as the Chinese soothsayers consult astral charts to plot a safer future, Irish republicans consult old calendars to do the same. Fifty years: a nice historical ring to it.

There was a not a single point where their minds or their vocabularies could have met. We know now, but really did not know then, what was going on. Mutually baffled, mutually angered, the two sides soon parted, the IRA to prepare for war, which it relished, and the British to prepare for whatever it is they do as they fumble their way to failure.

But it was by this time, emphatically, no longer a largely two-sided war. Now there was a serious third force, though there was, everywhere, a huge reluctance to accept the reality that the leviathan of Protestant opinion was turning to the bomb and gun, as dead Catholics were being found most mornings in loyalist areas. I made a television news item about the series of lethal attacks on Catholic bars, which RTÉ then refused to run because I couldn't 'prove' that they were by loyalists. After all, no one had been convicted, had they?

The desire not to detect the shadow of a Protestant Caliban slouching into the room was ubiquitous, and united the IRA with the British army and government. The atrocious bombing of McGurk's bar in which fifteen Catholics were murdered was blamed by the British, ludicrously, on the IRA. So too was the equally horrific loyalist bombing of Kelly's bar, just up the road from Henry Taggart Hall. In the ensuing multi-sided gunbattles between the loyalist paramilitary organizations such as the Ulster Defence Association and the Ulster Volunteer Force, both IRAs and the British army, five people – including another Tommy McIlroy – died. The idea that a major loyalist terrorist offensive was under way was simply unacceptable to the British.

As it was to republicans. The idea of a concerted and armed Protestant resistance to an Irish Republic was ideological heresy; therefore this alleged 'loyalist' terrorism must be the work of the British. Not quite taking the same tack, a Northern Ireland Office spokesman told me in all apparent sincerity: 'What we haven't been able to work out yet is how the IRA is able to dump all its Catholic victims in loyalist areas.'

Protestant cleaning women in our offices had an answer to that mystery with their own version of the Catholic car-myth. Each night, they said, IRA cars – dark blue Cortinas, because they were almost invisible – full of the dead bodies of IRA men killed fighting the British were driven around loyalist areas, where the corpses would be dumped, so that the innocent Protestant communities – which of course never did any harm to anyone – could be then blamed. On a quiet night, the myth continued, there were so many IRA casualties that the Cortinas couldn't cope, and you could even hear the sound of monks in Clonard Monastery digging graves for IRA corpses, using spades with their blades wrapped in blankets, while nuns mumbled the rosary, and muffled bells rang at two in the morning, to toll the secret dead.

As in every war it has ever fought, the British army believed that it was killing more of its enemy than it was actually was. Therefore, in the absence of many public funerals in the North, it believed that secret republican burials were occurring in the Republic. But the same story was told the other way round: IRA men were also convinced that they had killed more soldiers than had been acknowledged, and that in English towns soldiers were buried without ceremony, the local press sworn to secrecy. These myths became, remained and persist as abiding 'truths'.

The IRA ceasefire occurred on 25 June 1972; and far from the tension easing in Belfast and elsewhere, it dramatically increased. The various ghettoes erected barricades, and outsiders approached those borders at their peril. Two who did were Gerald McCrea and James Howell, both Catholic car dealers. They were captured by the Ulster Defence Association somewhere around the lower Shankill Road where they had – unbelievably – gone to sell a rather special car that McCrea owned.

Gerald McCrea's body was found near the loyalist Forthriver Road. He had been hooded and shot. James Howell's body, also hooded and shot, was found in the back of Gerald McCrea's car, a powder-blue Mercedes. McCrea had bought it from Susan McIlroy, whose husband Tommy – yes, my taxi driver – had been killed while changing batteries. He of course had bought it from an insurance company after its previous owner had been killed. Gerald McCrea and his best friend had been murdered trying to sell it.

The car was now unsellable in Belfast. It was advertised in a Dublin newspaper at a ridiculously low price, and a man caught the train up to buy it from the McCrae estate. It would have been the bargain of his lifetime if, in his exuberance at getting such a high-powered car so cheap, he hadn't try to get home too quickly. He lost control on a bend near Drogheda, hit a tree and was killed.

Belfast was now like that Mercedes: cursed from on high, and violent and terrible death awaited the unwary at every turn and every hour. There was a stampede out of the city centre each evening, before the various vigilantes established their little empires, within which stragglers caught away from home could – and often did – face torture and death.

Each morning brought a harvest of bodies of the stupid, the unlucky and the gullible who had died terribly. Protestants and Catholics were equally likely to fall victim to this lethal mood. An Englishman called Paul Jobling was picked up and murdered by the UDA merely because he was staying with a Catholic. Two Protestant brothers, Malcolm and Peter Orr, set out to meet their Catholic girlfriends, in Malcolm's newly bought car. It wouldn't start. So they walked from their home on Alliance Road, and were captured and shot dead by men of the Ardoyne IRA. This was the same group that had been responsible for the first double slaying of brothers when they had murdered the three off-duty Scottish soldiers.

I spoke to the Orr brothers' parents shortly after these murders. They were decent, quiet and incredulous: the worst thing in the world had happened to them, and they behaved with an extraordinary dignity and courage. They didn't have an idea who had murdered their boys – they even thought it was possible that loyalists had killed them because of the lads' friendship with Catholics. I wanted to believe that loyalists were responsible. That the IRA would murder two such blameless boys because of their religion seemed in violation of everything that Irish republicanism was supposed to stand for. This merely indicated my naivety, and almost everyone else's misunderstanding of Irish history. Murdering people for their religion was what Irish republicans had always done, especially in their most celebrated period, 1919–22. Only the successful seizure of Irish historiography by republicans had concealed this vital truth.

Yet strangely, the terror of these times was associated with a heady jubilance and a giddy sense of self. In Protestant areas, UDA men proudly took to the streets in a garbled version of identity. They adopted desert-warfare slouch hats, but their attenuated view of their military self had come through the filter of American television programmes. Despite their almost universal claims of having served time in the armed forces of the crown, their many, many lieutenant-colonels pronounced this rank as 'lootenant-colonel', thus failing the first shibboleth of true, militarily aware Britishness.

I took Laura to a UDA night rally in east Belfast, introducing her as Lill, daughter of an army officer. I was invited to walk a line of UDA men under the command of an individual called John Haveron, the sort of despicable insect that times of distress sometimes propel to power. Laura had the poise and self-confidence to become perhaps the only working-class Catholic girl from west Belfast to solemnly inspect the ranks of the UDA, pretending to be a Protestant with army connections. Just about every 'officer' we met was a 'lootenant' or a 'lootenant colonel': no NCOs, no majors, no captains, and all demanding British rights, without understanding how British 'lefts' are pronounced.

On the nationalists' side, the ignorance was comparable about their parent identity. Almost no one in west Belfast who wanted a united Ireland could have named a single Irish government minister of the time. Irishness was a mental tribe, a sense of self that was almost entirely free of mere documentary detail or dogged, diurnal duty.

And this sense of identity was rising in intensity, reaching into a feverish lunacy. Laura took me to a vast beer hall in Andersonstown, where long-haired youngsters with their pints of lager were celebrating the musical rituals of their tribe. One ballad went,

> *British soldiers came to Belfast to shoot the people down,*
> *They thought the IRA was dead in dear Old Belfast town,*
> *But they got a rude awakening from the rifles and grenades,*
> *Of the fighting first battalion of the Belfast Brigade.*

At which all members of the IRA's first battalion in the drinking hall would rise, and with one finger raised in the air, sing,

> *Glory, Glory to Old Ireland. Glory Glory to Old Ireland.*
> *Glory, Glory to old Ireland and the Fighting First*
>   *Battalion of the Belfast Brigade.*

The next verse would belong to the second battalion, with their two fingers, and so on. This was a giddy mixture of a regimental mess night and an identification line-up, but surely not the birth of a deadly guerrilla army. For British intelligence purposes it could scarcely have been bettered – though I think that British intelligence at this time was still in the traps.

'Even if you couldn't speak a word of English, you could still hear the hatred in that man's voice,' the wonderful fiddler Frankie Kennedy once said of one the most popular ballad singers of the time, Eamon Largie. It was true. When Largie sang 'Boolavogue', his voice trembled with an uncontrollable loathing of England, which of course explains his popularity – at that time far greater than that of Frankie Kennedy, who was unusual in being both passionately engaged in Irish culture, but aloof from and even disdainful towards the insane republican agenda.

Through the weeks of that hot and terrible summer I would drink in the Old House, just off the Falls Road. On weekday evenings the company of working-class people there was as intelligent and as well read as any I have met since, and on Saturday nights, in the upstairs room there was music and a defiant sense of gaiety and fun. It was not – I would gather – the giddy heroism of the London Blitz, to be sure, nor anything like: but its emotions, and pleasures were kindred ones.

One evening, a girl rose from the audience to the platform, and at the first note from her throat, the pub went silent as ice, almost stilled by the will of God, while she sang 'My Lagan Love'. I have never in my life heard a singer so captivate an audience, and afterwards, having missed her name on introduction, I fought my way through the crowd surrounding her to request it. 'Rose McCartney,' she replied, smiling, before turning to acknowledge her other admirers. There were many.

Such nights could not conceal the other drumbeat realities that were daily gathering, though we knew nothing of either the IRA talks in London, or their failure. A dispute erupted over the relocation of a Catholic family into a Housing Executive – that is, a publicly owned – house in a Protestant area in the new and leafy suburb of Lenadoon. Loyalists objected, republicans insisted, and a stand-off ensued. A republican convoy tried to move the family into the house but was stopped by a loyalist barricade.

At which point Seamus Twomey, the senior IRA figure in Belfast, appeared. In my report on RTÉ television, I identified Twomey as an IRA man – unusual for that time – but to my enduring shame I said that the ceasefire had broken down 'despite' his presence. In fact, it had broken down *because* of his presence. He sought war. He had warned that if the British used rubber-bullet guns, which were riot-control weapons, the IRA would return fire with real bullets, which were battlefield weapons. So the Provisional IRA actually wanted the ceasefire to end. Even the Official IRA – supposedly now on ceasefire – wanted war. Moreover, Northern Irish loyalists also wanted war. The vote for hostilities was unanimous amongst those people with guns: and those without were not consulted.

That July day in Lenadoon the first victim of the secret ballotless vote was an unarmed soldier who was leading negotiations. As he stood there, trying to put the British army's point of view to the republican delegation, one of the latter suddenly produced a golf club from behind his back, and in violation of every rule governing talks between opposing sides, smashed the young officer across the forehead, instantly felling him and inflicting irreversible brain damage. At the same time the Belfast summer fête was being officially opened. Rioting spread across those pleasant gardens and open green spaces, and soldiers were felled with carefully arranged supplies of bricks, as mothers ushered away screaming children. Next, squaddies were firing rubber bullets and CS gas canisters, followed by gunfire in vast symphonic waves as scores of gunmen tried to kill soldiers, and vice versa, bullets hammering against the armour-plating of the army's personnel carriers.

I should have been appalled but wasn't. That afternoon was exhilarating. Gunbattles are intoxicating: the whiff of cordite, the tang of testosterone, the roar of war. And so, with ecumenical consensus, Northern Ireland returned to its usual habits. Within an hour or so, in Ballymurphy, the Parachute Regiment was conducting another little massacre, killing their second priest within a year and another half dozen residents, and a few days later, in Andersonstown, I ran into the tragic ambush that opened this memoir.

The man really responsible for the renewal of hostilities was Twomey. I had met him but once, in a house in Riverdale in Belfast to do an unbylined interview for the Dublin magazine *Hibernia* a short time before. He was a uniquely revolting individual: crass, ignorant, bullying. He glared constantly, his face corpse-white beneath the slick of greased and alarmingly black hair (dyed locks at this time being de rigueur for even the most ancient and withered of terrorists).

He denied the possibility of a loyalist backlash, and said that the British were responsible for everything being blamed on the 'so-called loyalists'. For example, he barked, uniformed British soldiers had been seen carrying a bomb into McGurk's bar, where fifteen Catholics had been killed.

'Uniformed? Why were they wearing uniforms?'

'They were bluffing,' he snarled, in the only variation on the barking tone he used throughout the interview.

'Bluffing?' I said in a small voice. 'What kind of bluff is that?'

Twomey's pink eyes flashed, and his teeth, all crossed and fang-like, briefly ground against one another. 'Because they're British, and they realised that if they wore British uniforms, dupes and eejits like you would say, British soldiers wouldn't wear uniforms doing something like this, so they must be people *pretending* to be British, aye, *pretending,* and then people – aye, eejits and dupes like you – would blame the Protestants and say it's the backlash, BUT THERE IS NO BACKLASH BECAUSE DEEP DOWN THE PROTESTANT PEOPLE WANT A UNITED IRELAND,' – a brief pause as his anger subsided and his voice lowered – 'only, they don't know it yet.'

This was like talking to a man who thinks that Martians run the post office, and are stopping his mail. Irish republicanism has since acquired the telegenic veneer of suited respectability, but this was its raw product: a man indoctrinated in the ways of death, who had repeatedly and casually caused men to be murdered. These deeds meant nothing to him: his eyes were not cold but angry, as if he lived his life in a permanently homicidal rage. His soul knew no pity, his conscience no sin.

But in *Hibernia* I didn't have the nerve to describe the raving lunatic as I had found him, so I used the information he had given me in a general description of how the IRA stood in its campaign. I wrote a sound assessment, the IRA was in good shape.

I soon learnt that Twomey exploded in wrath when he realized that he hadn't got the interview he had hoped for: no doubt he had expected a profile of the gallant warrior-gentleman, with a steel glint in his eye and a merry quip on his lips. Some time later RTÉ got an approach from the IRA: would it like to do an interview with a senior IRA figure, but conducted not in Dublin (where such interviews normally took place) but in the very heart of British-occupied Belfast, the interviewer being anyone RTÉ liked, so long as it *wasn't Kevin Myers.*

Liam Hourican did the interview, and came back afterwards with the glazed look of a bullock a moment after it has been hit with a humane killer. 'It's over,' he said simply, once he'd been brought round with a cup of coffee. 'The man is a psychopathic clown, a raving nincompoop, a certifiable lunatic. With him as leader, the IRA campaign is finished. Finally – thank God! – I can get back to reporting on flower shows.'

It was the opinion of the young soundman, Sean, which interested me most. Sean was from the edge of the Ulster drumlins and I had worked intermittently with him for over a year, during which time he had never uttered a single word. Indeed, I had no reason to believe he could speak: and now, finally, he did, in the strange Lallans dialect that Scottish settlers had brought to Ulster. He was uniquely agitated. 'Have ye ever ran intill thon eejit, hey?' he suddenly asked me. 'Have ye? The like of him, I never did meet. Shite for brains, and a fucking thug forebye. That's me decided, well. Them there Sinn Féin boys can go and fuck theirselves for good and all.'

He then fell silent, probably for another decade or so, confirming my feeling that the IRA was being run by a cretin, and that any campaign with Twomey at the helm was doomed. Moreover, the IRA had begun fighting an almost conventional war in Belfast, using hundreds of men to fire on British army positions. The night of 15 July the IRA directed many thousands of rounds at British army bases. I was in a pub with Laura on the Falls Road shortly before the battle began. Two Russian journalists were present to report on the cruel oppressiveness of the British government, and there was no shortage of locals to agree that Britain was the new Third Reich, and Ted Heath Hitler reincarnated.

The Russians and myself happened to be simultaneously

using the urinal – a rather grand name for an open, unplumbed yard: there was no toilet as such, Belfast publicans having a touching belief in the retentive power of their male clientele's bowels – when a sniper opened up from the roof three feet above our heads. I was used to gunfire, and all this did to me was to cause a mild inaccuracy in my flow. But my Russian comrades leapt fifteen feet into the air, wild urinary arcs cascading all round them. When they returned to earth they had very visibly, and very copiously, pissed themselves.

I later learnt that, unable to get a decent shot at the sentry post he was firing at, the IRA 'sniper' on the roof above decided to fire from the other side of his protective chimney. With the next shot the sideways-ejected cartridge removed his eye. For though he knew nothing whatever about guns, he was the kind of innocent the IRA leadership was arming and sending out to fight the British army.

At ten, Tom Slevin the publican stopped serving drinks and allowed no one out. We hunkered down in silence for hours while bullets hammered against the walls like a horde of frenzied, metallic alcoholics. At about four in the morning a local silence descended and I drove home, the sound of gunfire rising again from almost every section of the city, a rolling, brittle cacophony that must have cost the IRA a fortune in ammunition.

The British army's death toll from this financially ruinous frontal assault by the IRA on their fixed positions? None. There were no casualties, aside, that is, from an eye, and two pairs of Russian trousers in a single pub. No, the IRA was going to have to do better than this; indeed, it – and dear Seamus Twomey – had something rather special up their evil sleeve. For the drumlins on the southern edge of Ulster are not large, but their shadows are long, and the pools that gather from the ceaseless Atlantic rainfall are tinged with red.

Eight

LUNCH TIME that July day in 1972, and I was sitting in the main RTÉ reception area on the twelfth floor of Fanum House when the building murmured to itself. A fraction of a second later, a huge explosion pressed itself against our blast-proofed windows.

That was big and that was close. We rushed to look outside. A sullen grey oily plume was shimmying upwards as if bounding up a ready-made staircase, and people on the street below were running away from the seat of the explosion, back towards town.

Then came another more distant boom. And another. We stepped back from the windows. Then another, this time closer. Minute by minute as we gazed across the city, fresh, angry billows repeatedly boiled upwards. Almost at measured intervals, bombs were exploding, all of them major enough to have been the lead story on most days.

It being lunchtime, I was the ranking (in other words, the only) journalist in the office. With a heavy heart – and I say this without irony – I decided. Danger lay out there, but so did duty, and we had an obligation to tell the truth. Right, I said to the camera crew, we're doing no good in here. It's time to get out on the street.

I can't remember who the cameraman was. He was up from Dublin and replied, very amiably: 'Fuck off. I'm not going out there. I'm just not. That's that.'

A bomb exploded nearby. I'm a poor authority figure at the best of times, worthless with plumbers, a comic turn to electricians and, worst of all, utterly wretched with cameramen. This was not the best of times. 'But you've got to,' I protested lamely. 'This is our job.'

'Do what you fucking like, but I'm not going out there, I've a wife and kids and that's that.'

'So what in the name of fuck are you up here for? Why didn't you become a wedding photographer rather than a fucking news cameraman if your wife and fucking kids are so fucking important to you?'

Bombs were going off closer now, so I knew – oh fuck, I knew – he had a point. I relented. 'You're right,' I said. 'I'm sorry, I shouldn't have said that.'

Funnily enough, he seemed to understand my argument. 'No, *you're* right. But I'm not going out. Why don't we do it from the roof?'

We were on the top floor of just about the tallest building in Belfast. A fire escape led to the roof. We went up there, and looked around us. Smoke rose from almost a score of spiralling columns. The city was a bedlam of sirens, of loosened sheets of glass exploding on the ground, and most of all, of the wailing and the shrieking of the maimed and the hysterical, rising up above the streets in a chorus of atonal dementia.

Still the bombs continued to explode; in the distance a visual puff, followed a second later by a boom. We agreed I should do a piece to camera (PTC). Just as recording started, I was about to say to the cameraman, 'Keep filming when I've stopped talking and do a wide angle shot over the horizon', but stopped myself, because he surely would know to do that anyway.

I did my PTC: 'It's ten to three here in Belfast, and already well over a dozen bombs have gone off in the city …' I said (or something on those lines). I finished my piece, and the cameraman promptly turned off his camera. The moment he did so, the building behind me vanished in a fireball. That clip of film – initially made against my wishes: but oh if he had kept on filming – is now a standard archive piece on the 1970s Troubles.

To witness what happened to Belfast that day from above was like seeing the hand of a terrible god, whose wrath was unquenchable and his means inexhaustible. The figures of ten dead and hundreds injured do not begin to capture the horror of that long-lost era. Nothing can.

Later, alone, I walked through the city centre streets. The last sonic boom of trinitrotoluene gases had departed to the hills, and the city air now carried sounds of sirens whooping at one another like primates in a forest. Plate windows were still tumbling from their frames; people of all ages cowered on broken glass in now-unglazed doorways; everywhere adults were comforting weeping children. Families had gone out for a day, only to be ambushed by nearly two dozen bombs around the city, catching its inhabitants in a hideous vice where a wrong move might mean death or mutilation for the children of parents utterly untutored in such choices.

In the Royal Victoria Hospital, Laura had been rushed from her cardiac duties to deal with the scores of injured being brought in. She never told me then, nor did she for many years afterwards, that the entire casualty area smelt like a burnt roast. To this day, whenever she is downwind of a barbecue, she is brought back to those long hours futilely applying various medicinal marinades to the charred limbs and sizzling torsos of Bloody Friday.

Where do we go from here? We go on, as we went on back then, as we had to: the world didn't end with two dozen bombs: ask Coventry, London, Berlin, Dresden, Mannheim or even Belfast, which in a single night in 1941 lost two hundred times the number of people killed on Bloody Friday.

And that's what in part troubles me. Both Seamus Twomey and that other stalwart leader of the IRA in 1972, Joe Cahill, had been through the Belfast blitz in 1941. IRA units had actually shone lights up at the Luftwaffe bombers, to guide them accurately to their targets. Did some residual sense of the power of bombs inform their tactics in 1972, and did their memory of the vast charnel heaps of 1941 thereby make them immune to the moral consequences of the far lesser catastrophe they invoked in 1972?

Or is a question of age? Do men in their fifties usually wish either to validate the choice of youth, or do they wish instead to repudiate it?

Meanwhile, the blade continued to slice through the air, reaping those I knew. A couple of days later, the bodies of a man and a woman were discovered, shot many times, in a car in the Glencairn estate, in Protestant west Belfast. The man's name, Patrick O'Neill, meant nothing to me, but the girl's most emphatically did: it was Rose McCartney, the singer of a couple weeks before.

The last night of their lives was also the last of Joseph Downey's, the simpleton who had been imprisoned for shouting 'Up the IRA' in reply to a loyalist mob shouting 'Fuck the Virgin Mary.' This poor half-wit had joined the IRA upon release and, drunk, had one night gone out with a revolver, apparently to take on the British army single-handedly, and was promptly, and I imagine rather easily, shot dead.

He is commemorated today on an IRA mural as 'Volunteer Joseph Downey'. You can call this sad creature by such titles if you wish, but he was not a volunteer for anything. Most of us are carried by a rush of history so broad that we never feel its power upon our keel. But Joseph Downey's rounded hull, keeled by neither wit nor wisdom, was powerless before the tidal powers of bigotry and ruthlessness: all these dispatched him to the edge of the weir, and after a moment's pause in jail, hurled him to his doom.

That summer of 1972, the language of Belfast shifted. 'Dry

your eyes,' became the standard sneer – in other words, feel no pain, mercy or remorse. To execute someone at point-blank range was to 'nut' him. The dead were merely called tatey-bread, and the verb 'to romper' entered our vocabulary. This was a satanically mordant wordplay on a BBC children's programme called *Romper Room*: but in loyalist paramilitary parlance, a rompering was now a truly terrible beating that was given to a man, usually a Catholic, before he was murdered. Each dawn revealed a new batch of bodies in loyalist areas, the rompered remnants of imprudent or unlucky Catholic men.

The IRA was now abandoning its mass-attacks on secure army posts, and instead switched to sniping at foot patrols, a far more effective way of killing soldiers. These unfortunates now barely registered on our consciousness: they were nameless, numbered uniforms. Their bodies were dispatched back to Britain unseen and unmourned in Northern Ireland, to the cursory ceremony of the firing party and the last post in the local cemetery at home in a north-country mill town, some briefly bereft Scottish glen or a grey London suburb, soon to be commemorated only by the invisible grief of parents or widows.

The overwhelming majority of soldiers stoically did their duty within the law. A few did not. One evening in September 1972 I drove up the Whiterock Road to see Laura. As I got out of my car, some paras emerged from the hedges. A huge moustached Scots sergeant was in charge. He asked me who I was, and I told him I was a reporter with Irish television.

He put his face an inch away from mine and said: 'Well, Mr Reporter from Irish television, your fucking television news will be reporting how one of their fucking reporters got fucking shot dead in Belfast for being where he wasn't fucking wanted. You've got a minute to get out of this estate before we shoot you fucking dead. You got that, you cunt?'

I wasn't being brave when I replied, 'Can I tell my girlfriend we're not going out tonight?'

'You fucking can, but your minute's ticking away.' A couple of the paratroopers laughed. I walked to Laura's front door, hammered it, and cut Laura short as she opened it. 'The paras have told me to go and I'm leaving.'

No further explanation was necessary. I turned, and walked back towards my car. A drunk across the street was walking in the half-light towards two soldiers. He was humming to himself. Wordlessly, one of them drew back his rifle butt, and smashed him across the head. He instantly fell into a heap. The soldiers began to kick him with savage method, while the Scottish sergeant laughed approvingly.

'Sergeant, you've got to stop that,' I said.

'Fuck. Are you still here? Your minute's nearly up. You want to be fucking careful, or you'll end up like this poor fucking cunt here.'

He ambled over to the figure on the ground and kicked him very hard.

'This is not right, and you know it,' I repeated to the sergeant. 'You can do what you like to me, but I'm taking that man to hospital, and if you shoot me, my girlfriend will be my witness about what happened here.'

The sergeant looked at me and, after a moment, said, 'Take him wherever you fucking want. But if I ever see your ugly fucking face around here again, you cunt, I personally will shoot you fucking dead. Have you fucking got that?'

The drunk filled my car with blood, which flowed incessantly as I drove him to the Royal Victoria Hospital, where I carried him into casualty. 'What happened to him?' asked a nurse.

'Army beat him up.'

'Well, if he's going to make a complaint, I'm not admitting him.'

'Not admitting him? Jesus. Look at his head.'

Blood was pouring from deep wounds in his scalp. She looked at them cursorily, sniffed and said, 'He smells of drink. If soldiers did this to him, he must have deserved it. We'll stitch him up, but we're not admitting him. And he'll have to wait his turn.'

Four hours later, John Kelly – as I discovered his name was during my long, long wait – emerged from casualty with about twenty-five stitches in his scalp. He should have been admitted with such serious head wounds, yet such was the polarization within Belfast that even medical decisions were being influenced by tribal politics.

It was long past midnight when I drove John back up the Whiterock Road, on the way giving a lift to a teenage hitch-hiker. Surely the paras would have retired for the night by this time? As I approached my turn, just opposite the City Cemetery, paratroopers emerged from the shadows and waved me down.

'Well look what we've got here,' cried a Scottish voice. 'An old friend. A very fucking stupid old friend.'

The three of us were taken out of the car at gunpoint, and were made to lean against the cemetery wall, resting on the tips of our toes and on our fingertips. The sergeant cocked his gun and put it against my neck.

'Is there any reason why I shouldn't blow your fucking brains out? Didn't I fucking warn what would happen if you came back? And now you're back, you cunt, with this here cemetery nice and handy.'

'I've rung my office, and told them what I was doing and where I was, and they've already told the watchkeeper with 39 Brigade what I'm doing,' I improvised frantically, using language I'd overheard army officers use. 'If any harm comes to me, it'll come to you too.'

Paratroopers were giving the two other men a terrible kicking on the ground: the poor devils – including the already beaten John Kelly – yelping like dogs, but I sensed that like all true bullies, my sergeant was a coward. Those words, '39 Brigade', would have brought a chill to his squalid heart.

'Stay as you are,' he whispered in my ear; and so I stayed like a hypotenuse against the wall, and every time my fingers or toes trembled – as they did a lot – he kicked my ankles. But the seed of doubt was in his mind, and after about a quarter of an hour of this, he told me I could go.

'I'm taking them with me,' I said.

He looked me in the eye. 'I see you a third time, you cunt, *I – will – personally – kill – you*,' he measuredly intoned. 'That is a fucking promise. You understand, you cunt?'

I dropped off John and the other fellow in Ballymurphy, and I took a complex but safer route home, thereby avoiding my sergeant friend. Liam Hourican and I later both wrote formal letters of complaint to the GOC Northern Ireland. I got a reply from a junior officer, which began 'Dear Myers', suggesting that the matter was one for the RUC, with whom I should take the matter up.

Yours faithfully, et cetera.

This was the official army command I was dealing with, and I was not some republican troublemaker: so much for the rule of law.

I never ran into my friendly sergeant again in Ballymurphy, but as it happened, we met again in Leicestershire, nearly fifteen years later, in December 1986. I had called a taxi, and as I got in, I recognized the driver. Of course, he didn't recognize me. His name and taxi number were displayed on his permit. I chatted away with him amicably enough, and as we arrived at my destination, I complimented him on his military demeanour. 'Aye, I was in the army for twenty years,' he sniffed proudly. 'You don't forget some things.'

'Some you do, and some you don't. You've forgotten me, sar'nt,' I said, deliberately using military pronunciation. He blinked in surprise. 'I don't forget you, and believe me, the people of Ballymurphy don't forget you either.' I patted his shoulder encouragingly. 'And better still, now they know where you work. Why, they can even ask for you by name and number.'

His eyes vanished in terror into the fat of his cowardly face, and I bade him goodnight: I trust that even now, if this vile wretch is still alive, he starts awake at every sound at night.

That, at least, may seem to be a 'satisfactory' conclusion. But it is not generally the way of Northern Ireland, and nor unfortunately, is it the way of the rest of my tale. The reason why the paras were so particularly violent was because the previous night one of their number, eighteen-year-old Private Frank Bell, had been murdered by an IRA sniper. Paratroopers later arrested an entirely innocent local boy called Liam Holden, a chef who was trying to make the most of an otherwise unpromising life. He was ruthlessly beaten. He later confessed and was sentenced to life imprisonment, going on to serve nearly twenty years for a crime he had nothing to do with.

Nine

AMIDST ALL THIS VIOLENCE I had a social life that was almost totally centered on west Belfast, and Laura's extended family, which though not being in the IRA, tended to favour the left-wing, semi-Marxist Official IRA, now on an intermittent ceasefire, rather than the Provisional IRA, which had become an engine for war and was now roaring out of control.

Strange to say, these were not unhappy times. Even amid all the tragedy of war – and perhaps because of it – it was possible to enjoy yourself. The people of west Belfast were the most outgoing, gregarious people I have ever met. And though their tribal appetites had been sharpened by conflict, they remained profoundly witty, and often unpredictably intelligent.

An elderly man wearing barely better than rags once stopped me as I entered The Old House. He knew who I was. He asked: 'Son, you're the fellow to tell me this. Who was the finer tenor, Beniamino Gigli or Jussi Björling? Forbye Björling couldn't speak Italian, he had a finer tone. Did you ever hear his 'Angels Guard Thee'? Magic, pure magic, and better sung in English than the original French. But Gigli was incomparable at Puccini, incomparable.'

One night in another pub, Laura introduced me to Seamus, a remote connection to her family. He sat down shyly and didn't say a word. I looked at him carefully. Could it be him? Yes indeed. He was the bone-thin youngster who I had seen shoot the soldier on Shaw's Road a few weeks before. Of course, he didn't recognize me. A careful, non-probing conversation followed, in which I asked nothing but – I suppose – like a psychiatrist, still tried to exhibit a mute personal interest in my companion. We got on well, despite his youth. He drank only Coke. Once he had put himself at ease, I found that he was both intelligent and amiable. He certainly wasn't Joe McCann, but of course he was far younger, and moreover, was good and likeable company.

And, obeying the special Belfast rule that local people should feel completely uninhibited about telling Kevin Myers anything, after a while he informed me he was in the IRA – indeed, he had fired the first shot that had formally ended the ceasefire in July at Lenadoon. After a pause, I told him I knew he was in the IRA. Indeed, I had seen him shoot the soldier on Shaw's Road.

His eyes narrowed in disbelief. 'You seen that?'

Yes, I said. 'Aye, well, that's dead embarrassing, so it is,' he said.

'You're *embarrassed* that I saw you shoot the soldier?'

'No, not that. All that cheering and dancing, that bloodlust – that's against orders. We're supposed to be doing a job, not enjoying ourselves.'

He was perfectly, perfectly serious. I asked him if he had ever shot anyone before. 'Aye,' he replied, 'I done one once before.'

When he was fifteen – and he was only sixteen now – a member of the IRA had called him from his home and told him that he was going to have to 'nut' someone. There was a man up an entry (alleyway) and he was to shoot him twice through the head. The boy was given the gun, and immediately did what he was told. He related the story as he might his first kiss.

I was silent for a while. This was the worst thing I had ever heard in my life. Keeping my voice low, I said: 'Holy fuck.'

He stirred uneasily in his chair. 'Excuse me, Mr Myers, but I don't like talk like that.'

'Like what?'

'The f-word. I don't like it.'

I blinked for a minute or so before clearing my throat and phrasing the next, carefully curse-free sentence. 'It's Kevin. How did you feel about murdering a man like that?'

'Me?' He was both incredulous and indignant. 'I didn't murder no one, so I didn't. I'm a member of the army. I obeyed an order to shoot a man. So I shot him. I squeezed the trigger. That was all. The IRA killed him, not me. It had nothing to do with me, didn't know his name nor nothing, and it was none of my business neither.'

Even more perplexing, he was a lovely young man: charming, shy and polite. Was this it? Was Belfast now the home to armies of charming, polite teenage killers who never swore and sailed through life with a radiantly clear conscience every time they sauntered back from 'duty', a smoking gun in their hands and a huddled corpse left behind them in an alleyway? Later, Laura asked me if I'd liked Seamus. I replied, very much, adding that he'd told me he was in the Provisionals.

'Aye, mad isn't it, what with them killing his da.'

'*What*? The IRA killed his father, but he's still a member?'

'That's my point. Shot him. Mad, isn't it?'

'Shot him? Why?'

'A wee accident.'

Seamus had not forgiven the particular IRA gunman responsible for his father's death, but he certainly didn't blame the IRA for it.

I felt no such generosity towards RTÉ. I was working a seven-day week, and for each eight hours of overtime, I was being paid just £8 – about €10. Boredom filled my working days, and indifference to RTÉ filled my heart, as indifference towards its Belfast office filled RTÉ's institutional heart.

So much was wrong: ludicrously so. Thus RTÉ continued to employ a cameraman as inept as Hughie McAlinden. About half of his film was overexposed or underexposed, and often destroyed because his home-made camera – yes, his home-made camera – leaked in light through its poorly welded joints.

He refused to film riots, because of the damage done to what he called 'may bock possudge' (my back passage) by a bombing no one else could remember him being present at. There was one particular major in the Guards, terribly pukkah, who regularly gave media interviews and who would start tugging at his collar whenever he saw the approaching cameraman was Hughie.

'Agh, major, what about you,' Hughie would joyfully cackle, a prelude to an unstoppable torrent of words. With a wild, broken look in his eye, the major would begin to back away, mumbling incoherently, and still plucking at his throat.

'Let me tell you, major, cause I know you're interested, may bock possudge is STILL playing me up something shocking, so it is, something shocking. It's never been the same – so it hasn't – since that explosion up the Grosvenor. Come here. You ever had any trouble with your bock possudge, major? No? Don't, is my advice. Once you get troubles with your bock possudge, major, your stools is never quite the same.'

Perhaps the most bizarre individual in the RTÉ news organization was its head, Jim McGuinness, a former IRA man of 1939 vintage. He told me that, as a matter of principle, one unit of Catholic boys had staunchly refused to handle bombs that used acid-containing condoms as timing devices. They were not certainly going to imperil their mortal souls to blow up Londoners.

Jim was a kindly man for whom terrorism was not a natural calling, and who had abandoned his career in the IRA for journalism. However, he had not abandoned his republican genes entirely, banning the use of the term 'gunman' in connection with the IRA, on the grounds that it was pejorative. I was grateful to him, for he had been largely responsible for my getting a job with RTÉ, against much opposition.

In a conscious act of ecumenism, Jim had chosen to give a job to our deskman Bob Hume, a genial old and moustached veteran of RAF Coastal Command during the Second World War. When asked his religion, Bob would gruffly reply: 'Matrimonial Catholic': in other words, he was a Protestant who had become a Catholic in order to marry the woman he loved.

He was already slow when his wife was still alive. She died early in 1972 and was buried in a small graveyard on the Black Mountain, overlooking Belfast. The RTÉ newsroom came up from Dublin in force for the wake and a ferocious drinking session the night before. Drunken obsequies were what RTÉ journalists really did best.

Next day, I arrived at the church late, with a hangover that felt like a blacksmith had set up his anvil just behind my eyes. The church was full, so I stood outside, swaying in the flat, icy wind. Liam Hourican suddenly erupted from within, bright green around the gills, and proceeded to vomit a voluminous and matching verdure. A haggard John McAleese, his face the colour of withered lichen, then came weaving up from the graveyard, with a shovel in one hand and a cigarette in the other. 'The gravediggers are on strike, and I've been digging the frigging grave alone. Jesus, I'm fucked. It's your turn.'

Too miserable to argue, I took the shovel and tottered down to the half-dug grave. The ground was an iron ice-field. I scrambled into the hole in my best, my only suit and began to dig, pausing occasionally to disgorge the last whiskey-reeking contents of my stomach. I made little progress, and was still in the hole as the coffin made its appearance, borne tremulously by a quartet of whey-faced ancients from Dublin: they looked as if Bob's wife should have been carrying them instead of vice versa.

They halted at the graveside, their knees buckling beneath

their burden, while I struggled to get out of the hole before the coffin and its bearers toppled onto me. I had actually made it onto the clay parapet around it, but then I slipped right back, into the bottom of the grave, and the whiskey-flavoured stomach-contents with which I had so thoughtfully been lining it. While above me the pall-bearers continued to tremble miserably beneath their load, a brace of broken fellow mourners, their eyes red as sunsets, hauled me up from the grave, whereafter the service approximated to canon law.

Following a suitable period of mourning, poor Bob Hume returned to work, but had ceased to function: and by 3 pm, he ceased even to pretend to, as he sidled off to the pub, to console himself with that lethal Belfast combination of Mundie's sweet South African sherry and pints of XX Guinness. An incoherent, babbling fool might totter into the office at around six to collect his hat and say good night, or equally, might not.

This was the most important news operation in the history of independent Ireland, yet we were working on a pauper's budget, and were hopelessly understaffed. RTÉ was still unable to process film in Belfast, so that – for example – the day the ceasefire broke down in July, I had driven at lunatic speeds (with the two lanky Deasey brothers aboard and screaming, their long thin limbs twitching in galvanic terror) the hundred miles on country roads to Dublin with footage of the gunbattle.

Meanwhile, the blade of death continued to whistle by my ear. I had just left The Old House on Albert Street one evening when a derelict building simply blew up beside me, as if hit by napalm. I ran over to it. There was no way of getting in. Through its window, in the heart of this instant inferno, I could see the naked bodies of two men rolling across the floor in a strange, slow motion, backwards and forwards, as if wafted by the roaring flames around them. Their clothes had been instantly incinerated by the explosion, and their pink skin was now bursting like pork crackling. In their perpetual, swaying motion, they were surely dead.

Local men instantly materialised beside me on the street, and they gallantly kicked the doors down to reach those within. But that merely fed fresh oxygen to the flames, and the house was turned into a steel smelter. The courage of these would-be rescuers was nonetheless astounding, and utterly characteristic. We stepped back and watched as the house collapsed. Three young men – John Donaghy, eighteen, Patrick Maguire, twenty-four, and Joseph McKinney, seventeen – died in their own IRA bomb factory.

The next day my landlord, genial William Staunton, was shot and critically injured by gunmen as he dropped his daughter off to school not far from where those three men had died.

I was lucky I had Laura. I had many acquaintances, but few close personal friends, the closest being Bob Moon. I'd seen less of him in recent times, largely because of Laura. In her presence, he tried far too hard to be interesting – no doubt hugely aware of the differences in age and religion. He succeeded in being boring and often irritating, and – I felt – sometimes sensed our irritation, but not always: he once treated us to a two-hour description on how to get a ship into a bottle, in which not even the first minute was interesting.

Yet Bob was an interesting man who did not always succeed in being interesting. Belfast – actually – was usually a boring place that did not always succeed in being boring. Boredom was repelled by the simple expedient of going to pubs. One night in The Old House I ordered a pint, but when I attempted to pay for it the barman said, 'It's paid for.' The same happened for my second drink. And my third. Also my fourth.

'What the fuck's going on here?' I asked the barman. He replied, 'He says, "Sorry".'

'Who says sorry?'

'Him over there.' He pointed to a figure in the corner. It was Barney Cahill, my interviewing-nemesis, now released from internment, smoking his pipe and looking as bashful as I would ever see him – which wasn't very. Naturally I joined him, but only briefly, for soon he had to leave: so we arranged to meet the following night in The Beehive, another bar on the Falls – one I'd never been in before.

Faithfully I turned up at The Beehive, but there was no sign of Barney. Fortunately, I knew the barman from an Irish language course I had briefly enrolled in, simply to confirm my membership of the Irish nation. After an hour or so, two men approached me and began to question me, in low, urgent tones. One bent forward to enable me to see inside his jacket: he had a gun under his armpit. They were IRA, they told me, and they found me very, very interesting indeed. Just who the fuck was I?

I told them who I was, and I suppose my easy manner reassured them. The barman asked me was everything okay, and I said yes, and everyone relaxed a little. We chatted for what seemed like a year or two, while they told me they were on the look out for undercover British soldiers who the IRA knew were now visiting pubs. Finally, with still no sign of Barney, I decided to leave. My companions asked me if I could give them a lift up the road: of course, absolutely, anything to oblige my dear friends in the IRA.

I drove them to Andersonstown, where I stopped. We were just saying our farewells when there was a tap on my window. It was a soldier, with an entire foot patrol in the dark behind him. I lowered the window.

'Good evening, sir. Any ID please?'

I showed him my press pass. We talked for a while before he remarked. 'You've got an English accent.'

'Yes. I was born in Leicester.'

'Leicester, eh? Mind me asking, was you ever in the army, sir? Only you seem sort of military.'

The temperature in the car became mildly Arctic. I laughed dismissively. 'In the army? Ha ha ha. No, never.'

'Are you sure, sir?' He leant forwards ingratiatingly and declared: 'Only I can usually tell officer material, if you don't mind me saying so.'

You could have chiselled lumps of ice from the silence emanating from my two companions, and which now filled the car. I replied in steady, measured tones that I had never been in any army whatsoever.

'Go on sir, pull the other one. Never been in the army. I like that one, sir, I really do.'

The roar of my companions' hackles thundered in my ears.

'Corporal, you surely have better things to do than this.'

'Corporal, eh? You even say it like an officer.'

The soldier cheerfully gazed back at me, and then at my two companions, before the smile on his face faded and was replaced by a look of horror. 'Sorry, sir, that was really fucking stupid of me.' Rising, he called to the rest of the patrol: 'It's all right lads, they're ours, they're plain-clothes SAS.'

With his penetrating intelligence, no doubt he went on to become Chief of the General Staff. Such otiosity could well have been fatal: people really did die for far less in Northern Ireland. A couple of days later I ran into Gerry, one of the two IRA men, on Great Victoria Street. I asked him to join me for lunch.

'Lunch?' he said dryly. 'Lunch. What the fuck's that?'

We went to a Swedish cafe where I often ate and where the manager was clearly and resoundingly unionist. That day it was almost empty. We talked about the soldier's misunderstanding the other night: my, how we laughed. Well, I did anyway. Gerry continued to study me with doubtful, unwavering eyes. I had booked a taxi to come and collect me, but because no car could ever be allowed be left unaccompanied, the system was that the driver would merely sound his horn outside, and a member of staff would find who his passenger was to be.

That's what my taxi driver Liam did on this occasion; and the manager went out to discover his fare. Being Protestant, he had probably never in his life knowingly met a Kevin – a Gaelic name in origin which in Northern Ireland is confined to Catholics, and in Belfast, is pronounced as Cavan – but he even misheard this.

On his return, he approached my table in a series of writhing undulations, his hands rubbing together like copulating octopuses. He cleared his throat before declaring in a stage whisper, 'Captain Myers, your driver awaits you outside,' his nostrils flaring with pride. 'And may I say what a pleasure it is to be serving one of our armed forces. And undercover too. So brave,' he sobbed. 'So very brave.'

He took my bill and ostentatiously tore it up as he walked away, as Gerry glared at me incredulously.

'Come with me,' I hissed, rising to leave. Our benefactor was holding our car door open and quivering to attention: he just about managed to repress the urge to salute us as we got in.

'Liam,' I gasped. 'Tell Gerry here who the fuck I am.'

Ten

IF FRIENDSHIPS were limited, they were nevertheless lasting. There was one double-friendship that proved the most loyally enduring of all those I made in Belfast. I first met these characters in the summer of 1972, when I was walking down one of the back streets of Belfast. The tenements crowded in on me, their Victorian red-brick oozing murderous melancholy. Rain drizzled down from the Black Mountain, and I was cold and wet.

The men appeared out of nowhere. They were masked and armed and said not a word. Both raised their guns, but only one fired at me, hitting me neatly in the neck, and down I went, on my back. I knew I was doomed, that the wound was fatal. My spine was severed, and my trachea torn open. The two men walked over to me to finish me off, as I felt the cold rain fall on my face, and I wanted to say, 'Jesus, lads, don't waste your bullets, I'm done for, just give me a couple of moments to order my thoughts before I die.' But as I began to speak, the air merely bubbled through the bullet hole in my trachea, splattering boiling hot blood over the ice-cold rain on my face. Then they fired.

Now, that's a dream to get you sitting bolt upright in your bed in the middle of the night, and it was now a constant in my life. As girls had told me, I often screamed in my sleep, and would not know why the next morning – perhaps those were a variety of the common-or-garden, lesser-spotted unmemorable dreams; but this dream was truly the greater-crested nightmare, guaranteed to haul me from the very deepest of slumbers. Thus woken, I would lie there, facing the ceiling, my head on the pillow, feeling my neck, to make sure that this time the dream wasn't real. Because, when a dream comes to haunt you night after night, you come to think of it not as a nightmare, but as a premonition. This is your end, and aren't you the lucky one to be given a nightly dress rehearsal of it? Yet one day, it will actually come to pass, and better still, unlike all the other victims of the Troubles, you will know your death, down to the very last detail.

I soon christened my two visitors Jimmy and Seamus, in a suitably ecumenical cross-community gesture: but possessing Christian names made them no more Christian in their conduct, except in the drumlins' interpretation of the creed of Gethsemane and Calvary.

Events reflected my dreams, and grew steadily more atrocious as an acceptance of depravity seeped through the two communities. One night loyalists left a bomb beside a Hallowe'en bonfire, killing two little Catholic girls, aged six and four. True, in terms of youthfulness, this didn't quite match the IRA's earlier achievement in shooting dead six-month-old Angela Gallagher, but as atrocities go, it wasn't bad.

But this double murder didn't reduce Protestant support for loyalist paramilitaries, any more than Angela Gallagher's death had diminished Catholic support for the IRA, or Seamus's support for the organization that had killed his father. Anything was possible now: anything, as the murder of the harmless Catholic simpleton Patrick Benstead in east Belfast soon afterwards showed. His loyalist killers had burnt his hands and the soles of his feet, and branded IRA and the sign of the cross with a red-hot poker across his back – not on the chalkboard of a cadaver, but on the flesh of a living man.

As matters on the island grew more serious, and the threat of violence to all institutions north and south grew graver, the government in the Republic introduced the Offences Against the State Bill. This was condemned by opposition parties, and even as the issue was being debated in the Dáil, two bombs exploded in the centre of Dublin. The opposition to special measures immediately faded, and the bill became law.

In November 1972 Kevin O'Kelly, an RTÉ reporter, interviewed the IRA chief of staff, a deracinated English sociopath with the self-styled name 'Sean Mac Stiofain'. But for his limitless appetite for blood, this former RAF fitter was directly out of *opéra bouffe*. His qualification for Irishness was a single Irish grandmother – a northern unionist, as it happens, and he had joined the IRA before he had ever visited Ireland, subsequently acquiring a Hollywood Darby O'Gill brogue that he apparently considered to be Irish.

Government regulations didn't permit the broadcast of interviews with IRA leaders, so Kevin O'Kelly read a transcript of the interview with this ludicrous, posturing butcher on radio. The government promptly ordered the RTÉ Authority to discipline Kevin O'Kelly, and it refused, insisting that he had stuck to prescribed guidelines. The government then sacked the RTÉ Authority.

I didn't particularly object to the prohibition on broadcast-interviews with IRA leaders, because in the early days of the Troubles IRA leaders had been regularly fawned upon and fellated by RTÉ interviewers in Dublin. It had been gruesome, debased stuff. On the other hand, journalists cannot be expected to second-guess governments, which must legally define what they want and not expect more. Kevin O'Kelly had stuck to the legal definition, but that wasn't sufficient.

I now better understand the position of the government – that it felt the rush of water beneath its keel, and it was not going to be drawn by the rip tide of terrorism into a flood of others' making: but that is irrelevant. At the time, I felt indignant that news broadcasting should be subject to such gross and arrogant interference; broadcasters couldn't do our job if we had to worry about the government's opinions of how we did it.

There was much talk of mass resignation, and I genuinely believed that other journalists would honour their promises to one another and leave. How little I understood the gap between word and deed in Irish institutional life, especially for those safely berthed in the unchallenging harbour of state broadcasting: for when I resigned in protest, I did so alone. Others grumbled, but even 'ardent' republicans in the station felt able to control their ardour, and their pens, when it came to writing their letters of resignation. One hero even told me that you should never resign on principle until you'd found another job.

But I didn't give a damn. I genuinely did resign on principle, but I also was happy to find a pretext to leave. I had taken extraordinary risks to report stories, had served astonishingly long hours without extra pay, and worst, without any thanks whatever. (My efforts during internment had merited no praise at all – merely the criticism that I had filed only once from the phone-less inferno of Ardoyne, and that in one report I had missed a Mac – from a name.)

I had no plans, no ambitions, and no professional contacts to speak of: the single project that I had in mind was to stay in Northern Ireland until the Troubles were over, which must be reasonably soon. No previous period of violence had lasted more than five years, and these had been going on for four. So I began 1973, unemployed and free: and I celebrated by squandering almost every penny I had on a used Fiat 128 and a colour television.

Lill, a Protestant cleaner in Fanum House who had taken a shine to me, told me she knew a leader of the Ulster Volunteer Force, the only illegal loyalist terrorist organization. At that time, the UVF was almost completely invisible, with no contact whatever with the press. I asked whether she could arrange an interview with the UVF for me. Two days later she rang and said we had to meet. She gave me a piece of paper containing instructions: failure to comply with those instructions, they stipulated, would mean death. I was to stand at the junction of Conway Street and the Shankill Road the following Wednesday at 8 pm precisely.

Such silly, cheap melodrama, I thought: poor lad's been to the Gaumont once too often. I arrived a couple of minutes early. A car drew up at eight, the rear door opened, and a mountain of flesh gestured me in to the back beside him. Mount Fatmore drew a pistol, cocked it and put it into my ribcage. 'You were told eight precisely, and you were two minutes early. That is the last time you disobey orders. You know the penalty. Get out of this car now if you don't feel able to stick to your instructions. If this is a set-up by the police or army, I will kill you. Do you understand that?'

I did understand it, perfectly. I didn't look at him. I didn't have to. He was and remains indelibly cast in my mind. He was young and simply enormous, but his was the fat of the very strong man, rather than the indolent. He wore a black leather pork-pie hat, a black leather jacket, and a black polo neck, and comical caricature though it might seem now, it really wasn't. Some men with guns: you just know they've used them, and he was such a person.

In time, I got to know his name – Bunter Graham, one of the few truly formidable men in the UVF. He made me wear taped-over spectacles and I was driven for some distance, with lots of turns so I couldn't work out where I was. Then I was led into a room, where masked men were sitting at a table covered in the Ulster flag and the Union Jack. Thus I got my second interview with senior terrorist leaders, and let me relate what I didn't realize then, but time has since taught me.

Everyone in Northern Ireland lied. Everyone, without exception: republicans, loyalists, soldiers, police – everyone. Lying is easy in such a place. It is the default mode to which everyone turns when there is no consensus about truth. In the absence of an agreed reality, truth is whatever you're having yourself.

So they told me palpable nonsense about the UVF being a peace-loving organization that was merely preparing for a possible doomsday situation, when Ulster would have to fight to defend itself.

'But what about all these sectarian assassinations of Catholics?'

They exchanged appalled looks. 'Assassinations? Of our Catholic fellow Ulstermen? By us? Never! Not the UVF. We are peaceful. We deplore all violence.' Their heads were shaking in incredulous dismay as they contemplated the distressing notion that I might think them guilty of violence.

So who was killing all these Catholics found in Protestant areas? Ah, they replied, for the most part the IRA, but they had to accept there were rogue elements within the Protestant community responsible for some unfortunate deeds: but woe betide them – oh woe betide them! – when the UVF finally caught up with them. Jowls shook as they nodded in a more-in-sorrow-than-in-anger agreement, while I dutifully scribbled down every word that I could.

'Can I see your notes?' asked Bunter finally, his gun resting on his lap.

I passed him over the frantic longhand scrawl with which I had in vain been trying to faithfully capture their pious and vacuous effusions. He stared at it blankly for a while before declaring, 'Shorthand. Very impressive. Now read back what you've written.'

He passed me back the notebook. It was as illegible to me as it had been to him. 'The UVF is a peace-loving organization that extends the hand of friendship to its fellow Ulstermen, whatever their religion,' I extemporized frantically. 'The UVF has raised, armed and trained the menfolk of Ulster solely against their common enemy, the Irish Republican Army, and its allies in Rome.'

'Very good. You've got it spot on,' said one of the UVF men, who I later learnt was Tommy West. 'You got my bit about Rome. Thought you'd missed it.'

I laughed a gay laugh. No, I said, I thought it was a very telling point – though in fact, he'd actually said no such thing. They had recited to me what they wanted to believe, and I had thrown similar gibberish back at them: and everyone having assented to a lie, it thus became the truth, and the world was a happier place.

Only it wasn't. The UVF had shown me extensive military files of IRA men and women, and maps of Belfast, identifying IRA houses. These were official British army documents, in the hands of loyalist terrorists: this was a serious leakage. Even if for the most part these men were fools, such intelligence had no business being in anyone's hands but those of the security forces.

That the rule of law was sliding further and further beyond human grasp was confirmed with the death a couple of days later of my amiable landlord William Staunton from IRA gunshot wounds of months before. And to this day, I still haven't found the single verb where Damon Runyon slipped into the past tense.

Bob called round a couple of nights later, and found me despondent about the killing: did I fancy going up the Shankill with him? I suspect I was possibly the only person at the time who was regularly drinking on both the Falls and the Shankill. 'Go on, it'll do you good.'

We went to a loyalist club where Bob met an old associate, an Ulster Defence Association man called Sammy Flatface, who was actually wearing a UDA blazer. (What other terrorist organization in the world would have its own preposterous regimental blazer, complete with gold badge, but an Ulster loyalist one?) When Sammy was in the gents, Bob whispered he was a bit of a wrong un: he'd put both his wife and his daughter on the game. The two girls worked tricks together, if I was interested, he observed mordantly.

'Jesus Christ. Why do you hang around with such filth?'

'I don't. But this is Belfast, and you don't make needless enemies of anyone.'

When Sammy returned, he suggested we go down to a pub in south Belfast where the Guinness was pulled by real barmen, not these clowns – look, girls some of them. So off we went, and as soon as we arrived, who did we happen to run into? Only the local UDA commander Rab Brown.

'Is that right, your name's Kevin?' he said to me, after the introductions. 'His name's Kevin,' he called out to two young male companions, who exchanged glances. 'Let me buy you a drink, Kevin. Never bought a drink for a Kevin before. A pint of Guinness, aye?'

'Is your name Kevin for real?' asked one of two wiry, long-haired young men, looking at me very hard. 'You a Fenian?'

'A Fenian? Me? Ha ha ha. No, not a bit of it. Kevin's a common name in England. Me, a Fenian indeed.'

'Never thought I'd be drinking in here with a Kevin,' said Rab. 'What do you do for a living?'

'I'm a freelance journalist,' I said.

'A freelance journalist, eh? Freelance means you can work for anyone, is that right?' I nodded. 'So who do you work for at the moment, Kevin?'

'Right at this moment? Well, right at this very moment, no one actually.'

'No one actually? Is that right, actually? Which actually means that you're an *unemployed* freelance journalist. Sounds just like a Fenian to me, Kevin.'

Everyone roared with laughter, except Bob, who had been looking on anxiously. He spoke up: 'It's all right Rab, he's with me. He's no Fenian.'

'That's right, he's not,' said Sammy, who didn't know what I was.

'Look lads, I wouldn't give a fuck if he was,' declared Rab with sudden warmth. 'I don't judge a man by his religion. All that sectarian shite. Catholics and Protestants together, that's what I say.'

The evening progressed superbly. Sammy headed off home, as Rab and I got on better and better. Late into the evening, he asked me, what did I think of sectarian assassinations? Because, speaking personally, he was against them. He just wanted nothing better than to live in peace with the Catholics in the nearby Markets and Grosvenor Road areas. Excellent, I said: sectarian assassinations were an evil monstrosity and those responsible should fry in hell.

'Very true, Kevin,' said one of the young men with long, greasy locks. 'Kevin's right, isn't he?'

'Aye, Kevin's dead on, so he is.'

Rab and his friends pursed their lips and continued to nod in solemn assent. Some time after 2 am, I was just finishing a long and pleasant piss in the urinal, musing what a delightful bunch of people I had fallen in with, when Bob slid in beside me.

'They're going to nut you,' he whispered. 'The guns have just arrived. Do as I say or you're dead. Slip out the side door there. Get behind my car. Do not move until I come out. Now GO!'

Instantly sober, my fly still open, I turned and walked out of the side door onto the street where I hid on the far side of Bob's taxi, gazing through its windows at the pub door. The two young men ran out, with revolvers in their hands. They scouted immediately around them, but just feet away, still missed me.

'Fuck, he must have gone back inside,' spat one, and the two ran back into the pub. Bob emerged from the shadows, and like a catly dark wraith came silently gliding towards the car. He got in, and began to drive away. Crouching alongside it, I ran in a strange little hobble, as within Bob leant sideways and opened the door, even as he continued to drive. I scrambled in, and he put his foot down on the accelerator.

'Jesus,' he said, 'did you not see me trying to shut you up?' All that ould shite about sectarian assassinations. He's the fucking worst of the lot, you not know that? I'd never have took you there if I'd known you couldn't keep your fucking trap shut.'

Even before I went to the toilets, Rab had sent out for a couple of guns. Bob had twigged what was going on, and risked his own life to save me.

'Christ,' I whispered. 'Will this cause you problems in future?'

'It's one thing to kill an unemployed taig. Quite another to kill a journalist with a posh English accent. No, when he sobers up, he'll be grateful to me.'

'No chance of popping back for a nightcap, I suppose?'

'Very fucking funny. You could have got us both fucking killed with your blather, you know that?'

That was a Friday night–Saturday morning. I know now that the following Monday, a group of Rab Brown's 'men' killed a fifteen-year-old Catholic boy, Peter Watterson, in a drive-by shooting on the Falls Road. Having got a taste for teenage blood, two nights later they abducted a small, frail, asthmatic fourteen-year-old called Phillip Rafferty, took him to a beauty spot outside Belfast, hooded him, bent his little body at the waist, and shot him dead. I had been supping with a devil.

Eleven

BY THE MYSTERIOUS alchemy of gossip, Bob Chesshyre, the usual London *Observer* man to pop over and report from Belfast, had heard I was available for work, and he was looking for cover for when he couldn't manage it. Had I anything of interest?

Well, by happy chance, I had: my UVF interview. Journalists weren't given interviews by the UVF in those days, and even now I still don't understand why an unemployed journalist with the Irish Catholic name of Kevin was granted one. I gave my account to Bob Chesshyre – most of it an imaginative though spiritually accurate reconstruction from the baffling hieroglyphs of my notes – and *The Observer* was impressed. They used it: would I be interested in doing more for them?

Of course I was. Happy circumstance had brought me a new income and unexpected opportunities – not least because working for a Sunday glossy in those days was regarded as the very height of journalistic fashion. With barely a pause I had leapt from broadcast journalism to a British national Sunday. All I had to do was to take life seriously, and I had a real newspaper career opening up before me.

Laura and I had now been going out for a year. During a

trip to Dublin I had met a young American with whom I'd had a brief but passionately wonderful affair. I didn't tell Laura about Barbara, but the power of the connection I felt with the young American warned me that whatever existed between Laura and myself would not last. I ended our relationship one evening in early spring, and I immediately felt desolate for having done so. But I knew my decision was right and Laura's relatively swift move to another man, whom she later married, confirmed this was so.

So, I would go alone to The Old House, where one evening I found myself talking to two drunken sisters in their mid-twenties. When they indulged that curious female ritual of going to the toilet together, the barman warned me: one of them was married to a senior IRA man who was serious fucking stuff. Don't fucking go near her. Don't fucking think about it.

Not a chance. What do you think I am? Mad? The girls came back, one considerably the worse for wear. Her sister explained: she'd earlier had a row with her boyfriend Sean, it was her fault, and she felt guilty about it. When it came time to leave I offered the sisters a lift home. The barman gave me a look of deadpan warning, but that was okay, because I intended to do absolutely nothing.

I drove the girls up to a housing estate, and the unmarried sister who was in the back, got out and went inside. She was very drunk indeed. I looked at the woman beside me and we started kissing.

'This is mad,' I said, lust grasping me warmly by the groin while common sense tapped on the window of my brain in vain.

'Come in,' she said, 'and have a cup of coffee.'

'Do you mean a coffee or a fuck?'

'Can't promise the coffee.'

'I'm having neither. Jesus. Where's your husband?'

'Shh. He's gone down the state [the Republic] on business. Won't be back till Monday.'

'Are you sure?'

'Fucking certain.'

We went inside and – surprisingly – she began to make coffee. I turned the kettle off. We kissed, and lightly, hand in hand,
she led me upstairs. The bedroom floor was covered in huge
barbells and weights.

'He's a weightlifter! Jesus Christ almighty!' I cried. 'I'm getting out of here.'

'Shhh. He's a weightlifter, aye, but a weightlifter in Dublin
for now. It'll be fine.' She kissed me again, and we hurriedly
undressed one another, and soon were at work. After about a
minute, she said, 'Am I doing something wrong? You haven't
come yet.'

Ah: was that what the poor thing was used to? So much for
IRA weightlifters. Which is why I so diligently and retentively
toiled at my labours as long as I did – but such ostentatious
endurance was my undoing. The very second – *the very second*
– I had concluded business, a car drew up outside, the front door
opened, the footsteps came pounding up the stairs and reached
the landing. In a single movement I rolled out of the blankets,
grabbed a handful of my clothes from the floor, and slid under
the bed as the door opened.

'Fucking hell this place is a fucking tip,' a harsh male growled.
'Jesus, I'm fucked so I am.'

'What the fuck you doing back? Jesus ye scared the shite out
of me there, barging in like that.'

'Scare the shite out ye, did I? Aye, sure I did, with your fancy
man under the bed and all.' He clearly enjoyed his little joke,
this muscular comedian of ours. My face sideways on the floor,
I watched his size-twelve feet move around. His shirt descended
to the floor, thoughtfully covering my own shirt. His shoes and
socks came off, followed by his pants. Splendid! Now I was in the
company of a nude weightlifter.

The nude weightlifter also turned out to be a very heavy
weightlifter, as he sat down hard on the bed directly over me,
pressing my head into the floorboards. I felt strangely able to

repress any cries of pain or indignation, and I said nothing, but – pinioned firmly to the floor – waited for a bit of female initiative from above. It came only after a very considerable wait, during which my ears grew approximately half an inch closer together.

'I'm dying for some tea,' she said. 'Go and make us a wee cup.'

'Fuck off, I've been driving all day, you go and make it.'

No, you go and make it I silently screamed through a mouth crammed shut by the huge weight of his muscular frame. He shifted in the bed, apparently reaching towards her.

'Jesus, you're all wet. You been at yourself?'

'You fuck away off with yourself, and go and get me some tea.'

'I'm fucked, you make it. Here. Why are you in your nude?'

'Maybe you'll find out if you make me some tea.'

'Not interested, so I'm not, I'm fucking bollixed.'

'Make her some fucking tea', I mouthed through crushed cheeks and pouted lips.

And so it proceeded, her nagging and his bluster, until finally it concluded with him going downstairs to make the tea. I rolled out from under the bed, scooped the remains of my clothes from the floor, and without kissing my girl of the night farewell, hopped into the only other bedroom, where the sister was drunkenly slumbering. I had no choice but to slip in beside her, and hope she didn't notice.

Alas, she did. 'Sean,' she sighed. Ah. Sean: the boyfriend. Quite. She snuggled against me, and I unsnuggled myself, backing away from her. 'Sean,' she repeated, and taking my hand put it against herself.

Oh dear me. Oh dearie dearie me. I suppressed a small whimper of hysteria. The one thing I could not afford was for her to wake up indignant at Sean's failure to administer to her needs. So gallantly, with – in the circumstances – admirable delicacy I counterfeited another's digital skills, just as she sought: a small gasp, a little whimper, *Sean,* and thus content, she fell deeper asleep. Hmm. I should have been forging cheques for a living. Next door they were still arguing. I lay rigid as a roof joist.

At long last, silence of a sort descended on this domestic idyll. Not even daring to get dressed, with my clothes in a bundle in my arms, nakedly I stole out of the house, nakedly I got into my car and nakedly I drove home. Once there, I discovered that in addition to removing my own clothes, I had also made off with my involuntary host's underpants, shirt and a single sock. What a baffled morning he must have had, scrabbling around on the floor, looking for his personals, trying to work out what had happened the night before: and as for his sister-in-law…

I went to London to meet the editor of *The Observer*, the extraordinarily dapper David Astor. He was a true gentleman such as I had never met before, nor since. He was a Whig, an English Brahmin who was driven by the (often difficult) obligations of his peculiar caste. Pain in the dispatch of his duty would unquestionably have been far less than the agony of its failure. That is to say, his Savile Row suits notwithstanding, he worried, and worry was written on his face. No joy lit his features when he offered me a contract, merely pain at the knowledge of what perfect beasts men could be, and I was unfortunate enough to be a first-hand witness to it all.

He was helping organize the first British-Irish conference to discuss the crisis in Northern Ireland, and he suggested I meet a fellow organizer, Lady Henrietta Guinness – of the brewing family – for lunch. We had a moderately pleasurable meal, illuminated by the occasional shaft of Astorian melancholy, and after David departed trailing clouds of patrician gloom, Henrietta stayed on. We got mildly drunk. Henrietta paid, and we retired to her double-mews off Sloane Square.

She was uneasy about my undressing her. She happily revealed her breasts, but was reluctant to open her blouse below them. I gently unbuttoned it, and saw why: her stomach looked as if she had been clawed by tigers. Years before, she had been subsidizing a good-for-nothing boyfriend, who had crashed her Jaguar in the south of France. A nurse had found her unconscious body on the road, and beside it her liver, which she had shoved back inside as best she could, and so Henrietta survived. However, she had also suffered massive brain injuries that every six months or so propelled her into deep depressions that invariably required her to be hospitalized.

She was a profoundly troubled, highly sexual, extraordinarily lovely woman: heaven knows what would become of us had I lived in London, but I lived in Belfast, which is where I had decided my life, for the moment at least, should continue.

Not long after I had returned to Belfast, Bob Moon rang me. This was fucking ridiculous, he said, but he'd had pains in his heart and he'd been admitted to the City Hospital, from where he was ringing me. Would I come and visit him?

By God, I certainly would. I hadn't seen him in a while. The American novelist Leon Uris was writing a book about Ireland and had very sensibly employed the best taxi driver on the island for the duration of his stay. Moreover, I was going to enjoy seeing Bob in a hospital. Super-fit Bob – who could hold himself horizontally and unmoving from the steel awning uprights outside the Wellington Park Hotel – now with pains in the heart! That would teach him to show off how fit he was.

When I turned up at the hospital, he was having tests; the nurse asked, would I come in to see him the next day?

I arrived the next day: Mr Moon was not able to receive any visits. I went back the following day, still not knowing what was going on, with some girlie magazines wrapped inside a copy of *The Newsletter*. I found Bob, looking catastrophic, and beside him Lill, his wife.

Bob had that same curious Belfast complexion that Tommy McEvoy had had: a deep, deep, dark which now for the first time seemed to risen from its sub-cutaneous lair and now coloured his face. He had trouble speaking. 'I had a fucking heart attack,' he said.

Lill hissed in disapproval at the language. He seemed barely able to move, his head deep in the pillow. His face lay strangely upon his skull. I put the newspaper and its worthless contents beside the bed.

Slowly, he explained what had happened. He'd had chest-pains and his GP had sent him to the City, which had run some tests, and had instantly admitted him, whereupon he'd had a massive heart attack.

He smiled the terrible pillow leer of people unable to move their heads. 'I was fucking lucky, so I was. I'd probably have died if I hadn't been here.'

There was another disapproving noise from his wife. But soon, she had to go, and Bob and I sat together. I don't know whether I have invented the memory of him being on a drip, but I know his hand was across his chest. I reached out and took it. He squeezed my fingers.

'I brought you some magazines. That was stupid.'

'Aye, it was,' he laughed thinly. 'You may take them with you when you leave.'

I dumped them in a bin near reception. A couple of nights later I met Harry McCormack of the RUC press office for a drink. *A drink*: what a lie that term was in Harry's company. Harry, like Bob, was a refutation of the Ulster Protestant stereotype. He was a charming, courteous, funny man, enormously good company but, like Mike Burns and Sean Duignan, an utterly lethal companion with alcohol.

He drank Bushmills whiskey and pints of beer – lager, I think – and expected those in his company to match him drink for drink. It was like sparring with Muhammed Ali. Oh he had a drink problem, and he knew it. His wife Phyllis had threatened to throw him out of the house after he'd come back drunk once too often: but she knew the devils that gnawed away at him from within.

He'd had a break from the press office, and become a scene-of-crimes officer for a while. But he'd seen such terrible sights, of men tortured and killed, that the only way to repress the memory of them, to eliminate any thought of what suffering had preceded death, was in alcohol. 'There's two sorts of officer in my job. The teetotal and the drunkard. You'll hardly ever find the moderate drinker.'

Harry had a big round face, with lovely soft eyes: he was about as suited to crime scene horrors as he was to pulling a sled to the South Pole. We finished the night at an elderly Catholic lady's house, where she kindly made tea and sandwiches and sobered us up. 'Just what the doctor ordered,' said Harry cheerfully. 'That's me on the wagon for the next wee while.' Harry was an unusual drinking companion for me – as unusual in his own way as was Henrietta Guinness in hers. She was visiting her cousins the Dufferins at Clandeboye not long afterwards. She took me to lunch in the Europa Hotel, and as always there the food was wretched, but the wine was – I believe – a Chateau Mouton-Rothschild '53, and was simply astounding. She was fascinated by everything I told her about west Belfast – and so, made buoyant by her generosity and the wine, I decided to take her to The Old House, on the Falls Road, to meet the natives.

The Old House had not granted its hospitality to such as Lady Henrietta Guinness in its entire history. We joined a group of men I half-knew, and Henrietta looked around her at the filth, the dirty walls, with a manic if apprehensive interest – an anthropologist among Amazonian headhunters, wondering what the local sentiments are towards anthropologists.

She had to go to the toilet, or what passed as such in The Old House. She returned, pale and wide-eyed, like a nun who has just been flashed by the Pope. 'What a perfectly ghastly place, an absolute nightmare,' she whispered incredulously. 'No seat, no loo paper, a door that doesn't lock and, oh, the smell! And there I was, absolutely hovering and trying to aim straight, when this utter harridan, a beastly woman, walks in and glares at me for simply yonks, before declaring at the top of her voice, "That's right dear, never you sit on a public pot, you never know who's coming after you". Yes, actually coming *after* me. I mean, really!'

Henrietta took a mouthful of gin from a glass still bearing the imprint of the bright red lipstick of a previous user – who might well have been several customers ago – and shuddered deeply. To take her mind off her recent experiences, and her eyes off her glass, I introduced her to the rest of the company. 'You see that stuff you're drinking there?' I declared cheerfully. 'The Guinness? Well, that's who Henrietta is. She's one of the Guinness family.'

I sat back, smiling broadly, filled with triumph at my unique range of social contacts. A titled Guinness, no less, and on the Falls Road, of all places! Oh very pleased with myself, I was.

'You really a Guinness?' asked a middled-aged man with the gauntly grey cadaverous features of one of those lifelong, day-long Guinness drinkers, for whom Vitamin C is an ocean off Haiphong. Henrietta smiled prettily, and said she was.

'You are? A Guinness? A fucking Guinness!' he snarled, slamming down his glass on the table. 'See you! See your fucking family! You been exploiting me all my fucking life, living off the back of my labour.'

'That's right,' declared his friend, angrily 'See you? See me? People like me have been the making of people like you. And *you*,' he continued, accusingly to me, 'with your Lady fucking Guinness. Sure who the fuck do think you are anyway?'

'Hold on,' I chimed in, the voice of sweet reason, to these two fine fellows who had never knowingly done a tap of work in their entire lives. 'No one made you drink Guinness. It's your choice, after all.' And then I delivered the knockout blow. 'And Guinness are very good to their workers – free health, and a swimming pool, and so on.'

The silence that followed was of the strangulated kind, such as a consistory of vegans might evince upon being told of the spiritual benefits of eating infant seals. Finally, one of my companions managed to speak, or rather roar. 'KIND TO THEIR FUCKING WORKERS? DID I HEAR YOU RIGHT? DID YOU SAY THEY WAS KIND TO THEIR FUCKING WORKERS? FUCKING CAPITALIST BASTARDS IS *EXPLOITING* THE WORKERS, AYE, *EXPLOITING* THE WORKERS. WHAT! KIND TO THEIR FUCKING WORKERS, MY *ARSE.*'

I somehow sensed that a meeting of minds was now unlikely to happen, and I ushered a rather relieved Henrietta away from her first and last encounter with the proletariat of west Belfast. I drove her back to the Dufferins at Clandeboy, and I think she shuddered gratefully when the huge manorial doors clicked oakenly behind her. We made a promise to renew our acquaintance as it had been in London: and then my life returned once again to the other end of the social stratum, mixing with republican-minded people in west Belfast.

This was where I had first met Róisín Hamilton at a party some time before. No one would have said she was beautiful, but to me she was stunningly attractive; her eyes were large and merry, which matched her humour: and she had a large, filthy laugh. She was with another man, and I was still with Laura, but I certainly remembered her. She was a medical student, and drank, smoked and cursed like a man. She had small, neat features, large, classically Irish blue eyes and curly brown hair.

I ran into her again during an afternoon music session at the Old House one Saturday shortly afterwards. We liked one another, and I drove her home. She invited me in and we discussed feminism. She showed me a British magazine which she had just been given, and opened it to a page showing a close-up picture of a woman's genitals.

'You know most women don't know what they look like?' she said. 'They don't even examine themselves. Jesus, some even have to be shown how to do it.' She turned a page to a picture of a woman using a mirror to look at her vulva. 'What the fuck happened to women to make them scared of looking at their own cunts?'

To have shown me such a magazine so soon after meeting her was both a statement of confidence and intimacy. Moreover, in her feminism she was both earnest and humorous. We laughed a lot together, and there was a physical ease between us that buzzed with potential. I think we both knew almost from the first moment what was happening, and we relished the unfolding process of discovery. I kissed her and left. She was smiling: a warm, crooked smile. I turned. She raised a hand and wagged her fingers in farewell. Only one outcome lay ahead of us, and I revelled in its imminence.

We met again a couple of days later. 'What about you, our Clark,' she bubbled. Clark? What did Clark mean?

'Clark Kent,' she explained. 'Superman off duty was a journalist, remember? Wouldn't mind seeing you on duty.' She fixed me directly: few men in Belfast ever looked directly at you, and even fewer women. Her pupils were tiny and penetrating, and her look could rest on an object and hold it unwaveringly.

'You hear the one about the couple sitting dead broke in a pub?' she asked. 'The woman's got colossal tits, fucking whoppers, and the man goes off to the bog, and this drunk comes up to her and says, "I'll give you a fiver if you let me kiss those tits." And she says, dead prudish, "Go away you horrible little pervert." Her boyfriend comes back, and she tells him what happened, and instead of getting up and giving the drunk a dig, he says, "You fucking mad or what? Jesus, we're broke and you're turning down a fiver as easy as that. I'm going back into the bog. If your man comes back, take him out the back and give what he wants.'

'So the drunk returns, and offers her the fiver again, and she says, Aye, and he takes her out the back, and she gets her tits out, and he starts licking them and sucking and rubbing them and

133

slobbering. She goes, "Aren't you going to kiss them?" and he stops,' – she imitated the man, cupping the woman's vast breasts and looking up at her, 'and he says, "Can't. I'm fucking broke."

Róisín erupted with laughter, tears rolling down her cheeks. 'The joke's only half the point,' she gasped. 'I was having a drink with a couple of medical professors and half the hospital consultants last night, and I told that joke. Jesus, the fucking silence after I finished. And the worst thing you can do is explain a joke, so *naturally*, I began to explain the fucking thing, and the silence just got deeper. And then this consultant, Sir High and Fucking Mighty Unionist, looked over his glasses and says, "Enough Miss Hamilton, enough, lest your career perish in this putrid swamp of proletarian humour."'

She loved the joke, she loved the reaction to it amongst the strait-laced, and she loved her own blundering into social disaster. Within days, I was utterly obsessed by her, and it seemed, vice versa. We didn't go to bed until we were sure that this was serious. What happened between us there was proof that something really important was under way.

Róisín came from a politically divided family. Her father was a senior civil servant, and though a Catholic, was essentially loyal to the Crown. His mother, Róisín's grandmother, even had a picture of the Queen Mother in their house in republican Ardoyne. But Róisín's mother was ardently – sometimes shrilly – republican, and Róisín had been strongly influenced by her. When she was a little girl, and was having her hair shampooed, she would imagine she was the bewigged patriot Robert Emmet, giving his famous speech from the dock in 1803 en route to the gallows. Her two brothers had felt the imprint more deeply: one was in the Provisional IRA, the other in the Official IRA.

Now that I no longer kept office hours and was working from home, I was freer than ever to shape my own life. I began to see more of Barney, my broadcasting nemesis, and – as I was already beginning to discover the night he hadn't turned up in the pub – one of the most unreliable men I have ever met. He was a builder, built like an ox, and intuitively good with money. He had also been a friend of Joe McCann's. He was wise, too: 'Well fuck. If they can make a hero of Joe McCann, they can make a hero of anyone.' I didn't know what he meant. But like Joe, he was very intelligent and entirely self-educated. He loved history, old books, and Victorian architecture. He had left school at fourteen.

Barney had lost his business when he was interned. Now he was living on the outskirts of west Belfast, making money in the mysterious ways of a city that no longer seemed to manufacture anything, but was nonetheless able to conjure money out of the skies, or the British taxpayer – both, if Barney had his way. He was always working moves: always. His mind was a machine whose cogs never ceased to click and whirr.

Róisín and I soon spent all our time together – so much so that she almost abandoned her studies. We would spend much of the day in bed, and when not making love, we would drink in The Old House with Barney and a few friends. Occasionally I ran into Seamus, my young gunman: always polite, fresh-faced, boyish, already with an engaging blush at the drop of a cunt or the hint of a fuck.

I'd found the perfect existence. I was doing occasional free-lance radio reports for Westinghouse Broadcasting in the US, and I would normally manage to cobble together an article for *The Observer*, without any serious research, though often enough drunk at midnight, after an evening's drinking with Róisín. My only concession to professionalism was that on Fridays I returned to my flat alone.

It was a semi-hippy existence in the middle of a profoundly grubby war. I was without any ambition for my life, merely content to be in love with Róisín, staying in touch with the Troubles, but meanwhile doing as little actual work as possible. Indeed, I had even ceased to think of myself as a professional journalist:

instead, journalism was how I got money to get by. It was incidental to my life, not its core, and this was reflected in how I socialized, which was hardly with journalists at all, but primarily with the participants of the Troubles. I regarded myself as an avid witness to events and but not as a serious chronicler of them.

I cannot explain why I seemed almost immune to what should have been the obvious gravity of what was happening all around me. In part it was a supposedly principled lack of ambition in life: 'careerism' was one of the gravest allegations you could make in the left-wing circles I had mixed in while living in Dublin. The culture was even more pronounced in nationalist west Belfast, where to rise above your class was to betray it.

Meanwhile, terrorists were testing the bonds of loyalty of the tribe, and generally finding that they held. Four off-duty soldiers were befriended by some women in a pub near Belfast. They agreed to meet again, and at this second meeting the women invited the soldiers to a party. They duly went to the house on the Antrim Road, beneath the Cave Hill, and found candles burning, a fire lit, and a buffet supper awaiting them. One of the girls popped out for a moment: seconds later, gunmen walked in and made the four soldiers lie on a bed. They were each shot in the back of the head with a Ruger .45 pistol. Three were killed: the fourth had his jaw and tongue blown away, but he nonetheless survived. Only years later did I learn that the woman who had set up these murders was the sister – no less – of the man who had organized the killing of the three Scottish soldiers early in the Troubles.

A by-product of such rampant wickedness was the steady increase in casual violence in a city in which personal violence had been commonplace before the Troubles. Bruisers such as Stormy Wetherall and Silver McKee were famously hard men in the city, curiously both feared and revered in working-class areas for their violent ways. I once met Silver, then in his sixties. He told me how in the old days people would pay him to beat strangers half to death. He had once broken a homosexual's arms, legs and ribcage merely because his particular paymaster didn't like 'queers'. He realized his era was over when a scrawny teenager pulled a gun on him. He never hit another man again.

Others were less restrained. At a wedding party in The Old House, quite early in the proceedings even before anyone was drunk, I saw a man break a beer bottle and drive the long shard into the groin of another male guest merely for talking to his wife. In other societies violence usually escalated in predictable steps: in Belfast, the final solution was often the first resort, and this existing culture of violence co-existed with and was reinforced by the intensifying political violence.

One afternoon I was in a pub on the Glen Road meeting a very clever, thoughtful IRA intelligence officer called Paddy. I went to the men's toilets and there lying on the floor was a man, a pool of blood, a wig and, sitting by itself in a Daliesque declaration of what is really possible in this life, a human eye.

I swivelled on my heel and strode with panicky nonchalance back to where I'd been sitting. Paddy was gone but our drinks were still there. I sat down and waited, my desire to bolt matched only by my desire to discover the truth. Finally, Paddy returned and cut across me as I opened my mouth: in the way of the IRA, he already knew what had happened. Three men were using urinals, one of them wearing a wig. A fourth man had come up behind him and plucked the hairpiece from his head. The man had stopped pissing, turned, smashed the wig-thief several times in the face, stuck a finger into an eye socket and scooped the contents out, in full view of the other two, who were still urinating, but by this time, I imagine, rather less accurately than hitherto.

The IRA, incredibly yet almost naturally, had almost twigged what was going on and had instantly taken over control of the situation. Paddy told me to stay where I was. I watched Gerry

Adams walk into the bar; he listened attentively, his head cocked, as events were explained to him by a couple of men.

'Leave,' said Paddy, 'now,' and I obeyed: as I walked past Adams, I heard him say, 'Shoot him.' I got into my car, and waited. Paddy joined me after a few minutes. 'They're going to shoot the fucking bloke who took the eye out. Not a word about this now. Not a fucking word.'

However, since no one was reported killed in Belfast that afternoon, I presume that the culprit was merely kneecapped. This was an IRA area. No police existed here. Order was IRA order, law was as laid down by the local IRA chieftain. Shortly afterwards – unrelated to this incident, needless to say – Adams was arrested and interned.

My encounters with the UDA leader Tommy 'Tucker' Lyttle were rather less dramatic. I'd spoken to him a few times on the phone, and we seemed to get on. He invited me up for a chat and a few drinks. I met him face to face for the first time in the Salisbury Bar on the Shankill Road. He was sitting at the bar, his hair in the 1950s cow-lick that Protestants still regarded as fashionable, and introduced me to the barman, Alex, as if he were a personal servant.

He directed me to a table, led by his regulation-issue pot belly, so we could talk in peace, and he conjured Alex to serve the next round with a mere nod of the head. In the course of the ice-breaking I told him about my encounter with Rab Brown. I hoped our meeting wasn't going to end up like that, I jested.

Tucker smiled. 'You were lucky. Thon creature's an animal so he is. Sure he nutted Duke Elliott for nothing, for fucking nothing.' (Duke Elliott was a famous UDA leader who had been shot a couple of months before I had met Rab Brown.)

'He shot Duke Elliott?'

'He did aye, his best mate and all. And just over a borrowed weapon. The worse thing was he didn't cover it up so as we could blame the Provies. If you're going to nut your own side, you got to make it look as if the Provies done it. Rule number one. You were right lucky, so you were. Rab Brown's a fucking nutting-machine.'

Thus began Tucker's confessional career with me. Within a few weeks I was a repository of who had done what in Protestant west Belfast. Some confessional catharsis within him occurred whenever we met. He told me many things, most of which I have forgotten, but not all. He had been present – he told me gravely – the night Rose McCartney was killed, as indeed had most of the UDA leadership on the Shankill Road. The UDA had picked up Rose and her boyfriend Patrick O'Neill after he had gone on the run from the IRA, which was pursuing him for every kind of anti-social behaviour. He thought he had outfoxed the IRA by moving into a loyalist area, but this was like seeking the safety of the flames from the perils of the griddle. To Protestant paramilitaries, Catholics were Catholics and therefore prey, regardless of how the IRA regarded them.

His UDA interrogators tortured Patrick, breaking his hand in the process, but they didn't harm Rose. Instead, they closely interrogated her about her neighbours in Iris Drive, using information about them from British army sources. She failed to identify the occupant of one house as being a member of the IRA, which he was, according to the army files which the UDA had access to, and for that she was sentenced to death.

She was hooded, and various members of the UDA leadership came in to see her, out of both interest in seeing a woman who was about to die, and curiosity about her singing voice, which they knew about because they had found a membership card to a folk-club. They actually asked her to sing: initially, she tried, but she said she wasn't up to it, and ever the gentlemen, they didn't press her on the matter.

It was decided that all the senior UDA present should shoot her, in part because the complicity would ensure secrecy, and in part because none of them had ever shot a woman before, and they wanted to see what it was like.

They brought Patrick and Rose together for the last time – I'm almost relieved to say, the victims didn't suspect this – and asked them if they'd like a cigarette. They said yes. They were allowed to lift the hoods above their mouths in order to smoke. Rose reached out to touch Patrick's hand – the broken one, though she didn't know it – and he recoiled in pain.

'Did they hurt you?' she asked, worried.

'No,' he said, 'I thought you might burn yourself on my fag.' He might have been a ne'er do well up to this evening, but in the last minutes of his life he reached a particular glory.

They finished their cigarettes, and still hooded, were led to a car and put in the back seat, where, hand-in-hand, they were shot, the four or so leaders – Tucker included – having a go. Then the bodies were driven away to be left in Glencairn, where they were shot again, just in case. Lord: imagine the embarrassment if the entire leadership of the UDA had proved unable to kill a couple of bound and hooded Catholics in a car.

This sort of thing was happening night after night, and the UDA was governing much of Belfast with a reign of homicidal savagery, yet wasn't even illegal at the time. Indeed, a British army spokesman had declared that membership of the UDA did not disqualify men from joining the army's own Ulster Defence Regiment. The British government's refusal to confront the murderous realities of loyalist terrorism at this time had a catastrophic effect on perceptions within the nationalist community – then, and in the years to come.

Of course, the IRA campaign distracted the attention of the British government from the evil works of the UDA and UVF. Many British soldiers were being murdered doing their duty, and the forbearance and good cheer of the average squaddie, despite the direst provocation, were extraordinary. But there remained the sense that soldiers were immune to the laws that governed the civilian population. In Newry that March a twelve-year-old boy, Kevin Heatley, had, without provocation, been shot dead by a soldier. The soldier was charged with 'unlawful killing'. His trial-judge later ruled that the soldier's evidence was unreliable and unsatisfactory, and that his colleagues had lied before the court. He sentenced him to three years' jail.

The soldier appealed the verdict and was freed on bail. He was later acquitted by the Northern Ireland Court of Appeal, and was allowed to return to his regiment: Kevin Heatley's father Desmond drowned himself in Newry Canal shortly afterwards. Other men, in their anger and frustration at such legal outrages, chose not to kill themselves, but to kill others.

Did their lordships consider for a moment what they were about? Did affection for the forces of the crown, and their attentive regard for the finer points of law that led to the acquittal of a man who had shot dead an unarmed little boy outweigh their duty to a broader community, which needed law not just as an intellectual argument, but as moral ballast?

Thus the descent continued, fresh lows plumbed, darker horrors explored. Gary Barlow, a young soldier from Lowtown in Lancashire, got separated from his foot patrol in the Lower Falls, which unknowingly returned to base without him. Alone, helpless, not knowing where he was, he burst into tears. He was grabbed by a crowd and disarmed. Some women wanted to escort him to an army base, but others prevented them. A soldier helplessly watched from a distant watchtower as a teenage girl appeared to orchestrate the semi-circle that had surrounded and trapped the weeping soldier. An IRA man then arrived, drew a gun and murdered the helpless boy, while Belfast's vile Mesdames Lafarge, no doubt contented at their handiwork, watched on. Gary had just turned nineteen. There must be nearly a dozen grandmothers on the Falls Road today who can tell the rising generation of youngsters about their gallant contribution to the war for Irish freedom.

Though these events horrified me at one level, at another – not being actually present – I was able to distance myself from them. I felt myself able to. Had I not held Leo McGuigan's dead body, and seen Jack Lavery's tissue scattered over half a street? Moreover, life had to be lived to the full, and love had to be enjoyed in equal measure, and I intended to do both. Even Belfast at its most unspeakable could not diminish the passionate love that filled my heart and soul: I had never known such emotional power, never been subject to such tyranny. Every time I saw Róisín anew, my heart sat in my throat. I could not touch her enough or hold her enough or make love to her enough.

I had of course stayed in touch with Bob Moon. Some weeks before all this I had visited him again in City Hospital. There, at last, I learnt that his central problem wasn't his heart. All those roll-your-own cigarettes had exacted an even worse toll. He had lung cancer. The stress of this had triggered the cardiac arrest. He looked shockingly haggard, a lock of hair hanging over his grey, lined forehead.

'Cancer, eh? So how do they cure that?' I asked, almost cheerfully.

'They cross their fingers, Kevin, they cross their fingers.'

I laughed lightly. The bleak look on a face that spent all day gazing at the ceiling told me nothing. I was in love, and was immune to any sense of either death or harm.

I attended a British–Irish conference in Cambridge, and met Henrietta again. She was troubled: her eyes had taken on a wandering, sometimes vacant look. She was aware of what was happening; and she was looking at a return to the hell from which she had only temporary reprieve. We got drunk together. She told me she had to explain something to me. She took me to her room, removed her top, and mournfully re-examined her mutilated stomach in the mirror. 'This is exactly what my brain is like,' she said, pointing at the palimpsest of layered scar-tissue. 'Dear Christ alive. What the fuck am I to do with my life?'

Our eyes met in the mirror. Something passed between us, the realization of a chapter closing. She put away her breasts and her wounds, and we went outside, sitting in one of the quads through to the early hours, holding hands like brother and sister. We were never lovers again.

One morning, just as Róisín was getting up, the doorbell rang. I answered it. Standing there was Jim Hanna, an Ulster Volunteer Force paramilitary leader whom I had briefly met the night before in a pub on the Shankill Road. We had got on well together, but he hadn't asked for any details of where I lived; anyway, I told no one that, absolutely no one.

'Good morning Kevin. I trust you find this a pleasant surprise.' He grinned raffishly.

'Jesus Christ. How …? You better come in,' I said. I took him into the kitchen. I finished the question. 'How the fuck did you find out where I lived?'

'Asked a man in UDR intelligence. I usually find that's the quickest way.' Perfect: a man working with the British army was giving out my address to a Protestant terrorist. 'Ah, good morning, young lady. You must be Róisín.'

'How… ?' I asked incredulously, before answering myself in a resigned tone: 'The same source.'

He nodded agreeably while I introduced her to him. They spoke for a while, before Róisín, after giving me a long, quizzical look, left for the hospital. Jim said he was bursting for a drink: did I fancy popping round to the Wellington Park Hotel?

'Jim, it's 9.30. The bar doesn't open till eleven.'

'We'll see,' said Jim, and I followed him round the corner to the hotel. Jim walked right up to reception, and asked, 'Excuse me, could you open the bar please? I'd very much like a drink.'

'Certainly, sir,' said the receptionist, getting her keys.

This was madness, in utter violation of the licensing laws. 'At this time of day I like to have a brandy and Babycham,' he added conversationally to the receptionist as she walked into the bar.

'My young friend will have one too. We'll move onto the vodka and lemonades then, if you please.'

'Certainly, sir. If you don't mind, I've got to return to reception. Tell me how much you've had to drink when you're leaving.'

Jim Hanna had a charm identical to that of Joe McCann – indeed, they looked rather similar, though Jim had the shattered look of someone who always threw the cork away. We drank nearly a bottle of vodka in an hour, after which I was speechless. Once Jim had settled the account – plus, I think a lavish tip – he helped me home to bed – by this time I was speaking in tongues. Then, God help us, he drove off, looking for fresh company to squander his liver upon.

Later that evening Róisín agreed, that he was incredibly like Joe McCann – partly in appearance, but mostly in personality. He had a fatal charisma that compelled obedience. But there was more to it than that: both men had the mysterious aura of those who have been clearly marked out for a particular fate. In the company of neither did you feel that here was a man marked for congenial old age, bowls on the green and an evening drink on the veranda.

That summer Róisín and I briefly holidayed in west Cork, staying with friends in Goleen. We were only there a week, but those few days stand like a shining watchtower over the broad, bleak moor that, unsuspectedly, lay ahead. For Northern Ireland is not another version of Ireland, it is simply a place apart. My friends listened to Róisín and I talking of the violence, which we now took for granted in that place where we lived beyond the drumlins, in uncomprehending awe. The perverse truth is that at the time, we felt sorry for them: we felt we were living real lives, while they were enduring the boring and predictable world of utter eventlessness, in which each day would end with them going to bed without ever facing the possibility of death.

The two parts of the island knew virtually nothing whatever about one another. For example, one of the company, Gráinne

O'Malley, mentioned that in her childhood she had spent her entire time on horseback. Róisín declared innocently: 'I'd never have guessed someone called Gráinne O'Malley was a Protestant.'

For in Róisín's world view, Protestantism and horse ownership were exclusively synonymous. The Northern Ireland nationalist ghetto experience, potentially or otherwise, did not extend to horse ownership, which was the monopoly of Wendy, Hazel, Trudy and Gillian in their pony clubs. People north of the drumlins concocted stereotypes, and then lived their lives surrounded by these people of their own imagination.

At night we all got mellowly drunk, smoked dope and listened to music – Horslip's 'Paddy's Green Shamrock Shore' providing an anthem for that summer.

Each morning the scend of the sea on the brine-washed gravel woke us, and we inhaled the scent of the wrack in the clean Cork air. Gráinne took a posed photograph of the two us, gazing at the camera lens, Róisín looking uncharacteristically bashful, and demure, me looking cheerfully, confidently male. Why? Only minutes before we had sneaked away for some quick and quivering sex, unbeknownst to our companions, but the camera did not lie: the moods it caught were ones of post-coital joy, and most of all, enduring love.

Twelve

SO BACK to Belfast, and my most steadfast of friends. Being in love offered no protection from my demons. Jimmy and Seamie haunted my dreams, and I would wake up screaming so often that their absence would be more remarkable than their visits. I had seen people die, consorted with killers daily, and taunted death often enough for mortality to take offence at my impudence and to seek its nightly revenge. Surely, I thought, the Troubles must be close to peaking: the atrocities were so numerous and so terrible that the human spirit must weary of them, and some sort of solution would be found. Yet I did not ask what or how, nor did I wonder greatly at the exonerative moral machinery that enabled the different tribes to do what they did.

Men – and the occasional woman – were being killed because of their religion every day, yet no backlash against terrorists occurred within the communities in which they operated. That summer of 1973 the IRA blew up a group of elderly Protestants, pensioners who were on a shopping expedition to Coleraine, killing six and making as many again limbless or blind. Did this even slow the gallop of the IRA campaign? Not by a half step, for the butchered and maimed were merely Protestant.

Bob Moon had been released from hospital and was now at home in the Village, where I visited him, with a present of a recording of 'Mise Éire'. He lay on a settee in his little front room, surrounded by all the furnishings of a Protestant home: the lava lamp with coloured-wax globules moving to the heat of the convection currents, the three ducks, the portrait of the Blue Chinese Lady on the walls, the little beribboned brass bells and plaster cottages on the mantelpiece.

He was almost totally paralysed by the cancer, and had little power over most of his body. His face was sculpted from grey wax, with a black chisel of pain. I put on the record, and as the music washed over him, he closed his eyes in rapture, tears rolling down his cheeks.

'Like the sun rising, Kevin, like the sun rising, bringing me fresh hope,' he sighed after the music finished. 'Fresh hope. He waggled a few fingers at me. 'See?' he crowed triumphantly. 'Movement!'

He told me that he had been saved by the preacher Oliver Cromwell Whiteside. Jesus Christ had entered his life, and had rescued him from sin. The moment Pastor Cromwell Whiteside had walked in to the room, Bob had felt God touching his soul.

My friend's face was bathed in a glorious light, the sub-cutaneous dark irradiated by a strange glow. 'Pastor Oliver feels that I have God's blessings, and that I *will* be saved, *hallelujah!*'

'You will be saved, *hallelujah!*' declared Lill.

'Feel my hand, feel my hand,' cried Bob. 'There is life there – life! Before Pastor Oliver saved me, when I was a sinner, suffering from cancer and a weak heart from my sins, my limbs had no strength. None. Now they are blessed with the strength of the Lord! *Hallelujah!*'

I sat with Bob for a long time in silence, my heart breaking at this gibberish. As I made to go, Bob asked me to put on the sunrise music again, which I did. I looked at him, wanting to kiss that grey, lined forehead; but to have done so would have violated his sense of what is manly, and worse, it would have been to tell him that he was dying. So I left him with his eyes closed, his hand moving across the counterpane in slow-time to Seán Ó Riada's 'Mise Éire'.

Cancer of another kind rampaged inside Róisín's brother Mickey, a member of the Provisional IRA, now interned in Long Kesh. She passed on a message from him that he wanted me to visit him there. There were developments in the IRA he wanted to tell me about. Of course I went. This boy was still in his teens, yet the fire that burned inside him was as terrifying as that which had laid poor Bob low. His hatred was pure and unrelenting: he was engaged in an uncompromising war to the very end, bloody death or no bloody death. His life meant nothing to him, and nor did the lives of those inside the jail, either to him or – it seemed – to them. They were all dead men walking, in the flush of youth reconciled to death and loss.

If anything, he was grateful to be interned, just for the moment. It gave him time to think, to avail of the opportunity to draw on the extraordinary vitality that republican prisoners gained in jail. They tempered their steel there, making it hard and unyielding. They learnt of the folly of mercy towards oneself and the enemy, and of the virtues of political purity. The lessons they took from Irish history were that compromise only leads to British and unionist victory: the armed struggle would not be won by those with the larger number of guns, but with the greater stomach for the fray.

'What makes you think that the British haven't got the stomach for a fight?' I asked him. 'What makes you think you can make them dismantle the Union Jack? What sovereign country has ever reconstructed its national flag at the behest of terrorists?'

He hadn't actually thought of it like that, and certainly didn't regard himself as a terrorist. But no matter. A new group was emerging in the jail, which he accurately predicted would take over the IRA. They were young and left wing, and they were not like the

Catholic old guard, who were out of touch. Listen. He didn't want me to get him wrong. The young faction respected the old guard: it was they who had kept the struggle going when Stalinist reformists tried to turn the IRA into a branch of the Communist Party. Most of all, they had proved this truth: when it came to willpower, the Irish were far tougher than the British. History showed that. The English had buckled to the Normans. The Irish hadn't, which was why, eight hundred years on, resistance continued.

Never mind that the comparisons were ludicrous: the point is that the historical picture he painted was convincing to him. It was as intact in detail and whole in vision as an entire religion. From that picture, from the purity of the warriors within it, down through the centuries, he and his fellow republicans drew their mandate for war.

No such purity existed within the minds of Tucker Lyttle, Jim Hanna or Rab Brown. The Protestant tradition – such as it was amongst men who never entered a church from one end of the year to the next – didn't lend itself to sacrifice, martyrdom, or philosophical abstractions. Their conversations were never graced by theories of any kind. They were Ulster Protestants, and they were British, and their idea of a good night out was to go to a pub or club, where the name of Jussi Björling was no more mentioned than astrophysical equations, there to have their ears shattered by a rock and roll band.

No ballads, no traditional music, no lyrical sense of self or sorrow provided them with their nightly entertainment. Their expressions of identity were not confined to halls amidst consenting adults, but were celebrated publicly on the streets – often enough, preferably being seen by the rival tribe – in their Orange marches. The Orange Order held a key to the Protestant mind that I could never grasp. Tucker Lyttle would willingly tell me who had killed whom; he would personally admit to the most shocking offences, but he would never let me into the secrets of Orangism. That was only for believers.

I got to know Jim Hanna better through the summer. When I was low on stories for *The Observer* I might pop up to the vast loyalist club on Craven Street in mid-morning. Jim would just be surfacing from some improvised bedding, ruefully rubbing sleep from his eyes. He was called 'the Red Setter' by his fellow UVF men, because he resembled an Irish setter: but of course no Ulster Protestant paramilitary would allow himself to have the word 'Irish' in his nickname.

The sleepy Red Setter's normal breakfast was brandy and Babycham, or 'cornflakes' as he sometimes called it. Other UVF men talked of him with awe. One of them told me that one night, here in this very club, there had been an argument about the difficulty in bombing two particular Catholic pubs. Most of the UVF men thought they couldn't be done. Jim Hanna said they could. The disagreement grew fierce. Jim Hanna stalked off, in apparent anger. He rejoined them later in the evening. He ordered a pint, took a mouthful, and announced that he'd done them both. Soon word had gone round the club, and people were cheering Jim and his heroics.

'He did this to win an argument? No-warning bombs on crowded pubs?' I asked, astonished. 'And people were *cheering* him because of this?'

The UVF man telling me the story looked at me as if I was an idiot. Yes, in other words, to all three questions, with enormous implications: that the UVF had explosives so readily to hand, almost like bags of sugar, that a man might on the spur of the moment go up and blow up innocents merely to win an argument, that other people might cheer news of such terrible deeds, or that this all could be admiringly related, without a single doubt or moral caveat.

The moral contamination reached beyond paramilitary groups into the security forces. Jim Hanna told me that the UVF had penetrated the Ulster Defence Regiment totally, especially in the Armagh-Tyrone region. He arranged for me to visit a

UVF training camp between Portadown and Dungannon, and I went down with an illiterate UVF thug named Billy Marchant to meet over a dozen masked terrorists. They were equipped with standard-issue British army SLR rifles, and by the way they bore them, by their haircuts, and by their demeanour, I knew they were locally recruited, part-time soldiers.

Even more alarming was Jim's relationship with British intelligence officers. Because I was a journalist working on an up-market newspaper, he assumed that I knew the senior officers working in army headquarters in Lisburn. I didn't. But he certainly did. He named half a dozen men whom he met regularly. He had gone deer hunting with two of them, and one night, he said, the three of them had caught and killed a sheep, using an army knife or bayonet.

What was the point of their association, I asked him. They were just friends, he replied. But he was a leader of an illegal terrorist organization, and they belonged to the security forces – wasn't there something strange about that? No, he said, puzzled, nothing strange about it at all – have another pint.

He certainly didn't tell me that these men gave him information about the IRA or that they steered him towards IRA targets – anyway, not that Protestant paramilitaries seemed willing to take on the IRA. However, they were more than happy to kill any Catholics drunk enough or stupid enough to stray into their areas, or bomb Catholic pubs to win an argument, or even kill any Protestant who wasn't quite Protestant enough.

One night, while Róisín was doing some long overdue studying, I went to the Club Bar, not far from Sandy Row, where students and the professionally uncommitted used to hang about. The security man Ivan Clayton greeted me as he greeted all men: 'Good evening, old chap.' Ivan was scruffy as a tramp, but his voice possessed a certain refined air: gentility fallen on hard times.

I went inside and sat by myself for a while.

'You by yourself?' asked a large, bearded man genially, sitting at the centre of a small group of people. His smile matched his dimensions. I told him I was. 'Come over and join us,' he said, clearing the way for me. 'Your glass is empty. A pint here please Archie!'

My host introduced himself as Robert Armstrong. 'But I prefer my middle name, Sean,' he added, his eyes sparkling. His family was Protestant, he told me, but – he added – he was really quite republican, though in a peaceful way. This violence was insanity. 'Sláinte,' he said when my drink arrived. He was one of those remarkable people who made you feel good just by being in their presence. The bar closed before I could buy him a pint. 'Next time,' he said, smiling. As it happens, we were neighbours. Together we walked back to Eglantine Avenue together, he to his new wife, a Japanese girl he was anxious for me to meet. We promised to stay in touch.

A couple of nights later I was in my flat when I heard three shots, in a house nearby – very close indeed. Obviously, I didn't investigate, but stayed in bed, waiting for sleep and the nightly visit of my two gunmen friends, the cold rain on my face, the spouting hot blood on my neck.

The next morning's news bulletins told me that Robert Armstrong, he who preferred to be called Sean, had been shot dead. He had told one too many people in the Club Bar of his opinions, and Rab Brown had got to hear of him and them.

As vile and as violent as Rab Brown in south Belfast was the UDA commander in east Belfast, Tommy Herron. He was an uncouth and unlettered thug, who once said that one of his men had been 'decapitulated' – decapitated – by an army vehicle during a loyalist riot. Herron got it into his own, undecapitated head one day that his wife's brother, Michael Wilson, who was living with them, was giving information to the Official IRA. Never mind that this was absurd, for idle fantasy became concrete reality in Northern Ireland, by the simple expedient of acting on it.

So one Friday morning in June Herron sent gunmen to

kill his wife's brother in the very house they all shared. Michael Wilson was just eighteen when his brains were blown onto his pillow. In order to make this look like an IRA operation, Herron had already organized 'revenge' killings of Catholics, the first of which occurred the next day, when sixteen-year-old Danny Rouse was abducted from west Belfast and taken to a loyalist area, where he was shot dead. That was Saturday.

On Monday, a mentally retarded boy named David Walker on a work-creation scheme boasted – emptily – that he had been responsible for the Rouse murder. He thought all the boys he was talking to were Protestants, but one, with a strongly Protestant name, was actually a Catholic from Turf Lodge and a member of the Official IRA. He reported the conversation to his leader, who passed it on to the leadership in the city. The usual leader, Billy McMillen who would never have countenanced what followed, was not in Belfast, and command had devolved onto a subordinate, nicknamed the Fruitcake.

He arranged for David to be abducted from his place of work, on Thursday 21 June. The boy was taken to the Lower Falls, where he was interrogated by an IRA team led by a college student. Needless to say he confessed to a murder he was innocent of, because in Belfast you will, sooner or later, and with an agreeably large tolerance for error, tell your paramilitary interrogators whatever they want to hear: sort of. That's the way of the city.

The IRA leader didn't kill young David himself, and nor did the bright college student. Instead, they arranged for yet another mentally retarded teenage boy to do the shooting. He said he would only do it if there was proof that David Walker was the killer. Well, he'd confessed hadn't he? The boy did as he was ordered.

On Monday 25 June the Catholic politician Senator Paddy Wilson – a cheery, feckless fellow, well-liked by us journalists for his amiable ways – and a young Protestant civil servant were having sex in a car on the Hightown Road, north of Carlisle Circus, overlooking Belfast, not far from where, two years before, the three Scottish soldiers had been murdered. A group of UDA men, wandering the city looking for Catholics to kill in revenge for David Walker's murder – in their terms – got lucky. They found the couple, knifing Paddy Wilson thirty-two times, and Irene Andrews – whose sexual activities apparently turned her into an honorary Catholic for the night – nineteen times.

Remember: this sequence began with a smokescreen killing of a Catholic to conceal the true identity of the murderer who had arranged for his wife's brother to be shot.

As for the various participants, Herron was himself murdered by fellow loyalists within weeks. The Official IRA boy who squealed on David Walker joined a republican splinter group and embarked upon a full-time terrorist career that lasted decades. The retarded boy who shot Walker told everyone he knew about the killing and was soon doing life in prison. The college student who interrogated Walker went on to become a successful trade union official in Dublin. The Fruitcake, the IRA leader, became involved in rackets, and turned himself into a millionaire.

The UDA man who led the Paddy Wilson murder gang was called John White. When he rang a newspaper to announce the killings, he rather cleverly called himself Captain Black. One UVF cover name was Captain Long, because it was usually made from a pub called The Long Bar. Ah, such lively imaginations these people had: and how wonderful that these cover names defeated the investigative guile of the security forces.

Meanwhile, all sorts of strange consequences were now attendant upon the terrorist wars. Glaziers – who, because they were associated with the building industry, tended to be Catholic – were in huge demand simply because of the bombings. Even a small explosion could break scores of windows; a large one simply hundreds. Bloody Friday, in all its extravagant generosity, had shattered many thousands of windows. The British government footed the bill for the damage, and there was barely any serious auditing of glazier bills. What government department counts broken windows?

Since glaziers were being made rich by the Troubles, the IRA thought it only right that it should get some of the vast amounts of government money pouring through their coffers, so it did. Glaziers paid the IRA (and in loyalist areas, by the same logic, the UVF or the UDA) protection. So, the British government was effectively subsidizing the Troubles; the more damage that terrorists did, the more money they would get – and not just through glaziers, but the entire building industry. As a matter of pride, the British government insisted on bombed buildings being reconstructed. Then they would be rebombed. Then rebuilt. Then rebombed…

Moreover, this was the first war in history in which a single government paid and housed both sides. This was one reason why the Troubles continued for so long: the welfare state at its most prodigiously, deviantly, energetic as a deluge of money poured from Whitehall onto its paramilitary opponents from the very outset of the Troubles with an almost feverish indecency. It was drumlin-witchcraft.

Consider for a moment why IRA bomb-makers always made such artful explosive devices. Well, though there had been discrimination against Catholics in the Stormont civil service, there was none in what was called the imperial civil service, which was controlled from London and which included the Post Office's telephone system. This impartially recruited and trained Catholics, many of whom became the most sophisticated electricians in Northern Ireland. And what did some of these people do but reward the government that had trained them by becoming bomb makers for the IRA. In time an electronics lore infused the IRA's culture, so that its bomb makers became the finest of any terrorist community in the world, while the loyalists, supposed inheritors of Ulster's great engineering traditions, continued to make what were in essence big fireworks.

British largesse subsidized the war in many other ways.

Paramilitaries controlled allocation of housing, regardless of the intentions and the integrity of the Northern Ireland Housing Executive, which oversaw for the vast public housing sector in the province. And who had created the Executive, but the British government, in order to take the allocation of housing away from corrupt – usually unionist – local government.

All the terrorists whom I knew lived in handsome flats built by the British government and leased at ludicrously cheap rents. Most terrorists claimed the dole, and their families were in receipt of an extravagant range of benefits. Catholics in particular were welfare-scholars, PhDoles, some of them: they knew their rights, even to the very last follicle of some largely unknown *fiat lux* dating from Henry II or some hitherto undetected *escrow* in Magna Carta. Of their responsibilities to the state that fed, housed and clothed them, they were a little less certain.

Because people were on the dole didn't mean they weren't working. The building industry was overwhelmingly Catholic, and therefore was controlled by the IRA. The British government repeatedly tried to prevent men doing the 'double' – working and claiming the dole – with a complicated set of certificates, which the IRA was repeatedly able to thwart by forgery and intimidation.

Maddened at the losses it was incurring, the British government spent two years devising a foolproof multi-million pound system that would prevent fraud in the building industry in Northern Ireland. It was introduced on a Monday, and was mandatory in all government-subsidized building projects – which meant just about all building work in the province. By Thursday the IRA had cracked the system, and by the following week it lay in ruins.

To all extents and purposes, every single man working on building sites in Northern Ireland was not only being paid twice over by the British government, on the dole and through wages, but was, by the artful use of certificates, also avoiding paying tax. At the end of each working day, building workers would return to their government-built homes, to watch British television without paying licence fees, and maybe slope off to the local illegal drinking club where the drink was stolen and no duty was paid.

From relatively early on in the Troubles, people realized that there was a living to be made from compensation for shock and trauma caused by bombings. These are largely self-diagnosed conditions for which a sufficiently alert mind can concoct the necessary mental symptoms; and many did so. It was routine for some people to rush to the scene of a bombing and then wander round looking distressed: a helping hand into an ambulance, and the medical and legal system automatically looked after just about everything else. This arrangement was almost tailor-made for abuse, and of course, on some blessed days, such as Bloody Friday, one could be spoilt for choice.

Such cynical exploitation was only possible in a sea of genuine suffering that makes it all the more inexcusable. Hundreds of people were blinded in the Troubles; thousands lost limbs. Using this background of tragedy, people regularly sought and were given medical certificates by obliging GPs declaring that they were suffering from Troubles-related stress.

Such unmerited certificates were commonplace in west Belfast: much of the community were living embodiments of the dependency culture, as they also were of nationalist grievance and a remorseless self-pity. There were enough GPs who hated the British state sufficiently to have no qualms about assisting their patients with whatever crooked paperwork was necessary to defraud the government.

A mirror image set of comparably distorted values was present in the Protestant working-class communities of both east and west Belfast. The shipyard, whose workforce was overwhelmingly Protestant, was perhaps the largest outdoor relief operation in western Europe, and lost millions through the 1970s: the IRA campaign of terror alone kept it open. The British government continued to subsidize it simply because it couldn't be seen to be unfaithful to the Union.

Ludicrous work practices were retained by an incompetent and insolently complacent workforce with farcical expectations. For a while it appeared possible that a Japanese consortium might buy into Harland & Wolff. A trade union leader denounced even the possibility of such investment with the splendidly enlightened observation, 'Sure them Japanese is only a bunch of Chinamen anyway.'

As it happened, not even the most uniquely Japanese cultural appetite for self-destruction, which had given the world hara-kiri and kamikaze, survived a brief perusal of the yard, with its happy, chuckling cardschools, its chronic absenteeism and a system of recruitment carried out almost entirely through the unions and, thereby, the local Orange lodge. For in the minds of its employees, the shipyard existed as a Protestant, British right.

Co-existing with such self-regarding dysfunctionalism within the Protestant community was an almost racist disdain for Catholics. 'For a Fenian, Mr Hill, you're a very intelligent man,' a loyalist terrorist once told the Catholic barrister who had successfully defended him.

A Protestant woman I met in the Wellington Park Hotel once asked me which was worse, the UDA or the IRA? I dodged the question. She did not. The IRA bombed businesses, so it should be stopped. But loyalist paramilitaries killed Catholics, and since Catholics – she said – were mostly unemployed, they were a burden on the economy, and therefore society was better off with them out of the way. 'Are you a man or you going to buy me a drink or not?' she finished, as I rose with a wax-seal smile imprinted on my face and departed to the rain outside.

She was not alone. A physical dislike of Catholics was endemic amongst Protestants, at both organized and unorganized levels. When James McCartan from the Markets was trapped by a loyalist mob in a Protestant-owned hotel in east Belfast, the receptionists ignored his pleas for them to call the police. The poor lad was abducted in full view of the crowd, beaten with a pickaxe handle, knifed and finally murdered. Not one witness rang the police. This unfortunate wretch belonged to the most accursed family in Belfast: the extended McCartan-Rice clan had over twenty of its members murdered, mostly by loyalist assassins.

Hatred expressed itself in more spontaneous, individualistic ways. Broken bottles – presumably intended to castrate their victims – were routinely sunk into the sand of the long jump pit at a Catholic school in north Belfast. Razor blades, which would have filleted a child like a trout, were often embedded in playground slides used by young Catholics.

Catholics disliked unionists and detested loyalists, but usually had no feelings about Protestants as Protestants. Throughout the Troubles, apolitical, liberal and socialist Protestants continued to drink in Catholic areas, and if they were under threat at all, it was from loyalists for socializing with Catholics. Indeed, some of the most terrible ends were reserved for Protestants who mixed with the other side.

Within the Protestant folklore Catholics were immigrants from backward, southern Ireland, from beyond the drumlins – though that was a word most of them wouldn't have known – into prosperous Protestant Ulster. Catholics didn't keep their word, and were lazy and ignorant: and indeed there were elements of truth in the broadstroke mythologies.

For there was a dysfunctional quality to Catholic education. Catholic schools did not teach engineering, metalwork or mechanical drawing – and this in an economy which had traditionally been based on engineering. So, if a business was looking for a fifteen-year-old apprentice, which would it choose – the little Catholic lad with his Latin, or the Protestant boy with an entire array of technical skills?

To be sure, there was little enough evidence that engineering firms were thirsting to give jobs to Catholics: but the Catholic educational system actually made discrimination against Catholics wiser to implement. For Catholic schools had their eyes on the professions: low achievement for the unscholarly was a patho-logical norm within Catholic working-class society. One can loathe Martin McGuinness and Gerry Adams and their deeds, yet at the same time recognize that they are men of extraordinary intelligence and talent. Both left school without a single qualifi-cation, McGuinness to become an apprentice butcher, Adams to become a barman.

The tribal stereotype held true in other regards. Catholic homes were less neat and tidy. The Protestant palace – as it was called – was to be found alike on the Shankill Road and the salubrious suburbs of Holywood. The pathologically immaculate equivalent simply didn't exist on the other side. Working-class Catholic houses were distinguished, and not just in caricature, by children everywhere, noise, chaos, and dirty plates in the sink. It wasn't merely a domestic habit. Both Catholics and Protestants would tend to agree that Protestant tradesmen were more reliable.

Such caricatures only went so far. Perhaps the most efficient sector of the Northern Ireland economy was in the hospitality business, especially pubs and hotels, which was dominated by Catholics. When Catholics were driven out away from building projects in Protestant areas by loyalist terrorists, the Protestant communities simply didn't have enough skilled builders to build their houses for them.

To Protestant eyes, Ballymurphy was the epitome of Catholic ineptitude and inertia. When the Catholics moved there just after the war, the story went – as repeated to me by my dear Miss Cuthbertson – they were so backward that kept the coal in their baths, and chopped up their doors for firewood.

I don't know where the coal story comes from. Perhaps if you have never seen a bath before, as many of the slum-dwellers couldn't possibly have done, it might just look like a large white scuttle. But as for the story about the doors, it was true. In the great freeze of 1947, which began on St Stephen's Day (or Boxing Day) and lasted until the end of March, coal lorries could not get up the steep slopes of Springfield Road or the Whiterock. After two months with the temperatures below freezing, the only fuel available for the open fires came from the interior doors.

There was nonetheless a slovenly improvidence about many of the residents of Ballymurphy. From the very start, problem families had been dumped in the area and left to their own devices. 'The only thing people around here can be depended upon to get serious about, is starting up and running a drinking club,' a local priest once told me.

Leaping forward to 1974, I was looking into the 'disappeared' of 1972 and I went to the home of a relative of one of the missing. A vast, overweight and toothless slattern in a short, filthy shift opened the door and showed me in. She could have been thirty or seventy. There were no carpets on the floors, and there was human excrement everywhere, but – alas – no sign of used toilet paper. There were two items of furniture in the sitting room: a sofa of quite terrifyingly squalid demeanour and a vast colour television set, which of course was on.

On the sofa two completely naked children, a boy and girl of about ten or so, were masturbating one another, and didn't even pause when I entered. With my back turned resolutely to the children, I asked the woman about her missing relative, and she asked when he had gone missing. I told her 1972. How long ago was that, she asked. She had no idea of the current year, nor how many years had elapsed since 1972, nor indeed, as I discovered, any concept of time.

She turned and bent down to stir the fire, and her short shift rode up over her naked buttocks. The world is not yet ready for, nor am I quite up to giving, a description of the sight that suddenly unfolded before me.

Yet it was the poor people of Ballymurphy, disadvantaged by poverty, ill-luck, discrimination and some epically dysfunctional family histories, upon whom the most fearful wrath was visited – by the Parachute Regiment in particular. One battalion actually had a standard operating procedure of wrecking fifty Ballymurphy houses every time a shot was fired at it. This was a policy that might work in the short term: in the longer term it was food and drink to the recruiting sergeants of the IRA.

Most people in Ballymurphy, like anywhere else, got up in the morning determined to get through the day; and perhaps for a greater part of the adult population that was only possible with the consumption of vast amounts of tranquillizers. Northern Ireland was not merely a divided society: it was also a sedated one, in which each completed day was an essay in heroism and dedication, Roche and Valium.

Yet through the narcotic haze that helped Belfast people get by, there remained a compulsive generosity such as I have never met anywhere else. One never entered a home in Northern Ireland without being assailed with sandwiches and tea. Sometimes the hospitality could be ruinous for the host's children. On more than one occasion after I had been chivvied, bullied and blackmailed into feasting on a mountain of ham sandwiches, I discovered that I had eaten the family's evening meal.

Some of the finest individuals I have ever met came from Belfast, they were brave, witty and decent but it was their unbroken intrepidity that I was most captivated by. One such hero was a wino I got to know on Castle Street called Roddy McCorley. He had lost a leg – amongst many other terrible injuries – when loyalists had blown up McGurk's bar.

He didn't feel sorry for himself. 'For fuck's sake, why should I? Fifteen fucking people died there, and I come out alive.'

After his compensation had come through, he took all his friends to Birmingham, presumably because that was the most exotic location he could think of, and when his money was gone they returned home. He now got by as he could; and whenever he was completely out of money he would pawn his artificial leg, which was quite valuable because it had platinum parts. When he was in funds, he stomped around Castle Street, buying and cadging drinks: when he was poor, he was back on the crutches, still buying and cadging drinks with unbroken cheer. For sheer gallantry and goodwill in the face of impossible adversity, people such as Roddy McCorley were the real beating heart of Belfast.

Thirteen

WHEN NEXT I visited Bob Moon, he was lying sideways on
the bed, by now he was almost quadriplegic. Drool dripped from
his mouth. One hand lay on the quilt, the other on the mattress.
His eyes flickered with recognition.

'Pastor Cromwell Whiteside is on his way, hallelujah,' whispered Lill, sitting beside him.

'Hallelujah,' croaked Bob, before subsiding into a spiral of
soft, productive coughs. Lill reached forward to wipe his mouth,
and Bob's finger moved in appreciation.

'You see, he has power,' said Lill proudly, as if talking about
her son's first steps. 'God's proof that he will be saved.'

'I will be saved,' said Bob, though the only reason I had been
able to make out his words was that they echoed Lill's.

His voice was that of an extreme drunk or someone with
advanced neural decay. Stupidity of the pathological, bedside
variety took command of my brain. 'How are you Bob?'

He made a noise.

'Getting better, as you can see,' declared Lill proprietori-
ally. 'Stronger and better every day, thanks to Pastor Cromwell
Whiteside.'

Bob said something. Lill smiled. 'Pastor Cromwell Whiteside wants us to call him Pastor Oliver, and Bob does, so he does, but I just can't bring myself to, so I can't. If you hang on, you'll catch the pastor himself.'

Having just arrived, I had no choice. I sat down and talked to Bob with a fevered, almost frenzied inventiveness, unable to decipher his mumbling replies, for Lill – my interpreter – had gone to make tea. Finally, I understood: Bob wanted me to play 'Mise Éire' again. I put it on the record player. While we were listening to its glorious celebrations of the possible, the doorbell rang and I braced myself to meet the man I knew was making off with the Moon money, for God's holy cure does not come free.

I turned off the record player as Cromwell Whiteside walked into the room, his glossy mohair suit shimmering with electricity. 'Praise the lawd, brothas and sistas, hallelujah!' he intoned joyfully in accents that blended Antrim with Alabama. 'Gahd's word is ma word, and Gahd's word brings joy to this heeyah home, hallelujah!'

'Hallelujah!' cried Lill. Bob mumbled into his pillow, his eyes glowing dully.

Lill introduced me to the Pastor who held his arms open towards me, as if welcoming a disciple. 'Brotha Kavan, I am mighty pleased and proud to make yowah acquaintance, yes sirreee. Any friend of Brotha Bob's is ma friend too, and any friend of Pastor Oliver Cromwell Whitesides', is the Lawd's friend also, hallelujah! Tell me this, Brotha Kavan. Would you pray with me, would you do that small thang? Would you pray that Gahd enters this room and drives Satan from owah hearts and sin from owah souls? Would you do that small thang?'

He raised his voice. 'Oh let us praise the good Lawd, brothas and sistas, for we are but humble folk, and sinnas all, hallelujah! Sinnin' against the Lawd Gahd's commandments brought Bob to his sickbed, and Gahd's forgiveness is gonna make him whole again, hallelujah! Why Bob, ah can see you looking better already, so ah do! See Sister Lill, the grace of Jesus Christ owah Saviour is making Bob strong again. Ma Lawd, help Bob do what ah say. *Move yoaw hand, Bob, move yoaw hand!'*

Bob's entire hand moved. Lill gasped. Bob's eyes swivelled with a demented joy.

'A sign Lawd, thou hast given us a sign! Bob is gonna be made whole again! We shaw are grateful to you, oh Lawd owah Gahd. You are blessin' this house with a miracle! One of Jesus Christ's saving miracles! Bob will be cured! Hallelujah! Hallelujah! Hallelujah!'

On the bed, Bob was gurgling and sobbing, and Lill was close to hysterics. Pastor Cromwell Whiteside departed, and Bob and I – Lill couldn't understand it – listened to the sunrise music again, though I knew that no sun would ever rise on this vanishing life.

When it had finished, Bob mumbled again about his imminent rescue from death. I touched his hand, and left the house with boiling solder in my tearducts and a dark rage in my heart.

Yet what filled my heart that day was an emotion commonplace in Northern Ireland at the time, and which hour by carcinogenic hour filled peoples' souls. Only angers of a particularly virulent kind could enable people to do the deeds they did, without apparent repentance or regret. Hatred infected entire areas: it was this ruthless malignancy that gave them a common, almost reassuring identity. Politicians endlessly spoke of 'a tiny minority' of terrorists: yet for each active terrorist there was probably a support group of at least fifty non-terrorist individuals. These amounted to 'communities'.

Just at this very time, while Bob was hastening towards his certain fate, two Catholic boys were abducted from the Catholic church-run St Patrick's Youth Detention Centre. They were the twin sons of Daniel Teggart, a father of ten and one of the victims of the internment-day massacre by paratroopers at Henry Taggart Hall. At the time of their father's death they were aged thirteen.

Their father dead, their area in permanent tumult, they were soon in trouble, and were sent by the courts to the Detention Centre, from where one night in 1973 they were abducted by the IRA, on suspicion of being informers. They were now fifteen.

As the IRA car crossed the city, it was stopped by an army patrol. Suspecting something was not right, a soldier asked the two boys if they were travelling voluntarily. They said they were. Allowed to continue, the IRA men, and the captives to whom they were now indebted, went to a house in the north side of the city for interrogation. There, Bernard Teggart admitted to his heinous crime: some time before, seeing a group of IRA men hijack a lorry, he had shouted, 'I'm going to tell on youse.'

As the boys were identical twins, the IRA were unable to tell which of them had made the 'threat'. Determined as ever in its pursuit of justice, the IRA wanted to know which brother had said those words. Having admitted his 'guilt', Bernard then pleaded with his abductors not to harm his twin. What further menace this poor lad, with a mental age of eight, might have posed to the IRA it is hard to imagine: after all, he had just saved his captors from a British army patrol. The IRA nonetheless made this mere boy kneel down and then shot him dead, and later – in a rather impressive gesture of kindness – gave his brother 15p for the bus home.

That this utter evil didn't cause an uproar in nationalist ghettoes should have told me of the emotional and unscrupulous energy underlying the tribal identity, which with an unspoken ruthlessness was able to exonerate terrorists for even the most terrible deeds.

Yet – though without thinking too deeply about *why* – I still thought negotiations could achieve a conclusion to the Troubles: they could indeed, many, many years later, as the IRA finally faced defeat in the field, but not then. I thought I understood the place. In fact, I understood less than when I had arrived.

Which explains what follows. I had told Barney Cahill about

my little trips to the UVF, and one day he reported that the Official IRA would like to have talks with their loyalist counterparts. Could I arrange them? Well, I could certainly try. Why was I, a journalist, getting involved in the Troubles? In part because I suppose I felt I had lifted myself away from the body of journalists who worked in the city: I rarely met them. I felt I had become an impartial insider, a unique citizen who could ply back and forth between the various sides. I had secrets in my brain that were of no use to me as a journalist. I was an intimate of the Troubles, not an observer. So why should I not use that intimacy to help bring the Troubles to an end?

I went to the loyalist club at Craven Street, where as usual two UVF members clad in black leather playing the slot machines by the entrance glowered at me. One, a short, but enormously fat man, was the abominable Billy Marchant. I didn't know the name of the other: he was small and muscular with a long hard stare. Neither, clearly, wanted me about.

I took the proposal to Jim Hanna, Billy Mitchell and Tommy West. I always assumed that Jim would discuss it, not merely with them, but also with his many friends in British army headquarters in Lisburn – which of course made the world I was now moving in moderately complex.

A couple of days later I got word that the talks would take place. One UVF man, Jim Hanna, would meet one Official IRA man, with myself as go-between. The suggested rendezvous was the Europa Hotel, because security there was (supposedly) tight and all guests were body-searched on admission, so neither side could be armed.

I arrived first, and it was quite clear things were not going as planned. Both the UVF and the Official IRA had managed to secretly smuggle a number of armed men into the hotel. However, most of them had never before been in a 'smart' hotel, which is what in Belfast terms the Europa – rather tragically – qualified as, and they certainly didn't know how to behave there.

So some gunmen stood around, looking gauche and awkward; others gathered at reception, as if it was a bar, steadfastly ignoring one another, and trying to get the receptionist to serve them pints. Others were wandering around the first-floor bar, their jaws half open at the sight of the Poppets, the fabulously big-breasted, round-buttocked Playboy Bunny-type girls who served drinks there. All these guests were of course wearing large, ill-fitting crombies, anoraks and oversized bomber jackets to conceal their firearms.

In the main bar more awkward young men, similarly attired, were pretending not to notice one another, all whistling silently and gazing at the walls and ceiling. Jim and Barney arrived separately, and the three of us talked affably at a table away from the bar, before I rose, wished them well, and left. In the lobby a couple of young men dropped to their knees to do up their laces while a baffled youngster in a very large coat struggled with the revolving doors – the likes of which were obviously not often encountered on the Falls or Shankill Roads.

I had an unpleasant feeling between my shoulder blades as I walked out. Parked outside the hotel, three men were sitting in a civilian Austin 1800. Could that have been British military intelligence? Why not? It seemed everyone had got an invitation to this party. Excellent!

Further meetings followed. Agreements were reached over the safe return of drunks and fools who had roamed into one another's territories. Soon, the Provisional IRA got to hear about the talks, and that I had been instrumental in arranging them. They approached me: would I do the same for them? Naturally, naturally, said mister peacemaker.

So I went back to the UVF, whose leaders seemed moderately pleased with the way the talks with the IRA had gone. The Provisional IRA wanted to make contact: what did the UVF think? After a couple of days, they said yes, but they would need a guarantor of their safe conduct: would I be it?

Bursting with self-importance, I agreed. The rendezvous was to be just over the Border, in a hotel on Lough Sheelin, in County Cavan, on the southern edge of the drumlins. I was to travel down with the UVF delegation – of Billy Mitchell, Jim Hanna and Tommy West – after meeting them in the Loyalist Club.

I parked my car around the corner of the club and went in. It smelt filthy as always: old smoke, beer in the carpet, rumours of vomit. Jim Hanna was drinking brandy and Babycham, his face crumpled like clothes out of a washing machine. Billy Mitchell was reading a book: probably on Calvin and the evils of ultra-montanism, a word he loved, and used at every opportunity. Billy fancied himself as an intellectual: by UVF standards he was Isaac Newton.

Tommy West, however, never showed up – an ominous sign, since he was representative of the broadstream of north and west Belfast UVF. So just Mitchell, Hanna and I went together to Cavan.

There, we were met by the IRA leader Dáithí Ó Conaill and a man I know now to have been Brian Keenan, but who introduced himself as Brian Murray. Keenan was militarily the most important man in the IRA, then and over the coming decades. His presence made this a very high-powered delegation indeed. Introductions completed, I left and spent the day in a nearby fishing lodge while the talks took place. That night we all had dinner together, and then the whiskey came out. My recollections of the night are accordingly confused. I remember Ó Conaill, a skeletal, haunted figure, drank whiskey with an almost vocational purpose, as if outdrinking Protestants would show them what a man he was. However, he had lost part of his bladder in a shoot-out with the RUC in 1956, and now required an unmanly number of trips to the toilet.

Brian Keenan, altogether cleverer and more talented than anyone else in the room, felt no need to impress and got stuck into the whiskey, singing songs, telling tales and laughing hugely at his own wit, which was considerable. He remains one of the most powerful, intelligent and charismatic people I have ever met. He and Billy Mitchell ended up drunkenly – though needless to say chastely – curled up in one another's arms, asleep.

The next day, after binding (if hung-over and pink-eyed) oaths of secrecy were made by all concerned, with ruin and death promised to anyone who leaked anything about these talks, Jim, Billy and I drove in their Ford Cortina 1600E back to Belfast, and to the Shankill Road. The three of us walked into a bar, where we found Tucker Lyttle nursing a glass of beer. Jim bought a round of drinks and after a while he and Mitchell left.

'Well now,' said Lyttle cheerfully. 'How did them there highly secret UVF talks with the Provies go?'

'Talks?' I cried, aghast. 'What talks?'

'The three of youse come in here together, which means youse arrived together, which is what *ye* never do, *ye* always come in alone. That means youse were all away together. Hanna was smoking Major cigarettes, which means he was down South. Why would ye be with him down South, only to give him safe-conduct to meet the IRA. Which IRA? Everyone knows the Sticks [the Official IRA] and the UVF been having talks already. So it must have been the Provies. Elementary, my dear Watson.'

Which explains why Tommy was a UDA commander and not a spear carrier. I thought and hoped that the talks might be a prelude to peace, I obviously still didn't understand the beasts that I was dealing with. The IRA simply wished to discuss the terms of the loyalist surrender, and the loyalists wished merely to assure the IRA that they no intention of surrendering. Letters would have been as effective. Still, for a while after the talks the IRA stopped killing UDR men, so lives were saved because of them.

Some time later, Bob Moon died. I had tried to bring myself to see him on his sickbed again, but I simply couldn't. I had the physical courage to face death in the streets, and to test my mettle amid all kinds of violence. I did not have the moral resolution to see a strong and noble man being eaten from within. I think I would have felt like that even without the possible presence of the witchdoctor Cromwell Whiteside, half buffoon and a total charlatan, lifting both the Moon spirits and the Moon money with his bogus spells.

Bob's last hours were spent in agony. I saw him in his coffin, which was a mistake. My memories of him are thus confused by the images of him in decline, drooling and babbling, or of lying in the coffin, black eyelashes stark against the candlewax of his lids, his mouth closed and set in the undertakers' final moue.

Among the 'mourners' at Bob's funeral was my friend Rab Brown. He stared long and hard at me, as if trying to work out who I was. His presence there was not out of mourning so much as engaging in a neighbourhood tribal ritual. This, after all, was a 'community'. Oliver Cromwell Whiteside conducted the service. It was every bit as grisly an affair as I had feared, his voice implausibly wandering through the various cadences of the Confederacy. But it was not quite as long as it might have been, for he had feasted at this particular table, and now it was time for him to move on, as not long afterwards, it also was for me.

The first real pressing sense that my life was irreversibly changing then came with the early morning radio news that reported that a man had been shot dead in a car outside a loyalist club in Craven Street, and a woman passenger injured. Intuitively I needed to hear no more. It had to be Jim Hanna.

I was right. The Red Setter had been killed, clearly by his own people. I waited a couple of days, until after the funeral, which I most emphatically did not attend, and then rang his wife Susan. She asked me to come and visit her as quickly as possible. I went that afternoon.

She was composed: she must have known that Jim Hanna lived in a terrible world of half truth and murder, and so was in a sense prepared for something catastrophic. She apologized for her appearance; she was overweight because she had a medical condition which caused her to retain water and was exacerbated by tension. That was related to the life Jim lived, she thought. Now that was over, maybe she would lose weight.

She had two things to say. She told me I was now in danger from the people who had killed Jim. They knew where I lived, and they were anxious to eliminate anyone who might know about the talks with the IRA.

'But that includes Billy Mitchell,' I said.

She shook her head. 'He's too powerful, he's got the south-Antrim-UVF behind him, and he's on his guard now. He'll say nothing about the talks. But you, you're vulnerable. Jim told me about your run-in with Rab Brown. That's UDA men and UVF after you. You're in big trouble.'

Rab Brown, from south Belfast, who tried to have me killed in his local pub. Rab Brown who killed my neighbour Sean Armstrong on Eglantine Avenue. Rab Brown who had murdered his friend Duke Elliott. Rab Brown who had seen me at Bob's funeral.

'You know Billy Marchant?'

I did, very well: the thick, violent thug who had escorted me to the UVF training ground and who had ever since scared the living daylights out of me as he stood at the fruit machines by the entrance to the loyalist club, alongside that smaller, more muscular figure.

'Well, Marchant killed Jim. Even though they're UVF and UDA, he and Rab Brown are that close,' she said, crossing her fingers. 'If Marchant wants Brown to do you, he'll do you. I know where you live – and so do they.'

Suddenly, it looked as if my time in Eglantine Avenue was coming rapidly to an end. 'I've got something I want to give you,' she continued.

She went to a drawer and took out a picture. 'The morning

Jim was shot, before I even knew it, the policed raided here. They weren't looking for guns or explosives, but pictures. Jim had a lot of pictures of him with his army friends. That's what they came for, and that's what they got, all of them – except this.'

She handed me a picture of two men, smiling and pointing guns at the camera, clearly taken in the same room that we were now in. She identified them by name as British army officers who regularly visited Jim in the house here, and with whom he went on various jaunts, of which she knew nothing more.

She saw me to the door, and beneath the wallet containing the picture of the two soldiers, my heart was thumping with a wild terror. That very day I got a copy of *The Irish News*. I needed to move away from an easy-to-attack middle-class area, to somewhere that would be regularly patrolled by the security forces, far, far away from the reach of Billy Marchant or Rab Brown.

I found an advertisement for a flat in Atlantic Avenue, off the Antrim Road, within sight of the Cave Hill. It was on the edge of the strongly republican New Lodge Road, which meant that there would be a constant movement of army or police patrols in the area. I went to meet its owner, Miss Kane, who showed me around. It was a top-floor flat, and was an utter horror, an essay in dirty wallpaper, damp drabness and accumulated filth. The kitchen consisted of a cooker set in grease. Even now, the lavatory remains indescribable. It was perfect. I took it, and moved in that very evening. Over thirty years before, my father had turned down the chance of a life north of Carlisle Circus, and beneath the Cave Hill. Now I was making my home there.

Carlisle Circus. In its own way, it was the magnet of Belfast. It was here that one of the worst yet most paradoxical men in Belfast's history had been celebrated in stone. Hugh Hanna was the real inspiration to this city. He had made sectarianism respectable in the 1860s, and set mobs aflame with his anti-Catholic oratory. People died in the tumult he provoked, and hundreds of homes were burnt. He triumphed in hatred. Yet as Catherine Hirst has reported in her brilliant analysis of the time, he both drove and was driven: when he attempted to relent on his anti-Catholicism, he was denounced from the very streets that he had led into riots with nearby Catholic areas.

That is the truth about the world governed by Carlisle Circus. The leaders are led: the led are leaders; and all are absolved of moral responsibility for what they do.

That a statue could be raised at Carlisle Circus to such a creature says something of the forces that he had both manipulated and unleashed. The statue was blown up early in the Troubles, but Hanna's spirit lived on, seeping into the stones of the streets around him. How suitable that I should find a home so close to where his final monument had until so very recently rested.

Fourteen

THERE HAD BEEN many, many killings in the area I was now moving into – most terribly, that of Margaret Hyrkiewicz, who had been stabbed twenty-four times, once for every year of her young life, the previous May. Simultaneously, and quite mysteriously, her four-month-old son, who was living with his father in England, had died in his cot. A week before her death, her boyfriend Edward Coogan had been murdered in precisely the same place.

But this was Belfast, not Zurich or Lagos. I didn't expect perfect safety, nor did I believe in voodoo. I wanted an area with lots of police and lots of soldiers, regularly patrolling, as a deterrent to those who might want to kill me. At no stage since Jim Hanna's death had I thought about returning to Dublin: I remained fixated on being an indolent observer of the Troubles through to their conclusion, (which, I still felt, should be quite soon now).

Over the coming days I discovered that the flat below me was occupied by an English prostitute who worked God knows where, and that the ground-floor flat was occupied by two very republican girls from south Armagh. The occupants of the neighbouring houses were all working-class or lower-middle-class

Catholics who were soon fascinated by this relative exotic in their midst, but I got no curious visits from the IRA. I continued my work for Westinghouse and *The Observer*.

Not long before, a power-sharing Executive between the two communities had been formed, to the common and savage disdain of the paramilitaries on either side. The arrangement might just have worked, but it needed time. In his confrontation with the National Union of Mineworkers in Britain, British Prime Minister Ted Heath, called a general election – as it happened – shortly after I moved into the flat.

Unionists opposed to the power-sharing Executive overwhelmingly outvoted pro-Agreement unionists; an election about Britain's coal industry had turned into a local referendum on how Northern Ireland was to be governed.

Worse still, the wretched Heath was replaced as Prime Minister by the even more worthless Labour leader Harold Wilson. Tweedledum had given way to Tweedledumber. Worst of all, so out of touch was the administration of the province that the Northern Ireland Office was still convinced that the greatest threat to the power-sharing Executive came from the IRA.

When anti-Agreement loyalists, aided by loyalist paramilitaries, called a general strike, the British government was totally wrong-footed: and since Protestants had close to a monopoly of employment in the public service, especially in the power stations, there could be only one outcome if the new British government failed to act. It failed to act. The streets were surrendered to loyalist mobs, with their hundreds of 'lootenant colonels', and in Dublin and Monaghan, UVF bombs killed nearly three dozen people. The men behind some of the bombings were almost certainly the very men I had met in Portadown, but of course I didn't know that at the time. The Executive collapsed. It looked like the Troubles would be around for a while.

Atlantic Avenue was built for army officers from nearby Girdwood Barracks at the end of the nineteenth century, and suffered the same melancholy fate of so many such buildings, being brutally subdivided and partitioned without the slightest regard for whatever minimal character the houses had initially possessed. Róisín hated the flat, the house, the area, everything.

She was now working, and had bought herself a second-hand car – a Cortina, naturally – in which foolishly I was giving her driving lessons. The dynamics of telling someone what to do and what not to do behind the steering wheel of a car are as incompatible with conventional sexual love as the act of performing colonic irrigation on one another. Most other skills can be communicated between lovers. Not driving.

Our driving lessons led to some terrible rows, and worse for me, a growing sense that Róisín at times actually neither liked nor respected me. I realize now that I irritated her with my affectation of knowledge about Belfast. I spoke as if I were part of the city, rather than what I actually was: an outsider with an extensive but tenuous grasp of the realities of the place.

During the lessons we would travel up the sides of the Cave Hill, along the Antrim Road, as I would give tense instructions, and if she made an error I would apologetically clear my throat, to be followed by her grinding the gears and ferociously revving the engine in neutral. 'Don't say another word,' she would hiss. 'Not another fucking word. So. Where do we go next?'

Now here was a quandary indeed: silence or direction? I conjured mildness out of the air, and let it inhabit my tongue, a pleasing little smile – I hoped – playing on my face. 'Up here seems a good idea – what do you think?'

'Okay,' she snorted, indicating left and swinging into a street marked Ben Madigan Park South. We drove up around a dogleg, and to my right we passed Ben Madigan Park, before driving into Ben Madigan Heights.

To make conversation, I muttered, 'He must have been some fellow, this Ben Madigan, to have got all these streets named after him. Any idea who he was?'

Róisín came to a halt, and looked at me with amused scorn. 'Are you serious? Are you actually telling me you don't know about Ben Madigan?'

I was tempted to bluff, but didn't. 'No, I don't know anything about Ben Madigan.'

'Remind me to tell you some time.' She laughed out loud. 'Which way now, if you please?'

We drove off, with me desperately, hopelessly, pathetically in love with her. But mine was an insecure, undignified love, of the kind that knows no pride, for it endlessly senses imminent separation, like those early moments after the locking bolts holding two orbiting spacecrafts together have been released: habit and gravity alone seemed to keep her with me.

I sensed that she was developing faster than I was, socially, intellectually and psychologically, for I had retreated to a flat that would have better suited some scruffy, unwashed undergraduates. She was more highly placed than I in the hierarchy of individual charisma, that magical quality which raises leaders above the crowd. In company, if she spoke, people would listen; far lower than her in that pecking order, if I spoke – no matter how wisely – others would often cut across me, as if they were utterly unaware that I was speaking.

Intelligent and articulate people low in the hierarchy usually find such neglect and personal dismissal irritating. Sober, with time and wisdom, we learn to contain our irritation: in drink, we are often unable to. Thus I had become an embarrassing appurtenance to a young woman's life that was taking a wholly different and unrecognisable shape to the one I had first encountered.

Róisín only partly knew how scared I was after Jim Hanna's death, for I didn't tell her: the full truth would have seemed pathetically melodramatic. I was also scared of the demons of my own devising. I had walked up to death so often that it had established a little throne in my mind, from which it nightly reasserted its authority.

Jimmy and Seamie now visited me with unfailing loyalty, and since Róisín was working at night, I often slept alone. So, when I woke prodded by nightmarish visits from my two faithful friends, I would lie there, gazing at the ceiling lit by the street lights from below, hearing the cars hiss by on the wet roads, listening to the joists shifting and the house sighing, and wondering if tonight was the night when men would finally steal into my bedroom, put a gun to my head and end it all.

Meanwhile, all expectation that we had explored every permutation of murder was endlessly and easily refuted. Ann Ogilby, a Protestant woman, was beaten to death by nearly a dozen Protestant women in a house in Sandy Row, just round the corner from where Rab Brown had sought to end my days over a year earlier. The reason? Some suspected liaison with a married UDA man. Throughout the protracted beating, her six-year-old daughter screamed on the other side of the door – Ann's killers, with commendable sensitivity, having locked the child out. Half way through the beating, the women paused to have a cigarette, two of them sitting on their victim's body because there weren't enough chairs. Thus refreshed, they continued about their manual labours until Ann Ogilby lay pulped and dead.

Two of the women were the wife and daughter of Sammy Flatface, who had brought me down to meet Rab Brown at his local – the very ladies he had put on the game.

Murder singled out the virtuous, the honourable, the true. An honest judge named Rory Conaghan had with judicious care denounced the arrest and internment operation on 9 August 1971, awarding generous compensation to the victims of British injustice. His personal record was of an almost meticulous probity. He had even imprisoned the great Orange Monster Ian Paisley. One September morning the IRA shot him dead in front of his eight-year-old daughter.

I began to realize that I could no longer take the endless killings, increasingly meaningless, increasingly purposeless, increasingly cyclical. If the IRA could kill the good and noble Rory Conaghan, without any nationalist outcry whatsoever, whom would or could it not kill?

Ivan Clayton, the usually mild doorman at the Club Bar to which I still drove from the northside of the city, was unusually warm in his indignation at the murder of the judge. 'And him the greatest gentleman that ever sat on the bench,' he declared a couple of nights later, his neck grimy, his collar worn and frayed, his bearded stubble grey against his sallow skin. 'It's got to stop, old chap, it's got to stop. We've all got to do our bit, that's what I say.'

He puffed on his roll-your-own, a flaccid, sodden little tube, nipping out head between browned finger and thumb as he put the fag end behind his ear. He was at the door when I left, bidding me as always, 'Good night, old chap.'

Leaving at around the same time as me, en route home but on foot, was a young Catholic student called Gerard McWilliams. A little the worse for wear, and having lived outside Belfast for a few years, he was an easy victim. He took what he thought was a short cut to Andersonstown, but was picked up by Rab Brown's boys and sadistically beaten before being stabbed to death with some blunt and agonizing instrument like a screwdriver.

Ivan Clayton was incandescent at this. A little leprechaun of a man who apparently had not once washed in the forty-eight years of his existence, he had never before given sign of uncontrollable anger. He had talked to the youngster as he had left the bar, had told him to mind how he went – and now this blameless creature had died a terrible death.

Ivan decided that he would find out what had happened to the McWilliams boy. Convinced the victim had been followed out of the bar, he began to question customers about what they had seen that night. In due course his endeavours were appropriately rewarded: Ivan was shot dead by Rab Brown's boys as he sat at his little door by the side entrance to the pub.

I had always assumed that because of his name – which to sensitive Irish ears has distinctly tribal resonances – and by his attempts at gentility, that Ivan was a Protestant. Not so. He was a Catholic, and I attended his funeral in the same churchyard, high over the city, where nearly two years earlier we had buried Bob Hume's wife.

But long before this killing, I had already sensed that there was no logical end to this horror – that it had enough energy to fuel an utterly goalless war for years to come. Moreover, my relationship with Róisín was further deteriorating. The previous summer I had gone to Donegal to stay with friends. Róisín stayed in Belfast, working, and I felt the distance grow between us as her increasingly handsome yacht sailed out on its own, leaving my rusting hulk behind. Finally, I sensed then that my time in Northern Ireland might be coming to an end. I remained desperately in love with Róisín, but her increasing coldness and almost infinite capacity to be irritated by me made most contact between us painful.

In addition, my nightly visits from Seamie and Jimmy were wearing me down. Sometimes, the same hideous dream would return several times in a night, each time as compellingly believable as before. And overarching everything was the growing distance between Róisín and me.

So I asked *The Observer* management whether it would give me a job in London. I had not so far distinguished myself with the newspaper. I had been lazy and trite, which were the governing sins of my semi-hippy generation – yet I had nonetheless been sufficiently competent for the newspaper to reply by offering me a six-month contract. My chance to make a name for myself in a larger pool had arrived.

It was agreed that I would serve my time in Belfast while *The Observer* found a replacement for me. I felt excitement and great relief. In all sorts of other ways, things had been going wrong. My flat had been burgled, and someone had danced on the roof of my Fiat, shattering the back window. A few nights later a hit-and-run driver had rear-ended it. I was insured against neither.

My neighbours suggested I take the car around the corner to a workshop being run by a man nicknamed Joe Ninety. On my second trip there, I saw a Cortina drive slowly by. In the passenger seat was a man I knew well. It was Davy Payne, one of the men who had knifed Senator Paddy Wilson and Irene Andrews to death, and the author of many, many killings.

'That fucking's car's been going backward and forwards all fucking day,' said Joe, who I knew belonged to the greatest at-risk group in Northern Ireland. He was a Protestant convert to Catholicism.

The car had stopped, and the occupants were watching Joe. Payne hadn't spotted me because I was largely concealed by a raised bonnet.

'What the fuck are they up to?' said Joe.

'What they're up to is checking you out for a hit,' I said. The only way I could see of handling this one was to take the initiative. I walked out from behind the bonnet and sauntered over to Payne's car.

He was agreeably taken by surprise. He adjusted his spectacles, which is what he often did when he was trying to intimidate someone. 'What you doing with yon turncoat?' he asked.

'Getting my car fixed,' I said. 'And now that I've seen you giving him the once-over, you can't nut him, can you?'

He stared at me for a few silent seconds over the rim of his spectacles before saying, in the softest of voices: 'You know I've never nutted a journalist – yet.'

'You better be on your way before you get into trouble,' I said coolly. 'I'll be seeing you.'

'That's right, you will,' he called out to my departing back.

'Why are you smiling?' asked Joe, looking puzzled. I didn't tell him I would soon be gone, and be outside the reach of Davy Payne and his goons, and beyond the power of Carlisle Circus.

Fifteen

RÓISÍN WAS still coming to see me and though we remained lovers it was seldom through the night as before. Then, early one Friday evening in September 1974 she was suddenly taken very ill; an excruciating pain almost immobilized her. Strangely, though I remember much about this time, I don't recall whether I took her to hospital or whether an ambulance collected her.

She was given extensive tests, and over the next few days she was diagnosed as having rheumatoid arthritis, a progressive disease that attacks the joints and that usually leads to immobility, often ending in total paralysis. She lay in her hospital bed, her legs in frames, and who could say what the prognosis was?

I was beside myself with a number of emotions; one was despair for her and her future; a second was enormous guilt over Bob's death and my failure to be true to him during his last weeks; and the third and the mightiest was love – an overwhelming, unstoppable, all-commanding love, a protective emotion greater by far than anything that I had felt before, even at the height of our mutual passion.

I would sit for hours beside her hospital bed while other patients in the ward cracked jokes about young love, and our not being able to keep our hands off one another. She was dependent on nurses to do everything for her. It was impossible for me to leave her in this condition and go to London; quite impossible. If she was going to be dependent on anyone from now on, it was going to be me. There were to be no more Bob Moons in my life.

I hesitated about telling London of my decision, because management had been very considerate towards an only moderately useful journalist, and I did not want to seem ungrateful. Finally, I wrote to the managing editor, Ken Obank, to inform him that I was withdrawing my resignation as Belfast correspondent.

My hesitation was fatal. It was too late, he replied. My replacement had already been appointed, and since I had chosen to remain in Belfast, the job offer in London could not be kept open indefinitely. I had to make a choice. I did.

I visited Róisín as much as I could, not telling her of the changes in my plans. Finally, she was released from hospital and went to stay at her mother's, while I finished the last period of my contract with *The Observer*, which was to conclude the following January. I was now stuck in Belfast, and with my primary source of income soon to vanish.

Autumn became winter, and the rains fell from grey skies onto grey streets and grey people, as they made of their lives what they could. I regularly sent articles for *Hibernia* magazine down to Dublin by train. Great Victoria Street station had been bombed repeatedly, and was now home to the world's largest collection of maimed pigeons, broken creatures fluttering with one wing, half-blinded, hopping on one leg, wingless, yet still surviving: an avian Belfast.

An IRA ceasefire was in the offing once again, but by now I was too familiar with the dynamics of this evil place: there was no chance of that ceasefire holding.

Barney Cahill had split up from his wife, and moved into a flat in a tenement like mine up the road from me on Atlantic Avenue. Sometimes he and I would drink in the local bar, which

I didn't like, because it only sold bottled stout, not draught, and sometimes we'd go down to Catholic Markets area, to drink there. We would often sit in silence, because there was nothing to talk about, facing the door so we might have a little warning if some Protestant terrorist with a machine gun came in to do a spray job on the bar. He would be puffing on his pipe, and to wean myself off cigarettes I even bought a pipe and joined him. So we passed long winter evenings, drinking, silently puffing on our pipes, both of us watching the door, waiting for death.

Stoicism in the face of death had become an expected norm of all Belfast communities. A loyalist leader, Billy Hull, was visiting UDA leader Jim Anderson at his do-it-yourself shop in north Belfast that November. Hull was a vast man, with a mountainside of a belly and a girth the length of a finishing-tape. IRA men burst into the shop while the two men were talking and emptied their guns into them.

Hitting Hull was easy. Finding a vital organ in his mass, less so. But Anderson was a thin man, and the gunmen, in their excitement firing low, shot him in the legs, breaking both femurs, before shooting him in the stomach. Knowing his legs were gone, Anderson held on to the workbench as his assailants fled. Beside him, Hull lay spouting blood from a dozen wounds to his lungs and colossal belly.

'Are you alive, Billy?' wheezed Anderson, struggling to hold himself upright.

'I am, aye,' came a voice from the floor. 'Here, Jim. You wouldn't have a wee feg on you now, would you?'

They survived. The two Catholics shot the next day in revenge did not.

Meanwhile, miraculously, Róisín then entered a period of remission – so much so that one night shortly before Christmas, she was able to drive over to join me at Atlantic Avenue. I had been invited – rather civilly, I think – by Liam Hourican for the RTÉ Christmas party. I asked Róisín and Barney along, and accordingly drove them there. Liam, with even greater civility, heartily welcomed them.

We proceeded to get hammered. Barney knew the barman who was from the Markets and slipped him a few bob: in return, the barman slipped Barney a bottle of Pernod and a bottle of Bacardi, which he pocketed. On our way out, I saw a crate of Carlsberg Special lager, and I helped myself to a half dozen. I was just completing the theft when I glanced up and saw Pat Hourican, Liam's wife, looking at me in embarrassed pity.

Well, I reckoned for all those £8, eight-hour days, a few beers was the least I deserved. We dumped our haul in the car, and went to the Europa, where we had a few more drinks. And when that closed, we drove back to my flat, the better to consume our little haul.

There were soldiers everywhere on our road and houses were being evacuated. I asked a soldier what was going on. Bomb scare he said, pointing to Róisín's car: that vehicle's been reported stolen.

'It's not stolen,' she said indignantly – she did indignation rather well, actually – 'it's fucking-well mine.'

She got out of my car and stormed up to the ranking NCO to unleash one of her formidable Róisín rants. I drove on a few yards, and then Barney got out and went into the house while I parked. I locked the car and looked round. Róisín was coming back towards me. I passed a soldier at my front door and went into the hall.

From above, Barney suddenly came tumbling downstairs, head over heels. As he landed in the hall, the soldier at the front door turned away, raised his rifle and fired up the street.

The briefest pause followed. 'Jesus fucking Christ, you stupid fucking cunt, you could have killed me,' I heard Róisín scream from the street.

'Sorry, dear, I thought you had a gun,' said the soldier.

At that very same moment Barney, confused and drunk, put

down the two bottles of spirits and inexplicably kicked open the door of the ground-floor flat beside me. Worse, far worse, was what sat within: an entire unit of IRA men, who instantly rose to their feet.

I knew one of them. I stepped in, eyed him meaningfully, nodded my head sideways, and whispered: 'Brits.' He nodded, and gestured around him. The guns remained out, but lowered. I backed out into the hall.

The soldier who had shot at Róisín had followed her into the house, apologizing profusely, and was now followed by an NCO. They stood in the hall, feet away from the open flat door and the IRA unit. Inside the flat, Barney was growing soberer by the second.

I turned away, and faced the two soldiers in the hall. Róisín, cool as ice, said: 'What the fuck are you doing in this house? You nearly killed me there, and now you're trespassing. You know that, don't you? Now get the fuck out. Go on. Outside.'

'She's right,' I said, half hysterically, 'You've got to go.'

'What's in there?' said the NCO, pointing at the open flat-door.

I turned, and inside the room one of the IRA men rose and put his hand on the cocking-handle of his M1 carbine.

'Me,' said Barney, emerging, his lip bleeding from a ferocious cut. 'Look, fuck, I've just had a few, and I fell. You ever do that?'

The NCO laughed. 'Yeah. Course I have. You should get that lip of yourn to a hospital.'

'I'll look after that,' I said. 'Thanks sergeant.'

'And watch what you're doing with that gun of yours, you stupid fucking cunt,' Róisín said softly to the private soldier, who, looking sheepish, shuffled out.

I closed the outside door, and walked down the hall to the flat. As I said, I knew one of the men inside: Barney knew them all. It was an Official IRA unit that had been activated because it was believed a loyalist attack on the area was imminent that night.

The emergency with the soldiers over, Barney was suddenly

drunk again, and rambling. 'Get him out of here, and stop him blabbing, or I fucking will,' said the IRA leader in seriously menacing tones. I put Barney in the car, while he kept calling, 'Robbie? Robbie? Why did you do it Robbie?'

I drove him to the Mater, where his lip was stitched up, as he cried throughout, 'Robbie! Robbie!'

'Who's Robbie?' I asked savagely, hours later, as we drove back home. By this time he had sobered up sufficiently to remember what had happened. When he entered the house ahead of me, he had confused the middle flat, inhabited by Pamela, the English prostitute, with mine on the top floor, and had walked in – bizarrely, the door was unlocked.

There, having sex in what he thought was my bed, was a strange woman with – he thought – a Markets man he knew named Robbie Elliman. Barney was indignant, as behoved a good friend. 'WHAT THE FUCK ARE THE TWO OF YOUSE DOING FUCKING IN MY MATE'S BED?'

Pamela's friend had withdrawn from her fair body, and – not an easy task – had laid out Barney, who had not merely flown backwards out of the flat but had also fallen downstairs, holding, like any good Marketsman, the bottles of Pernod and Bacardi protectively next to his body throughout. When he stood up in the hallway, somewhat confused – for it had been a confusing night – he thought he was still outside the upstairs flat where he'd been punched. He carefully put the two bottles of drink down, and kicked open the door, to find the IRA glaring at him. He was lucky not to have been shot on the spot.

I drove back to our house, but in the confusion of the night I had lost my door key. For various reasons that might just be obvious, we could hardly rouse any of my housemates, so we made for Barney's, just fifty yards up the road. He couldn't find his key either, so the three of us sat on the stoop, broke open the drink and began our private little party. We were drunk again within minutes.

Barney rose to pee against a wall when a soldier suddenly emerged from the dark. 'What have you got there?'

'This,' said Barney, presenting him with his penis.

Róisín, Barney and I collapsed in hysteria; we rolled over and over on the ground while the soldiers gazed at us in baffled disgust before filing away. We probably spent half an hour there, in uncontrollable gales of laughter, before kicking in the front door of Barney's house and staggering upstairs, where we got stuck further into the Pernod, Bacardi and Carlsberg.

Then, fully dressed, we collapsed on Barney's only bed where we awoke many hours later to a perfectly terrible smell. We were covered in dog shit.

The one remaining puzzle of the night before was why Robbie Elliman had hit Barney: I knew him, and he was not a man who was free with his fists with anyone, never mind with Barney. As it happened, Barney's assailant wasn't Robbie, but an unknown double who will probably remember his night with Pamela for a very, very long time.

Over the coming weeks, it didn't really matter to me that I would no longer have a job. I had Róisín, and I had saved a reasonable amount of money. I was more in love with her than I had ever been before. I decided, without consulting her, to buy a house. This would prove to her what a serious person I was. We would get married and live there, and she would have her career and I would have mine. It was terribly, terribly simple. Barney and I toured north Belfast, looking at some of the tree-lined avenues off the Cave Hill Road. I caught sight of the little district named after Ben Madigan, and I remembered the conversation I'd had with Róisín.

'Who was Ben Madigan?' I asked. 'Why does he have so many streets named after him?'

'See you? You're a right geg, so you are,' he said, meaning

I was a joker. He repeated, 'Who was Ben Madigan?' and then laughed. 'Aye, that's a good one.'

He continued to drive towards the Cliftonville Road. We saw a For Sale sign, inspected the house, and I decided to buy it. Róisín knew nothing of this.

That Christmas I told my mother that I was in love, and that by the following Christmas I would be married. I was very happy.

Things started to go wrong on my return to Belfast. I suspect in part it was because Róisín had found a footing on the ladder of the male hierarchy, and discovered that I was beneath her in that hierarchy. The old irritations surfaced, and I found it hard to please her. I think she found the idea of the house purchase both ridiculous and intimidating. After all, I hadn't discussed sharing a house with her, never mind marriage: I had told her I loved her many, many times, but I had never told that I planned we should live together for ever and ever.

In the first few weeks of the New Year, on many nights, she found reasons not to see me. I had not yet moved to the house. One such evening I was in my flat, watching television. Outside, a heavy fog had fallen. Some time after midnight, I walked around the corner to the Chinese restaurant for a takeaway. The fog was now incredibly dense, the thickest I had seen since the old pea-soupers of my childhood in Leicester.

Then, next to me, feet away, an invisible gunmen opened fire. Bangs were as close as those by my Browning-man: flashes through the fog. Then choking sounds, from within touching, even breathing distance. Almost paralysed, I backed away slowly. Next to me, somewhere, invisible, were gunmen. I stood still, and heard footsteps coolly walking away.

I blundered blindly away through the fog, and was soon lost. So I stopped and began to inch forward, hands extended, until my fingers touched a wall. I turned and rested my back to it, and there I stayed, frozen with fear. At length sirens wailed and the blue lights of arriving ambulances gave me my bearings. I went back to my grimy flat, to freshly enhanced dreams.

Years later, I discovered the truth: UVF killers had gone out in the fog, looking for Catholics to kill, presuming that in this part of the city anyone they found would be Catholic. And in that fog, they missed me. But the first two men they found, they shot: one dead, and one wounded. Now, not even the densest fog was foe to the random assassin, but his friend and guardian.

The dead boy was Michael Convery. His wounded friend was shot in the scrotum, and lost a testicle. His sisters, with rare kindness and delicacy, in time nicknamed him 'The One-Ball Wonder'.

Assisted by a Dutchman and his van – what twists of fate had brought him from the civilities of the Netherlands to this satanic place? – I moved into my new home. I had now almost no money. Róisín, on the other hand, had just taken a flat in south Belfast, where her social life was blossoming amongst the professional classes. I grew increasingly tentative in her company, terrified of irritating her to crossness yet again.

Some time later she was discussing her plans for Easter: a break in Donegal seemed to be a good idea. I agreed – I needed to get away from Belfast. She and some friends were renting a house near Gweedore, and were stopping overnight in Derry first, she added. Excellent, I said. She was going in her car, she said. Fine, I said. No reason to take two cars, and the driving practice will do you good.

I got drunk at her friends' in Derry, her scornful glare across the room penetrating my inebriated idiocy. In Donegal, things got far, far worse. Her friend Carmel took endless pleasure in piling humiliation upon humiliation on me. I could do or say nothing without her ridiculing me.

A group of people up from Belfast were present that weekend, some of whom I was vaguely acquainted with: their jocular leader, palpably, was a small, enormously fat man named John

McGuffin. His was the most magnetic presence in any room. What we all had in common was the vapid leftism of the day. That Easter in Donegal, on our television sets, we watched the Khmer Rouge march into Pnom Penh and we rejoiced at this triumph over imperialism. We genuinely believed that freedom would result.

I had more pressing matters on my mind though. Anyone who has been in a declining relationship that they're desperately trying to hold onto will recognize the ignoble position in which I found myself. Each morning I'd try to impress Róisín by frying breakfast for everyone in the house, and would then be criticized by her and Carmel, for some culinary imperfection. One day, Carmel came to me and asked: 'Is that true? Did you really ask Róisín who Ben Madigan was?'

'So what if I did?'

'And here's you always acting as if you knew everything about Belfast.'

Their niggling would continue unabated throughout the day, the women exchanging looks and exasperated raising of eyebrows, until the final drinks of the night. My desperate desire to placate merely fed their hunger to humiliate. I began to sound out if anyone was going back to Belfast early, so that I could get a lift: no one was. I withdrew from Róisín, not daring to face her scorn, nor the endlessly reiterated contempt of Carmel. After some of the most terrible few days of my life, we returned to Belfast. In my heart I knew the worst, but I still needed it to be spelt out for me.

Róisín came over to the house, and it was *she* who was cross with me. In fact, she was white with anger, her pupils shrivelling into narrow points with something that was close to hatred.

'Look,' she scolded, 'you weren't even meant to go to Donegal. Carmel and I had planned the whole thing with *our* friends, and you were a gatecrasher everyone resented and nobody wanted, and that was that. It's not my fault that you've bought this stupid fucking house. Do you understand? It's over. You and me, finished.'

She glared at me with those unwavering eyes that I had loved from the start, aided by that unflinching way she had since developed: '*Over!*'

She said goodbye, more in anger than sorrow, and left me forever, so marooning me on an island of emotional devastation where I was to spend many, many years. As for the rheumatoid arthritis that had so changed my life, and had so completely steered me away from a career in Fleet Street – it had vanished.

Sixteen

IT WAS NOW spring of 1975, and my new house had no furniture or carpets, because I couldn't afford any. I had bought a second-hand bed with a revolting second-hand mattress. With the IRA ceasefire, my radio income from Westinghouse had almost totally dried up. However, the ceasefire only applied to the security forces, whereas both the IRA and the loyalists were now engaged in savage sectarian warfare, which was suddenly focussed in the area I had just bought into: that bloody and now familiar arc of the city, running from Carlisle Circus to the Cave Hill. In other words, I had sunk my entire savings into a house that had plummeted overnight in value, and was located in the most dangerous quadrant of the most treacherous city of Western Europe.

I had no job, no life, no skills, nothing. In the previous two years I had become a journalist with a good and noble newspaper, and had blown it. I had fallen in love and blown that too. I had bought a house that was now worthless. What possible future did I have? Some days I would not get out of my bed at all. Dawn and dusk met at noon: night and day resembled Belfast's season-less year, a grey continuum of monotony and melancholy.

Could it really be that Róisín was gone from my life forever? I had been so certain, so sure, that she would be my wife, that, even after it could not have been made plainer to me that it was not to be, it was still impossible to accept. This was bereavement in its purest sense, with a single exception: wherever I went outside of my pathetic new home, there was a good chance of running into Róisín and her scarcely concealed scorn.

After a while, and for want of any alternatives in my life, I was drawn into McGuffin's circle. He would hold court in the Bank Bar in the centre of Belfast, popping out occasionally to give a lecture at Belfast technical college, and then returning to down pints of Harp and eat cheese and crackers, all day long.

He was unique: a middle-class Protestant who unwaveringly supported the Provisional IRA. He won all his arguments by using logic, emotion, blackmail, intellectual distortion, and ultimately bullying and abuse. At the end of any argument that he had comprehensively lost according to the rules of reason, he would bellow, 'Ah shut up you fucking wanker,' his acolytes roaring in agreement alongside him. His set – and it was very emphatically *his* set – consisted of left-leaning liberals of both Catholic and Protestant backgrounds. Some were trendy, right-on supporters of the IRA. Some were not. But they constituted an altogether more interesting society than any other set I knew of. I passed some inward rite of admission to this group that summer of 1975 by choosing to grow a beard: I thus officially became part of Belfast's mediocre attempt at an alternative society.

It was a broad and morally relaxed group of people, for many of whom sex was a predictable part of a friendship; but my heart had been thoroughly cauterized, and sex was simply a physical matter that occurred whenever it did.

Only now, looking at photographs of myself of the time, do I realize that I was a good-looking young man. I certainly didn't think so then. Nor should I give the impression that I was endlessly depressed, as I wasn't. By disposition I remained outwardly cheerful, and though desperately wounded was far from spending my time brooding.

However, being outwardly cheerful required an effort. Facing the day required an effort. It was an effort to get out of bed. It was an effort going to bed, because halfway through the night I would invariably have my little rendezvous with Jimmy and with Seamie, who though thick and thin, in love and in lovelorn desolation alike, remained true. Knowing that I would meet them meant knowing that I would awake, heart hammering like horses' hooves, and have to have at least one cigarette. Each night I slept with ten cigarettes beside me.

At this juncture I had a couple of hundred pounds in the bank. On a good week I might earn £10, sometimes nothing. In my empty house I watched television and stared at the rain falling onto the dripping plane trees on the street outside and the reservoir beyond my back garden. What else was there to do? All socializing was now in ghettoes; the city centre was completely dead at night. Its only population was that of unfortunate soldiers fruitlessly walking the deserted streets in the rain, their hands cold and wet on their rifle stocks.

Barney Cahill remained in touch with me. He was now apparently out of all paramilitary involvement and was trying to make a living out of doing whatever his fertile brain could come up with. He had what we would now call a female mind: it could cope with several problems simultaneously, yet he also had a very male capacity to concentrate, and an extraordinary ability to understand the way other people thought. All of which explained why he was so good at business.

He read widely and voraciously, especially if the books concerned were mine. These he borrowed with an unwavering promise that he would return them, before passing them on to other friends, no doubt in exchange for the same vacuous undertaking he had given me. With him as an intermediary, I probably became the primary source for the second-hand book trade in Belfast.

I didn't care. He, in his own way, did. Barney's real glory to me was he stayed in touch. He would never telephone, but he might just turn up at the front door, swaying drunkenly with a couple of six-packs under one arm, and his pipe in the other hand, and an idiotic grin on his round bearded face.

In time I got to know the people Barney associated with from the Markets area of the city, which was where Joe McCann had been shot. They were dealers, every last one of them; they bought, they sold, and most of all, they stole. They had a code of honour, but I didn't know what it was, because they all professed to be dedicated Marxists who were even more dedicated to the profit motive. These carnivorous vegetarians were either members of, or tribally loyal to, the rump of the Official IRA, the strange deviant body that adhered to several contradictory policies simultaneously.

So they had guns, but were in favour of peace. They were on a ceasefire, but reserved the right to 'retaliate', which, in a city where people were being killed as a matter of daily routine, made their ethical position hard to define, and harder still to predict. They were cheerful, unprincipled rogues, with complex and impossibly devious minds. I was a child in their company, and I suppose they tolerated me because this English-educated public schoolboy felt and exhibited absolutely no moral or intellectual superiority towards them. And rightly so: they knew far more about the world than I did. They were equally versed in the ways of the gun and the manifold ways of theft: the leader of the Official IRA in the city, Billy McMillen, said despairingly of his Markets volunteers that they weren't a unit, but a wee gang.

A wee gang, maybe, but as with all of the paramilitary people I met, they genuinely believed themselves to be soldiers. It is perhaps hard to accept this, but the cult of the legitimate warrior was an authentic creed amongst all the paramilitaries, compelling in its conviction, and utterly liberating in its authorizations. For this allowed every participant, whatever community they came from, to lay claim to the morally unexacting concepts of 'military necessity', which could effortlessly – if unconsciously – be translated into criminal activity. For my Markets men, their intrinsic loyalties were tinged with treachery: their intrinsic treachery limited by fealty to the group. They laughed a lot, from early morning when they rose, to early next morning when they went to bed. Laughter was their anthem and their antiphon, even as they were cheerfully pocketing one another's wallets while fruitlessly searching for their own.

That summer I decided to squander my savings on a one-month holiday in an old rectory in Connemara, staying with some friends from Dublin, with me paying my pro-rata share. I was prepared to spend so much money because I was lonely. But in Galway it rained every day, all day, and I had little in common with my company. They had careers and families and a purpose to their lives. They seemed to know what they were about. I was flotsam on the running sea of other people's making. Each night we settled into drinking and arguing, with a vicious vehemence that can be a very Irish characteristic, if one seldom remarked on.

I had applied to the BBC for a humble job as a researcher in Northern Ireland for the UK programme *Nationwide*, an interview for which coincided with my holiday. My time in Connemara reminded me of the golden days of Goleen, and early on during my holiday I had abjectly written to Róisín, pleading with her to change her mind and join me there. On my return to Belfast for the interview, a letter from her awaited me on the bare floorboards of my home saying that would not be possible. It was tearful, but it was very, very final.

I returned to Connemara and the rain, and each day I would leave the wet Victorian rectory at about one for the local pub, hoping I would find a woman in whose arms and loins I could drown my miseries. I found none. At six I would walk back to the big house, replete with Guinness and with gloom, for another evening of food, wine and bitter, meaningless arguments. In the dank wardrobes, our clothes were rimed with a hoar frost of fungus.

I returned to Belfast, where a rejection from the BBC awaited me on the unvarnished boards in my empty, echoing house. August was hot that year. Each day in my back garden, I lay in the sun. I was twenty-eight, lean, bronzed and handsome, with a broken and steadily hardening heart and a soul that brimmed with despair. Failure now was not a possible fate but a continuing condition.

Compounding that failure was a deep moral despondency. At the end of July a bus carrying the Miami Showband from the Republic was held up by a group of men in British army uniforms who were in fact UVF terrorists. The Protestant terrorists intended to put a bomb on board the bus so that it would later blow up in transit, making it look as if the musicians were IRA terrorists who had been killed by their own bomb. However, the bomb exploded prematurely, killing three of the bandsmen and two terrorists.

The men responsible were almost certainly from the Ulster Volunteer Force unit that Jim Hanna and Billy Marchant had introduced me to near Portadown. But, in addition to being terrorists, I also knew they were members of the British army's Ulster Defence Regiment. I had told no one in authority that Jim Hanna had given me information concerning the penetration of the legal UDR by the terrorist UVF. This had been confirmed by my visit to the UVF training area. Information so acquired was 'privileged', and anyway, I was not an informer. Yet I had information that could have saved lives. Once again, I was a passive accomplice.

Other professional dilemmas caused me much introspection. One Sunday in 1973 Barney was walking down the Falls Road carrying a pair of shoes when he saw a car stop and a man with a Sterling sub-machine gun get out. Two postmen, Anthony Coleman and David McAleese, convenient Catholics both, were yards in front of him. He opened fire into their backs. Once he had cut them down, he emptied his magazine into the bodies on the ground. Barney ran towards the killer, hurling his only missiles, his futile shoes, at him. The gunman brandished his (probably empty) gun at Barney, got into the car and escaped.

Two years later in my house, Barney was looking at a copy of *Combat*, a magazine produced by the loyalist Ulster Volunteer Force. 'Oh, fuck me,' he whispered. His face had gone white, the hairs on his arms standing up like a phalanx of elf spears. 'See yon fellow? That's fucking him.'

He pointed his trembling finger to a photograph of a loyalist terrorist inside the Maze prison. 'He done them two postmen.' I looked at the picture: an uncouthly distinctive face that one would not easily forget. Barney was hyperventilating, with cold beads of sweat forming on his forehead. 'Are you going to tell the police?' I asked him.

He looked at me incredulously. 'You fuckin' serious? You think I'm a fuckin' tout or something?'

Thus the unuttered republican oath of *omertà* even extended its benefactions to the other side, who, without scruple or discrimination, routinely killed Catholics. But of course, the rule of *omertà* did not apply to me. What should I do? Go the police with the picture, and say that an eye-witness I knew had identified the unnamed killer from the photograph? But I had acquired the issue of *Combat* as a journalist, just as I acquired all sorts of information as a journalist. Was I to give the authorities some items, but not others? And how long could I stay alive operating on that principle?

Thus Frankie Curry, the killer of the two men, served his brief time in jail on another charge before being freed. He was never charged with these killings, and was himself shot dead by fellow loyalists over twenty years later.

As with the killing of Robert Bankier, there is no resolution to this kind of dilemma. Journalists are not intelligence agents; but nor are we moral theologians, able to tease out the ethical threads of consequence and responsibility. As journalists become enmeshed in a story, any story, we are no longer mere witnesses but participants. When that participation is merely political, the conscience can remain aloof: but when innocents die, especially when journalists have kept vital information to themselves, conscientious aloofness is no longer possible.

And there was I worrying about my duties to others, when those with far graver sins on their souls sailed through life. Occasionally, I still saw my young friend Seamus, the cheerful killer who didn't swear. He'd done some time in jail, and I'd attended his release party. Everyone there had long hair, and I knew neither one from another, but I would guess Bobby Sands was there. I don't know. I do know that Seamus's grandmother, whose son had been murdered by the Provisional IRA, kept shouting, 'Up the Provies!'

I still had some way to go before I understood the dynamics of Northern Ireland. I was even invited to Seamus's wedding to a girl barely out of her pram. I found myself sitting at a table of spare guests without partners, at which I was the solitary male. The convention at a Belfast wedding was that only men bought the drinks. So with the manic grin of a bather who doesn't want his children happily watching from the beach to know he's being eaten by sharks, I kept my cackling, hooting harem in large Bacardi-and-cokes throughout a long, long evening. They were thoroughly indignant when I declined to drive them all to their respective homes. 'See you? Call yourself a man,' sneered one who had been imbibing to the detriment of my bank balance all night. There were times when one's affection for Belfast women found a natural limit.

At the end of that summer, my fortunes took an extraordinary turn: NBC News in the USA was starting a 24-hour-nationwide radio news service. My name was passed to them, and they contacted me: I did a test report for them, they liked it, and I was appointed as their Belfast correspondent, to be paid strictly by reports used.

Coincidentally, I was invited to participate in a conference about Ireland in Amherst University, Massachusetts, that autumn, all expenses paid. Of course, I went, and of course, in the manner of all such conferences about Ireland, nothing was achieved. But seeing life on the campus there, those beautiful Americans with their perfect teeth and their flawless complexions, and their open, uninhibited sexuality, I felt a deep pang of envy. They lived in a land of clean seasons, of sunlit summers, of golden autumns, of winters of bracing cold and certain snows, and lush New England springs: they had no understanding of the grey rain that could fall for days onto the Black Mountain and Belfast Lough, and onto the maze of grubby red-brick streets that tumbled down the slopes of one to the shores of the other.

Gratefully, before returning I had a fling with a beautiful American: sex and marijuana in the open air on a sunlit afternoon – that is how other people lived in other lands, before returning to how and where I lived. Still, even though my neighbours in Knutsford Drive, off the Cliftonville Road, probably did not have sex in the back garden, or smoke marijuana, they were none-theless delightful people, resolutely determined to live as normal lives as possible. My closest local friends were the McWilliams family – the artists Joe and Catherine, and their children Jane and Simon, both now artists in their own right.

But living normal lives was a feat now moving beyond even the considerable means of the people of north Belfast. Pure ter-rorism literally thrives on fear: the single deed lives on in the minds of the target population like a wave circling the ocean, endlessly returning to the same shore. Moreover, nothing quite compares with the terrors of an imagination that events show to be fully justified in all its most atrocious speculations.

A gang – now known as the Shankill Butchers – had taken to touring my part of Belfast looking for stray Catholic males to abduct and torture. They would then indulge in a few hours of sadistic sport before killing their unfortunate victim. I know now that the leader of the gang was Lenny Murphy, the small muscular individual who used to glare at me whenever I went into the loyalist club.

One day Lenny Murphy led an attack on a wine warehouse owned by Catholics, round the corner from Carlisle Circus. Two Catholic women and two men were made to kneel on the ground and were executed by gunshots to the back of the head. Not far away, at Carlisle Circus itself, a Catholic photographer was murdered in his studio, which was then blown up. Twelve people died in a wave of loyalist bombings and shootings across the province in this surge of terrorism. My new employers were news-hungry: the more of my bulletins they used, the more I got paid; the more misery and bloodshed there was in Northern Ireland, the richer I became.

Northern Ireland's profligate generosity to the hungry journalist was not confined to tribal feuding: for there was often inter-tribal feuding, usually of a colourfully murderous squalor. There were three major armed republican groups and three major loyalist groups, and each could begin a feud over an incomprehensible piece of theology, which to republicans might mean the proposed date for a united Ireland, and to loyalists might mean who didn't buy their round. Rab Brown, for example, had shot dead his colleague and chum Duke Elliott over the late return of a borrowed weapon. He would have made an interesting librarian.

Republican feuds always tended to be more bitter and better organized. Earlier that year, Billy McMillen, one of the nicest of all the paramilitaries I ever met, had been shot dead by Gerald Steenson, who had joined a republican splinter group. Steenson was the boy-Rommel – then aged fourteen – whom I had seen in charge of the gunfire-spraying teenage gang on Divis Flats the day Joe McCann had been killed and Lieutenant Nicholas Hull fatally wounded. Steenson proceeded to become a serial killer: by the time of his death in 1984, aged twenty-six, he had murdered at least sixteen people.

Some time later, irritated by some Official IRA activity, the Provisional IRA launched a pre-emptive assault, designed to put it out of business forever. There were two and a half dozen attacks, in which seventeen men were wounded. One man was dead, in the Markets area. I went down with my tape recorder to do an *in situ* voice report. The Markets were terrifying. Once again all lights were off, pubs were closed, the streets deserted and soldiers and policemen everywhere. In the brief time I was there I discovered the identity of the dead man: it was Robbie Elliman, Barney Cahill's best friend, and a man I had had more than a few pints with.

I had to tell Barney. He didn't have a phone in his new home at the top of the Cliftonville, round the corner from me, so I drove over to tell him. It was the first time I'd ever broken such news to anyone, and it was terrible. Barney was a big strong man, as you'd have to be to run a building site as once he did, and with his fists if need be.

He broke down and wept, his knees buckling with the weight of grief. After about ten minutes, he said something quite appalling. 'I've got to get down there. Now.'

'Jesus Barney, there've been shootings everywhere, and the taxis are all off the roads. It's fucking dangerous out there. Stay here and go down tomorrow.'

'You'll drive me,' he sniffed.

'*What?* Are you fucking crazy?'

'You've got to. My car's fucked. If you don't, I'll walk.'

Ah. Moral blackmail at its most brutal. No sober person in his right mind would walk down the Cliftonville at midnight: no sober person would allow a friend do it.

'You cunt,' I said. 'Come on, let's go.'

'Howld on there, till I get my coat.'

Belfast was its usual haunted deserted self, only more so, as I drove Barney down to the Markets. A heavy river mist had rolled in from the Lagan, and I drove slowly through the city centre streets, to the edge of Cromac Square, invisible in the fog, where three and a half years before I had seen Robert Bankier die.

A soldier emerged from the mist and waved me down. He came to my window. He was an officer. 'I'm sorry sir, I can't let you through, no cars allowed past this point.'

'I'm just dropping my friend off, is that okay?'

The soldier nodded and stayed beside me while Barney promptly got out of the car, vanishing in the fog with unusual haste. I looked around, preparing to turn, and noticed Barney's coat on the back seat. 'Barney,' I called out through the open window, 'you forgot your coat.'

'Excuse me sir, you forgot your coat,' cried the officer into the bank of fog. Barney emerged from the mist and came back towards me. I half-heard the soldier talking to me, describing the night of chaos and bloodshed. I put my left hand underneath the folded coat and tried to lift it. It was ludicrously heavy. I shoved my hand deeper underneath the coat and lifted it again. The reason it was so heavy was that it contained a gun. The balance of the coat shifted as it rose, and I had to use both hands, now around the gun itself. The officer continued to talk to me, apparently enjoying the company. Barney reached in and I passed him the coat and the firearm. The soldier chattered on. Barney silently and carefully folded the coat over his arm, getting the centre of gravity just right, while icicles formed in my blood. Then, saying not a word, he walked away.

'Good night sir,' the soldier called to Barney, then turned to me. 'And good night to you sir, and you mind yourself. There's a lot of chaps out there with guns.'

On a bleak night in December shortly after Robbie's murder, I heard of a fatal pub bombing in south Armagh. Though it was close to midnight, I chose to drive down to do another *in situ* report. I had no maps of the area nor any knowledge of it, and by this time south Armagh had become a graveyard for this generation of British soldiers just as it had been for Mountjoy's unfortunates. I nonetheless drove into that dark night, into an apparently happy land that knew no law.

In every hamlet, the pubs were open, the revelry loud and uninhibited, even spilling out on the mid-winter, midnight streets. I had no idea how to get to Silverbridge, where the pub bombing had occurred. Lost, as many outsiders must invariably become in the capillaries of lanes and roadways, I stopped at a bar and in my English accent asked for directions to Silverbridge.

Unhesitatingly, people poured out of the pub to help me. A man gave me one route to the village, but then another man pointed out that there was an IRA ambush in preparation there. A woman began to propose another way to my destination, but then remembered: there was a culvert landmine under the road there, awaiting a British patrol. An animated conversation followed, revealing a communal and encyclopaedic knowledge of pending republican operations. One way or another, they were determined to get me to Silverbridge without precipitating my own premature end at the hands of the apparent legions of IRA men about their sleepless vigils on the hillsides that dominated the countryside. They were bizarrely charming.

One of the men killed in the loyalist attack on Silverbridge was an Englishman, Trevor Bracknell, who had married a local girl and then settled in this most republican of areas. He was likeable, kept his nose clean, and therefore was left alone. When I expressed wonder at this to a local man in the village, he made a wry noise. The mother of two of the leading IRA men in Crossmaglen was English, he said. Maybe that's why they loved freedom as they did.

South Armagh people have a gnomic logic and a gnomic humour, and a gnomic way of fighting a war.

Seventeen

NEARLY A YEAR had gone by since Róisín had left me. I was emotionally hopeless, with a dangerous streak of indifference to my own and to others' feelings. Yet I was still likeable and attractive enough to find occasional sexual partners, but on the other hand, in Belfast at the time, that was no great achievement. Cities that do not make it to the sixth commandment are hardly likely to pay much attention to the ones following it.

My remaining communication with loyalist paramilitaries was Tommy (Tucker) Lyttle. I would regularly pop up to see him in the Salisbury Bar on the Shankill Road. His habits were religious: half-pint glasses of beer only, which the barman Alex – an almost Jeevesian figure – understood perfectly. Tucker only had to flicker his eyes at Alex, and the half-pints would instantly appear. Tucker never got drunk, and he liked me; he even seemed to wish to please me. He would take me home to meet his wife and young children, and she endlessly insisted that I stay and eat.

Jimmy and Seamie remained equally true to me; and as death wandered the back streets of north Belfast almost nightly, I had cause to conjure back their attentions. After all, they were friends. Another friend was the dream of Róisín, snoring beside me, as snore she did. I would wake up and, half-asleep, lie there, looking across the bed in the dark and into the past of a year before, a sideways smile on my face before I would reach out to touch her, finding only a cold empty bed in a midwinter house in Belfast.

1976 began catastrophically with a republican bomb attack on a hotel in Armagh where Protestants were seeing the New Year in. Three of the revellers were killed. A couple of days later loyalists struck back, fatally shooting six Catholic men, two sets of three brothers. The IRA then emerged from the drumlins to deliver the ace of trumps when it stopped a bus carrying workers from a factory, separated the Protestants from the Catholics, and then slaughtered ten Protestants.

Northern Ireland was world headlines, and each massacre meant more news reports for the USA, and thus more money. How did I feel about this? I felt like filth for a day or so at such blood money, until a fresh wave of killings swept over us, and I lost all power of introspection or analysis, and returned to producing my perky little forty-second slots about mayhem and murder for NBC news across the USA. Drive-time entertainment from the drive-by shooting capital of the world, Belfast.

Meanwhile a new man had made his entrance to the lives of the people of north Belfast. A skilled locksmith and housebreaker, this loyalist gunman would arrive beside people's beds, wake and then shoot them where they lay. Which is why I don't think that Jimmy and Seamie were in any way unique to me: I suspect thousands and thousands of Northern Ireland people knew them too, and nightly passed through the same ordeal at their hands. In all our minds, the slightest nocturnal sound was the harbinger of imminent death. Restful, nightlong unbroken sleep was a luxury as rarely enjoyed as in a city under artillery bombardment; we all had our vigils of terror to observe as the moon sailed across the sky and we watched its light shine on the far side of our curtains, waiting for the shadow of a gunman.

Daylight brought no relief. There was a charming little village of shops at the top of the Cliftonville Road on its climb around the Cave Hill: a florist's, a butcher's, a greengrocer's, a small supermarket, a little ecumenical island in the midst of a dozen warring regions. It was as if everybody consented to the notion that some areas should be free of war – until the day I was walking there to collect my daily ration of lamb chops, and I heard an almost synchronized volley of shots. Two police officers on village duty had been approached from behind by IRA men, their brains blown out in a merciless instant.

No courage lingered in my heart. At the sound of gunfire, I turned around and went home, learning the truth only afterwards. And many years later I heard that one of the IRA killers – an Ardoyne man – was subsequently convicted of both those and five other killings, including that of a fifteen-month-old Protestant boy.

It was around this time that stories began to surface about collusion between British soldiers and loyalist terrorists. *Hibernia* magazine in Dublin asked me to write a story about what I knew. I did so, allowing for the broad considerations of prudence that my survival instinct allowed. Not merely did I name the officers Jim Hanna had become so friendly with, but I also used the photograph of two soldiers in Jim Hanna's sitting-room, pointing guns at the camera.

This was wildly – indeed shamefully – irresponsible, because I didn't warn the army what I was doing. At the very least, I should have doctored the photographs so the soldiers weren't recognisable. Had they been operating undercover at the time of publication, I could have brought about a terrible end for them. Without thinking then too closely of the consequences, I believe I did so with the subconscious desire to impress Róisín, who had become increasingly bitter and anti-British – and if I could add to my credibility in her eyes, so much the better. Moreover, the journalistic culture of the period was deeply anti-government of any kind. Had I been offered a scoop into a murderous scandal involving the IRA or one involving the British security forces, I

– and virtually every other journalist of the time – would have chosen the latter. No professional kudos attached to an exposé into 'resistance movements', as the expression of the time put it: that would be doing the work of the British government. Subconsciously, and sometimes not so sub-, journalists were working to an anti-government agenda.

At least I did not give details of the soldiers' home addresses, which bizarrely they had given to Jim and he, in another of those idle moments of compulsive confessionalism, had given to me. I wrote that whatever collusion had occurred was not authorized, was the work of individuals goaded by the terrorism of the IRA, and I knew – because I had spoken to him about them – that the GOC, a thoroughly likeable and decent man named Frank King, had told me of his loathing of loyalist terrorists. (My article was further marred by my idiotically misnaming him 'General Ford'.)

All journalists at this time expected their phones to be tapped – Róisín and I had deliberately had sexual conversations to keep our listeners entertained. However, this piece, and the possible compromise of the safety of British intelligence operatives, seems to have triggered another and higher level of watchfulness.

Joe Ninety had taken me to a car dealer outside Belfast in reward for my saving his life from Davy Payne, and the two of them proceeded to fleece me – which is how car dealers say thank you, rather as Swedish prostitutes say 'Excuse me' for 'goodbye'. The car was a Triumph 2000. It was older than the Fiat it replaced, yet I'd paid an additional £1000 in part exchange.

The previous owner may have had a terrorist connection, for at the first army roadblock I came across, I was stopped for an ID check. The same thing happened at the next roadblock. I asked the soldiers why: my car was on the P-check list, which meant its driver had to be positively vetted every time he was stopped. Then I met an ITN journalist with good British intelligence contacts: he warned that he'd heard I might be a target for a more thorough surveillance.

My car was the obvious place. I resorted to the simple expedient of taping a piece of paper inside the driver's door, leaving a 50p coin on the dash, and getting out of the passenger's side each night. One morning, I found the seal broken. The 50p was still there. I calculated that if the IRA had been doing the bugging, the men would have come from Ardoyne and would have made off with the money. So henceforth, I always talked in the car as if I knew I had a military audience. To this day, I don't know whether I had or hadn't. But far from making me cautious, the suspicion that I was being listened to made me fuck-you flamboyant and outrageous.

Even though I only saw Róisín by chance, her brother Mickey, now released from jail, seemed anxious to stay in touch with me. He was still driven by a pure flame of hate-filled commitment: the struggle was everything. His contempt for England was complete, even though he knew nothing whatever about the country, just the embittered folklore and myth of Irish republicanism.

'The English love nothing, only money and conquest,' he said in my car one day. 'They don't even love England.'

'English people love their country every bit as much as the Irish love theirs. They don't appear to feel the need to kill anyone for it.' On this occasion I wasn't trying to provoke any would-be listeners. A chronic failure to understand the English was what made the IRA campaign possible.

'That's a load of fucking shite. What about Bloody Sunday, or better still, Bloody Sun*days*, and take your fucking pick from half a dozen. What about Amritsar? What about the Black and Tans? What about Dresden? What about Aden? Jesus fucking Christ, don't talk to me about the fucking English. They don't love England, they love killing people.'

I was familiar with the unanswerable litany; oh by God, they must have had a really fascinating time in Long Kesh, reciting it backwards and forwards, like rogation.

'Mick, I know the English, and for the most part they love England, but they just don't say so very much.'

'No, no, no, they love their fucking empire, that's why they're clinging on to it the way they are. Well fuck, this is the last bit of it, if they want a fucking war to keep it, a fucking war is what they're going to get.'

On the night of my twenty-ninth birthday I was alone in the world, with no one to celebrate the arrival of my thirtieth year. I drove to the Club Bar, saw no one I knew, and utterly miserable, began to drink myself into a stupor. Late in the evening, a blonde woman materialized beside me. 'You're having a good time,' she said dryly.

'No,' I said, 'I'm getting drunk.'

'Really? Well fancy that.'

'Sorry. Not *getting*. Am.'

'You're not driving yourself home.'

'Yes I am.'

'No you're not,' said this stranger. 'See me? I'm Eimer Savage. You live round the corner from me. I'm driving you home. And see that there? That's your last pint.'

She rejoined her company and shortly afterwards presented herself beside me. 'It's home for you.'

She drove me there in *my* car, and I invited her in to listen to some music: Jussi Björling, as it happened. We drank tea before we started kissing. I opened her bra, and out fell her vast, stunning breasts, upon which would have feasted an entire consistory of homosexual Cardinals, yodelling with joy.

We went upstairs for – considering my condition – a surprisingly successful encounter. What reason had she for doing this? There was none. This was a city at war, and people made strange decisions: picking up a drunk was only one of them. Elsewhere in the city, other drunks were being picked up for other purposes. Later, she drove home in my car, and next day returned it, dropping the keys through the letterbox.

I remembered her name, knew the road where she lived, and telephoned her. Could we meet for a drink? Certainly. Her voice was dry, sardonic. When we met, she was watchful. I guessed the source of her unease. She'd had a calculated desire for sex the previous night, but she had a fiancé in Germany and didn't want to have a large emotional affair; not having a fiancée, and with other weights on my heart, neither did I.

'We can be friends who fuck,' I proposed. And that is what we became. What followed wasn't happiness, but it removed the edge from my terrible loneliness. Jimmy and Seamie, however, remained regular companions – an abiding loyalty such as theirs could certainly withstand a few friendly fucks.

As well as a taste for the latter, Eimer fortunately also shared my love of opera, and the Belfast Opera Season – the optimism behind which constituted gallantry of a ludicrously high order – was upon us. We went to a production of *La Bohème*, interrupted as always by spurious bomb scares, but which had to be taken seriously, as pallid, second-rate Italian tenors were shooed from the stage, and left to quiver on the street with the rest of us, before being ushered back to start all over again. Voices often tremble during Puccini operas; only in Belfast do they do so in terror.

Afterwards, we went to the Europa for a drink. In walked Róisín who looked around vigorously before seeing me and coming over. I started guiltily, and immediately began to make fumbling introductions, explanations and excuses. Róisín cut me short.

'Michael's dead. He was shot by the police this afternoon.'

As Eimer and I drove up the Cliftonville Road that night I burst into tears, and had to stop the car. What a tragic end to a tragically useless life, with so much promise and with so little to show for it. Eimer looked at me with one eyebrow slightly raised. 'You're not *quite* the hard man you make yourself out to be,' she said.

'I don't make myself out to be anything.'

'Really?' she said, as if she knew better.

Mick had been killed by police during a bungled bombing

operation. It was an entirely justified shooting, yet emotionally I felt it could have been avoided. I was not being sensible. The absence of sense is what makes wars possible.

I went to the Hamilton house the next day. Mick lay in his coffin. A long shank of hair lying across his forehead as Róisín caressed his cheese-like skin. Death's ability to steal life so totally and leave such a bad caricature of the living person behind always astonished me. This was not Mickey. This could not be Mickey. Where was all the passion, the vehemence, the anger? Not there; therefore not Mickey.

I attended the funeral not as a journalist but as a family friend, walking within the cortége. Róisín came over to me and asked me to help carry the coffin. I was delighted that she still felt enough regard for me to allow me be, if only briefly, a pallbearer. I wondered as I bore one-quarter the coffin's load, could this be the opportunity to start again?

A Sinn Féin steward asked if I was all right going round the roundabout. The roundabout? What a question. 'Of course.'

I understood the question within a few moments: as we circled, I came directly in line with a battery of long-range British army cameras. Oh perfect. Oh fucking perfect. The standard overflight of an IRA funeral by an RAF English Electric Canberra PR 9 photo-reconnaissance aircraft – curiously unsuspected by the IRA – duly followed as we gathered at the graveside. I gazed upwards and knowingly smiled at it. Needless to say my personal and professional compromises made no impact whatever on Róisín, who after the funeral remained as indifferent to me as she had been since the end of our relationship.

Eimer was already an habitué of the Bank Bar, so I found myself going in there more often, to be enchanted, infuriated, beguiled, disgusted, flattered, bullied, cajoled, manipulated and controlled by John McGuffin. His personal habits were appalling: he used to pick his nose and then eat what he'd found. He belonged to that common species, a socialist for whom socialism was a guide to other people's conduct, not his own. He never bought a round, but happily enjoyed other people's hospitality. He believed in feminism, but verbally and publicly abused Judith – his very attractive and highly intelligent wife – often badly, and sometimes appallingly.

It says something for his charm otherwise that such disgusting conduct could – on balance – be overlooked. He was a deeply manipulative person. Years before, he had persuaded Penguin Books that he was an important reviewer, and was sent hundreds of review copies of books a year. How such a patently fraudulent scam escaped the vigilant eye of the publishers was a mystery, but then much about McGuffin was a mystery. This middle-class Protestant boy revered the Provisional IRA and yet he was also a petty criminal. Not only did he run systematic insurance scams, he was also a Fagin-like character. From his corner of the Bank Bar he organized teams of teenage thieves who shoplifted for him in the large stores of Belfast.

And no, the IRA did not object to such theft, but it did violently object to the consequences; petty thieves when caught by the police could be, and often were, turned into informers. McGuffin was taking serious risks with his health and even his life with such behaviour, but in his own way he had a death wish: he drank all day every day, and the real miracle was that he was able to function at all as a college lecturer.

While I envied him his charisma, I rather think he envied my experiences, for all his reverence of the IRA never brought him anywhere near a riot or a gunbattle. I think he was perhaps the most physically cowardly man I have ever met, and his eyes opened wide with an almost sexual delight at my description of the shooting of the soldiers on Shaw's Road. When I told him I had a tape recording of it, he hungrily asked me if he could have a copy of it, as if it were a particularly tasty piece of pornography.

I never went near UVF bars, nor for that matter anywhere near Rab Brown. I always stayed in touch with Tucker Lyttle, not only because he told me things, but also because he genuinely liked me. A soft, almost affectionate look came into his face whenever we met.

Not having seen him for a while, some time before Mick had been killed, I'd rung him up, and we agreed to meet at the Salisbury. There was a new man behind the bar.

'Two Carlings,' said Tucker, ushering me away from the bar. We sat at a table.

'Where's Alex?' I asked.

'Dead,' he sighed. 'We shot him.'

'You did *what?*'

'Nutted him. Had to. He was an informer.'

'But holy fuck, but I thought you liked him.'

'I did, aye. He was a nice man, but – a very, very stupid one too, flashing all that there money around. For fuck's sake. Did his handler tell him nothing? The army these days. So. We picked him up and gev him a bit of a rompering, but he never said fuck all. Then we searched his clothes and found a piece of paper with a phone number. I rang it. Come here – would you believe this? Some fellow answers, "Major Brown, Tenant Street RUC station". Good night Josephine, or rather, good night Alex.'

'But he was a nice man.'

'He was aye. Dead on so he was. I'll miss him.'

'There's been no report on this,' I said puzzled.

'Aye, right enough, sure we only done him last night, and the body's not been found yet. See yon lad sitting drinking the orange with the ould doll? He done it. A good lad, and lovely to his ma there. Doesn't drink nor nothing, and cool as a cucumber. He done that Fenian milkman in Ballymurphy the other day. A lovely job, early one morning, sitting up on the milk float chatting away, going Seamus this and Seamus that, then bang. Here now – not a word to the peelers about Alex. Oh here you, for fuck's sake, where's our flipping drinks?'

Alex's body was found the next day.

As we moved into the summer the tempo of killings became more frenetic. Though I was reporting almost every one, I have little memory of them. Perhaps this is because of what happened in May.

Eimer and I had gone to the Club Bar, expecting to meet McGuffin. He wasn't there. We joined a group of McGuffin's cronies. After about an hour or so, as I got up to go to the toilets, a drunk accosted me.

'I hear you got Ann Shelton pregnant.'

'You what?'

'She's pregnant and can't make up her mind whether to have it or an abortion. You want to watch where you put that mickey of yours, so you do.'

The fool leered at me, a drool of saliva dribbling from his lip. He had lost two brothers to the Troubles, so people tended to tolerate him. As usual, he was talking rubbish. I pushed past him, and there was a huge *thwack!* at the door beside the men's toilet, through which I would have been passing if the fool hadn't detained me.

Bomb.

The ceiling fell on top of me, and I dropped to the floor. Around me women were screaming. But by now I was a veteran. As I rose I felt an icy calm fill me. I walked to the seat of the explosion. Dust filled the bar-room like hanging linen. I passed three tables of men, all of them covered in plaster, dust and rubble, who continued to drink and talk, as if nothing had happened – which, to their traumatized minds, was probably the case.

In the corner lay a jumble of separated limbs, and two dead men. Not friends of mine. Strangers – their white-powdered corpses still moving minutely as if posthumously seeking a position of final ease. I went back to our group, in which the women – even the strong, sensible Eimer – were still shrieking hysterically, and told Tony, a companion, to get everyone out, but not to let anyone into the ambulances that were even now arriving.

I went back to the scene of carnage and looked on helplessly. Unseen, inside the toilet the brother of one of the dead men lay with both his legs blown off. I waited, then crouching down, touched a body. Warm steak. Still no ambulance men.

On the street, crowds of hysterical girls were scrambling into ambulances. Tony was standing by looking helpless.

I walked to an ambulance-man and told him: 'There are two dead in there and a lot injured. Get these fucking wankers out of the ambulance *now.*'

I grabbed the wailing but uninjured women and ruthlessly expelled them, then led the ambulance men to the charnel house within. It was the only time in my entire life when I had actually felt and shown true power of command, for I was consumed with a uniquely lethal rage.

The two young men who had been killed were Paul Hamill, a student, and David Robinson, a clerk. My old friend Rab Brown, the man who had organized the bombing, certainly didn't have them as his targets, no, nor even me. The man he sent the woman-bomber in to leave her bag beside was the loud-mouthed braggart John McGuffin, who was at that point on holiday in Donegal. Unable to find her target, she had simply abandoned her bomb and gone home.

Meanwhile that night, several people who were safely in their homes nearby dashed out to clamber into ambulances, wailing and weeping, in order to present themselves at casualty in a condition of shock. And when he got back from Donegal, McGuffin – almost sheepishly – asked me whether I would testify that he had been there at the time so he could sue the government for compensation: since I wasn't suing, even though I had damaged hearing (as it happens, permanently) from the blast, I told him I certainly wasn't going to assist him in his fraudulent claim.

'You're just a Brit wanker,' he replied sympathetically.

This bombing was another turning point in my social life. The Club Bar was now no longer safe. Robert Armstrong had been marked there. Gerard McWilliams had been killed leaving. Poor Ivan Clayton had conducted his ham-fisted enquiries into Gerard's death there, and been murdered for his trouble. Now, the bombing was the final straw.

Tom Slevin, the proprietor of The Old House – which had since been demolished – had rather bravely opened a bar in the hitherto almost lifeless city centre, within the gated area. Its advantage was that it was safe, and some nights there was music. When my mother came to stay one Saturday, we took her there, and it was very pleasant. The next Saturday, Eimer and I and a few of her friends returned. That night the IRA leader known as the Fruitcake was there: with him a women known as the Black Widow, because of the power she had derived from her marriage to a now-dead IRA leader.

I was enjoying myself with Eimer and her friends when a stranger came over and whispered that the Black Widow and the Fruitcake were arranging to give me a hammering, and that I should get out. I didn't ask why. This was Belfast. That was why.

I got up, and flanked by Eimer and her friend Máire (sister, as it happens, to The One-Ball Wonder) I got to the door before my would-be ambushers were aware of my escape. They ran after me, with the Black Widow in their wake, screeching 'Kill him! Kill him!' Fear lends such fleetness of foot to a quarry, so I was easily first to the one-way swivelling gate on the barrier blocking access to the city centre area. Eimer and Máire got through, and then jammed the gate with an imaginatively placed high heel.

I whispered a rendezvous point to Eimer and I fled for my car, faster than I have run in all my life, for what was being held at bay was a lynch mob, with all the non-existent restraints of an alcohol-fuelled frenzy. I drove in terror back to where I'd left my rescuers, who were now standing on the corner, laughing in triumph. The frustrated howling of the gang, and the banshee wailing of the Black Widow, had attracted the attention of the police.

The girls, rightly, were delighted with themselves but I was in a palsy of terror. Not merely had people wanted to do violence to me, but I actually knew some of them: I even thought they liked me. When it came to following the remit of the tribe, contrary to all my illusions, I remained an outsider. Moreover, another pub was now out of bounds. Eimer shortly afterwards returned to her fiancé in Germany, and I to my life of solitude.

Eighteen

BARNEY TOLD ME that he was, once and for all, abandoning all contact with paramilitary activity. The last feud had finished it for him. As it had proceeded day after day after day, his band of fellow Official IRA men had gone from one safe house to the next, while the Provisionals hunted them down.

The moment of revelation came in a sordid house in the Old Park, when he and Tealeaf Elliott were sleeping on the floor. Barney was scratching himself a lot. 'I think I've got fleas.'

'Fleas?' said Tealeaf. 'Fuck, I'm like a frigging aircraft carrier here.'

So, that aspect of his life over, Barney came visiting one day and sheepishly said he had something to show me. We got into his new car, a two-seater open-topped Triumph Spitfire, and he drove to the Antrim Road, where he got out, opened the door to a Victorian house, and led me into the front room. He waved around him expansively. It was easily the most vulgarly decorated room I had ever seen, which was strange, because Barney had good taste.

'What do you think?'

'Hmm,' I said.

'Fucking cat, isn't it? Desperate. But that's the way they like it.'

'They? Who's they?'

'Punters. It's the future. Sex. This here is *my* massage parlour. First of a chain. My own wee sex empire. Look. Cocktail cabinet, a full bar, let them relax. Porn,' – he pointed to a table covered in girlie magazines – 'to get them going, and see here, a wee bell, when they're good and ready.'

He pressed it, and moments later, three ordinary looking young women came in, wearing short skirts and blouses, their hair up.

'Sorry girls, no business, this here is a friend of mine. Kevin, meet Hazel, Maureen and Sandra.'

Two Protestants and a Catholic, probably.

'Oh for fuck's sake Charlie,' said Maureen, 'we've done fuck-all today.'

'Just as fucking well,' said Sandra, 'near fucking broke me wrist yesterday. Punter wouldn't come. Fucking cat, I hate that, so I do, wank wank wank but fuck all happens. And here's me, dying for even a wee dribble, then, that's it mate, you're done.'

'Ha,' sneered Hazel. 'See me? I only have to touch my punters and they're pumping out the ould amber sole air.' She looked at me appraisingly. 'You're a bit of all right. I'll see the colour of your amber sole air for *nothin*'.'

'Not in my time you won't,' said Barney.

'Ye wee hallion, ye,' hissed Sandra at Hazel. 'Ye fucking scut.'

'Girls,' reproved Barney, gesturing me towards the stairs. 'Should have mentioned to you,' he whispered as we went up, 'they think I'm Charlie, you know, in case the taxman comes calling. Charlie Green. Name like that, could be a taig or a bluenose.'

He grinned proudly as he showed me in the first parlour. 'You'd be fucking amazed at the fortunes to be made out of a wee bottle of baby oil and a box of Kleenex. Bricklaying's a mug's game. This is the life for me. Now here's where you come in …'

'Me?' I yelped in terror. Barney my nemesis was back.

'Aye you. I need you write advertisements for me for the *Belfast Telegraph* and *Newsletter*. Sexy without being too explicit. You get my meaning?'

Barney was simply irresistible when he was determined to have his way. Naturally, there was no advertisement for the Catholic *Irish News,* which carried gaudy death notices glorifying the deeds of the IRA, but drew a pious line at anything that smacked of massage parlours, Kleenex tissues and the perfectly meaningless streams within. Of course, I capitulated. 'If I do that, then what do you do here?'

'Me? What I always do. Look fucking menacing to the punters. Otherwise fuck all. You'd better ask the girls about what they do.'

Sandra – she told me – provided manual sex, and allowed punters to play with her breasts only. Hazel provided manual sex and let them touch her anywhere. Maureen did everything under the sun and beyond it.

'Forgive me for asking,' I murmured diffidently to Sandra, 'but why would anyone want a woman who wouldn't let them touch everywhere?'

'Because the frustration gets them all going, see?'

'They *pay* to get frustrated? Why would they do that?'

'Jesus, don't ask me. That's what I'm always telling my husband, I'm here to get money out of them, not fucking understand them.'

As Barney was to inform me later, all three were married with children, and were dropped off in the morning and collected in the evening by their husbands. On quiet days, he said, two of them would occasionally pass the time having sex with one another, while the third watched, sometimes using a vibrator, or so they told him.

'You get to see all this?' I gasped.

'They say I can, aye, but only if I fucking pay. You ever hear the like of this? Fucking disgraceful, having to pay to watch *my* girls' – he tapped his chest – 'perform. For fuck's sake. There should be a law.'

'Have you paid?'

'Not yet. But I sometimes try to get a wee gander.'

I wrote a few advertisements for Barney, but he didn't really like them, and so my brief unpaid career in the brothel business came to an end.

That summer of 1977 marked the fifth anniversary of the introduction of internment, with the normal birthday celebrations of riots and gunbattles spread over several days. I was up in Andersonstown when I heard shooting, very close. I saw two men, one carrying an Armalite, running across open ground and get into a car, which sped away. From another street, a hitherto unseen army Land Rover suddenly appeared and gave chase.

The incident over, I was asked into a neighbouring house for tea by a waitress I knew from the Europa Hotel. About a mile away from us, Anne Maguire was pushing her six-week-old baby Andrew in his pram on Finaghy Road North. On her bicycle alongside her mother was Joanne, aged eight. Anne's son John, aged two, was toddling next to them. Slightly in the lead was Mark, aged seven.

The IRA car sped down Shaw's Road pursued by army Land Rovers. It turned right at Finaghy Road North, where it was hit by army gunfire. It careered across the road, smashing into the Maguire family, killing Andrew, Joanne and John, and critically injuring Anne Maguire, who was in a coma for weeks with broken legs and pelvis. Four and a half years later, she cut her own throat with an electric carving knife.

The responsibility for this must fall four-square on the people who chose to fight a guerrilla war in a densely populated city – the Provisional IRA. Jackie Maguire, the man who lost three of his children – and in time his wife – himself was to say of the soldier who fired into the IRA car that he was only doing his duty.

Unhappy the land that knows such duty. The uproar that followed these killings, and the colossal marches of tens of thousands of people in protest at the continuing violence, led by the newly formed Peace People, did not dent the inviolable sense of duty of those who drew their mandate from history and the dead generations before them. The Provisional IRA did not consult the living, only the past and the future: the present meant nothing to them, as it had meant nothing whatever to Róisín's brother Mick.

Yet the present counted enormously when the wrong was done by the other side. Four days after the Maguires were killed, twelve-year-old Majella O'Hare was shot and fatally injured by a paratrooper in south Armagh. Paratroopers abused her father as he held her, dying, in his arms, and for several minutes prevented a nurse, Alice Campbell, from going to her aid.

Alice had been laying flowers on the grave of her fiancé John Reavey, whom she had been due to marry that very day and who had been shot – along with his two brothers – in the January massacres in Armagh. So no matter what happened in west Belfast, Armagh had its drumlins and its war, and now it had the banner killing of Majella O'Hare to rally around, and to cite in cyclical justification of all it did.

North Belfast too was driven entirely by its own engine that would not be governed by events elsewhere. Two weeks after the Maguire deaths, a married Catholic couple, Joseph and Jeanette Dempsey, and their ten-month-old baby daughter Bridgeen were burnt alive in their home by UDA arsonists, just up from Carlisle Circus.

Other fires were raging in men and women's souls, and nothing could quench that anger, not in that decade, nor in the one that followed. Aided by *Lost Lives*, I roam back through those months, almost as if I had never been there, and no longer know what I surely once knew. Is it really possible that a seventeen-year-old Catholic girl, Pauline Doherty, was shot six times by loyalist killers at her neighbour's home, where she was babysitting just around the corner from where I lived, and that I have since forgotten her? Or Catherine O'Connor, who, aged sixty-eight, was stabbed thirty-six times by her loyalist killers, also close to my home, yet again I have no memory whatever of this?

No pain that I had ever felt in my life could remotely match that of Jackie and his son Mark Maguire, or the extended families of the exterminated, now forgotten, Dempseys, Dohertys, O'Connors, and, largely thanks to the IRA, the thousands to come.

A member of the John McGuffin set, Eamon McGinley – a witty, kindly man – was once talking to a colleague at work in the Short and Harland aircraft factory. They were discussing luck. Eamon spoke of the unluckiest man he knew: his car was endlessly driven into, his flat burgled, abandoned by his girlfriend.

Ah, said Eamon's workmate, let me tell you about the fellow who used to live beneath me. We left the bathwater running with the plug in one day, and his basement flat was turned into a swimming pool. His car was written off by a hit-and-run driver just outside the house. He could never get his replacement car to start. He lent money to a neighbour who vanished. And his girlfriend walked out on him too.

They were talking about the same man. Me. But in addition to the army of misfortunes that pursued me down these years, there was the latest, the most insidious and persistent: the P-check. This consisted of a car and owner being detained at a military roadblock until an army officer sitting beside a radio in a building somewhere or other authorized release. Being on the P-check list was a colossal bore, because it meant you were always being stopped: no journey was simple. Sometimes, where one army battalion area ended and another began, you might find two roadblocks within sight of one another, simply because the two battalions were unable to co-ordinate their operations.

I was being P-checked once at such a roadblock by Green Jackets, with another roadblock a hundred yards in front of me. I asked the soldiers to radio ahead that I was okay. They couldn't. Not in their power to do so. Thus I drove into my second P-check of Scottish soldiers seconds after leaving the previous one.

'This is fucking stupid,' I spat to the corporal in charge of the roadblock as the pair of us stood around awaiting my inevitable clearance. He sniffed and smiled equably. 'Everything's fucking stupid about this place, or haven't you noticed?'

We looked one another in the eye, two men in a foreign place, and instantly recognized we had something in common. We were joined by a small, chunky private, who fell into an amiable conversation, the way that soldiers – bored, lonely and driven distracted with sexual frustration – often did. They were clearly best friends. The corporal came from Dundee, the private from one of those strange towns whose existence is usually only attested through the Scottish Second Division football results – Cowdenbeath or Stenhousemuir, or some such place.

I was finally cleared, and I went on my way, three men briefly brought together by the accidents of the Troubles. But as it happened, this was just the beginning a P-check friendship, for I found myself repeatedly running into my Scottish corporal and his companion at roadblocks, where perforce we would spend some time together. They were Gordon Highlanders. The corporal was called Jock and the private Andy. The latter actually liked Belfast, mostly because he thought the girls were so attractive.

'Really?' I said.

'Och aye, compared to the gurruls back home, they're so byoootiful.' He was small and plain, and I imagine he had never been very successful with girls. The corporal was a more silent man. He was married, with one child, and lived only to get back to his wife who was pregnant. Driving most days into the Bank Bar, I would run into them often, and on each occasion they would with mounting regret and fervent apologies go through the meaningless P-check rituals.

I went to the Bank Bar so regularly simply to break up the tedium of my day. There were of course better things to be doing with my time, such as reading books, but Belfast seemed curiously antipathetic to scholarship. The Bank remained the epicentre of John McGuffin's empire. Loud, genial, lordly, he governed an entire corner of the lounge during the daytime. German and American revolutionary tourists came to pay homage to him there, and when he gave them a meaningful look, to buy him drinks.

For all his pretence that he knew the world, he didn't even know his own crowd. From my earliest days in his circle, I guessed that at least one of his companions was a British agent, and I soon learnt – because, remember, people told me things – that I was intermittently sharing the sexual favours of a female member of the group with a Welsh sergeant in the SAS called Vic. I even knew where he lived.

Of course McGuffin knew nothing of this. Though I wouldn't be surprised to learn now that McGuffin himself was an informer. He was greedy and wholly untrustworthy, and his house was never raided, though logically it should have been. It cannot possibly have escaped the attention of MI 5 and MI 6 that he had close connections with the Red Army Faction terrorist cell in Germany, which was itself intimately associated with Baader-Meinhoff.

He and some of his cronies – though not all – revelled in a celebration of carnage. One of his friends, Brendan O'Toole, used to write grotesque ballads that extolled and personalized violence. One verse ran, 'Power to the hand that shot Cecil Patterson down ...' Cecil Patterson was one of the RUC officers killed the night before I arrived in Belfast. McGuffin revelled in jokes about dead British soldiers. One concerned a woman in London who'd heard about a new singing telegram service and insists the telegram boy on her doorstep sings his telegram. He keeps refusing, but she insists. Finally he relents, and then does

229

a little mistral dance before singing: 'Your son's been stiffed in Crossmaglen, doo dah, doo dah.'

And would then roar with laughter, no matter how often he had told the joke.

Meanwhile, I learnt that during his stay in jail, Seamus, my well-spoken little IRA man, had been conducting interrogations of fellow prisoners during a colossal joint UDA–IRA intelligence operation against penetrations into both organizations by the British. Even he was shocked by the deeds about which his IRA-colleagues had told him, so casually, and so free of doubt. He asked them the same question I had asked him: Did they not feel guilt at their deeds?

Not a bit. Those deeds had been authorized by the IRA. If sometimes the wrong people had been killed, that was not the fault of the killers, but of the British presence in Ireland. If that logic didn't work, and on rare occasions it didn't, terrorists had gone to confess to certain select priests – in effect IRA chaplains – who assured them of the essential divinity of their deeds, and the moral righteousness of their cause. Eggs are broken when you make omelettes, the priests would say. War was war: theirs was a moral cause being fought by moral means against a mighty foe, as all Irish struggles had been fought. This poisonous, evil rubbish was only sustainable by a profound ignorance of Irish history, and a ruthless elision of uncomfortable truths.

Needless to say, Seamus concurred with the general senti-ments. He was nonetheless shocked that membership of the IRA seemed to confer such unconditional and all-embracing indul-gence upon its members for even the most appalling crimes. For immunity-to-consequence was both a by-product of the Troubles, and its fuel, rather as a nuclear reactor can run on its own waste. Northern Ireland had become its own crazed Sizewell running out of control, its cooling stacks glowing as its workers were fried, a plume of murderous contamination reaching down through the decades.

Never did that plume assume more grotesque proportions than in this UDA–IRA joint-operation against 'informers', the drumlins' answer to the Hitler-Stalin pact. This was too bizarre for words; but once the idea, from whatever crazed or Machiavellian source, grew that the British army had set up a third force to penetrate both the UDA and the IRA *jointly*, it became a truth confirmed under torture of members of both organizations, by both organizations. Alas, they were not so ecumenical as to allow one another swap interrogation duties, with UDA having the pleasant task of breaking IRA men, and vice versa, but the results were nonetheless monstrous, as each side confirmed its own worst fears by beating the daylights out of its own members until it got whatever fantasies it wanted to hear. Then, using that 'intelligence', they began a murderous purge of the guilty ones, who had, no doubt under interrogation, brokenly confirmed their own guilt. Northern Ireland's plutonium killed you all right – but often enough drove you insane first.

Thus Tucker Lyttle was able to tell me well in advance the names of IRA men on the run from their former colleagues who were going to be killed by the IRA – in addition to which, of course, he told me of UDA men on the run from the UDA, who would be killed once it had caught up with them. And it did, and they were, and so my passive complicity with murder intensified.

Genuine victimhood mingled with mythic victimhood in Belfast, their union ultimately becoming seamless. In the tiny nationalist ghetto of Short Strand, in east Belfast, I once heard a withered she-ancient abusing an English soldier, who stood there with a stoical, distant look on his face. 'Ye fucking cunt, ye,' the fishwife spat, while an approving crowd listened. 'Ye prick. What are ye? Only a bag of fuckin' shite. A heap of bollocks. An old cow's twat. Fuck off back to England where ye came from, ye filthy fuckin' hallion, ye cunt ye, ye fuckin' shitehawk.'

There is only so much of this even the most equable of men can take. 'Oh piss off, dear,' he said in a measured voice.

'DID YOUSE HEAR HIM? DID YOUSE?' she shrieked in transports of wrath. 'Did youse hear what he said to *me*, and me a grandmother a dozen times over, and him, using filthy language, the p-word, like that?'

'You want to fuckin' watch it, talking to an old woman like that,' chimed in a young man. 'An' her a granny an' all.'

Suspicion was the weft and the warp of Northern Irish society. Many people used to wonder at me. When in Knutsford Drive I went round to my neighbours' houses, suggesting we all exchange telephone numbers so that we could tip one another off if we saw anything suspicious, a Catholic neighbour assumed that I was an SAS man sent into the area to organize defence. A member of the Official IRA once asked me: 'Who are you really working for – the Brits or the Provies? 'Cause you can't be just a journalist, going round the way you do.'

Only those involved in intelligence can know who was doing what in Northern Ireland at that time. Since conflict zones are also legendarily inhabited by fantasists, the truth can often be impossible for the rest of us to ascertain. Early in my days in Belfast, a 'dental technician' in the Wellington Park Hotel told me he had a source for Kalashnikovs: as someone with good contacts, did I know anyone who wanted to buy any? I sensed a story. Could I get an exclusive about arms smuggling into Belfast? I smiled politely, and I said maybe. The next day I reported the conversation to Liam Hourican.

'You said no, of course?'

I explained what I had done, thinking I was very clever. I concluded triumphantly: 'What do you think?'

'What do I think? I think you're a cretin, that's what I think. Do you know *anything* about this world of arms buying, if that's what it actually is? No? No. Ring the RUC – no, Jesus, don't ring the RUC. That could get us into more trouble. If you see this fellow again, just ignore him. Where did we find you, do you mind me asking?'

I did see him again, in broad daylight. 'Any news on the business the other night?' he asked.

'What business?' I replied, amiably feigning drunken forgetfulness of the night, so prudently allowing the dental technician – spy or spoofer – to pass from my life.

I never knowingly met a British intelligence officer throughout my time in Northern Ireland, though I knew Colin Wallace of the army press office well. I actually liked him a great deal – but I liked almost everyone in those days. He subsequently became famous for having made allegations about a military conspiracy against the Wilson government, a matter outside my knowledge and beyond my power to comment extensively upon. I believe he was probably a fantasist – but who was not in this miserable hallucination of the drumlins, whose myths conjured poison from the soil, and whose embittered souls endlessly reinvented and reinvigorated those myths?

I used to wear a beeper, and on Sunday nights, with the pubs all closed, and usually mad with boredom, Barney and I would go down to a city centre club called Richardsons, where we would meet some of Barney's friends – Tealeaf Elliott and Josie McKee. Tealeaf was like Barney – a wide boy, always on the lookout for moves, a career criminal who also managed to be a paramilitary. Josie McKee was a nice, simple man, who always got things wrong: long after they were out of style, Josie wore flares and big-collared shirts, as if he and they were still the height of fashion.

His friends never teased him about this. Though they were stronger, cleverer, more powerful people, and though he was quite stupid, clan loyalty bound them all together, they never mocked him – even when he had trouble pronouncing his words, which he usually had. I had huge trouble understanding what he was saying, especially if I found myself alone in his company. He didn't so much talk as munch his lips noisily, as if speaking some almost vowel-free Borneo dialect. 'Nng chung mrng clung,' he would say conversationally. 'Whng ching blah nch. Ghng?'

Those who had known him from childhood could navigate these strange linguistic shoals, but I could not: and I dreaded his undiluted company, most of all because I didn't want to hurt him. He really hated that some people didn't understand what he was saying: he always finished every remark with a plaintively hopeful little smile on his face – which had been much punched in life, and now looked quite pig-like. Sentences borne on the melody of the indicative mood could be answered with a genial if non-specific affirmative: but, oh, how my heart sank when I heard a question mark.

Richardson's was, frankly, a desperate place, to which I only went because I needed the company. However, after a while one great redeeming feature was an enchantingly pretty waitress called Danielle. As I left one night, I found her at the door and asked her if she wanted a lift. She smiled and said yes, and I drove her to her home off the Falls.

'What's that?' she asked, pointing at my beeper.

I explained I paid an agency to notify me of messages and warn me of explosions and shootings.

'What do you do?'

'I'm a journalist. I need to know these things.'

She was silent for a minute. 'I'm sorry, but I told my local OC I thought you were a peeler. I gev him your car number and all. Jesus, I'm sorry, but you could be in real trouble here, you know?'

'You gave the IRA my car number? You followed me out of the club?'

She nodded. 'I did aye, last week.'

It was my turn to be silent. Finally I said: 'If you thought I was a police officer, why did you accept a lift from me?'

She looked away. 'Because I kind of sort of liked you, if you know what I mean.'

No, there's no making sense of that. The next Sunday she

was working at the club again – heavens, she was pretty – and she gave me a wink. 'I seen the OC,' she whispered, 'and you're dead on, so you are.'

'You want a lift again tonight?'

'I do, aye, but not so direct, if you get my drift.'

Once we got back to Knutsford – now fitted out with furniture – I asked her about herself. No, she wasn't in the IRA, but she did what she could for it. Meaning? Oh wee things, like holding open the flaps of letter boxes. What?

She told me that the IRA would remove the outer flap on a letter box, but leave the inner one in place. It would be attached to a piece of string, and girls such as Danielle would hold the flap open inside the house from a distance, using the string, while an IRA sniper deep in the hall would wait for a soldier to come into distant view down whatever street the letter box commanded. A single shot, and the girl would release the string, and the rest of the foot patrol would see nothing.

'You've actually done this?'

'Aye, a few times. It's very fuckin' borin', an' all, specially when fuck all happens.' she said, grumpily.

'You ever do this when a soldier got shot?'

'Worse luck, no.'

'Danielle, if you had, you know you would have been guilty of murder, legally and morally.'

'Me? Guilty of murder for holding up a wee letter box? Away and shite.'

I explained that as an assistant to murder she would be as guilty of murder as the man who had pulled the trigger. She looked wonderingly at me. 'You see, that's what we're fighting,' she said indignantly, 'British injustice like that there.'

I told her – as if this was news to her, and it probably was – of what an immense and terrible thing it was to kill anyone. The most appalling thing that had ever happened to me had been the death of my father, which caused me grief for many years.

'That's different. Your da wasn't a British soldier.'

'But my uncle was. And British soldiers' families have feelings too, you know.'

'Oh for fuck's sake, are you going to keep talking shite like this all night, or are you going to kiss me?'

She was a devout Catholic, a regular communicant, and most of all, an utter devotee of sex. The following Sunday, she caught my eye at the club and gave me a wink. I drove her back to my place again.

'See what you was saying about soldiers' families having feelings an' all? I been thinking about that, and you're dead fuckin' right. I shouldn't have said you were talking shite, because you weren't, I was, but, and I'm sorry. Now. That's over. Severed me links, blahdee-blahdee-blah. Anythin' else you want to talk about, wastin' my precious time, or have you something more interestin' in mind upstairs that might tickle a girl's fancy? Then upstairs with you. Me wrist's near wore off me, I been that randy these past few days.'

One girl only came home with me on condition that I set the alarm nice and early. Of course, I said, puzzled. We had a perfectly normal session in bed, and then we fell asleep. It was still dark when the alarm went, the girl rose and got dressed, kissed me goodbye, took her holdall and then set off.

I bumped into her long afterwards and she told me that there was good reason why she got up when she did: the holdall was for the gun that she was going to collect, and the man she and the rest of her IRA unit were intending to kill worked early shifts. Happily for him, he slept late that morning. His would-be killers hung around nervously for a few minutes and then dispersed.

Sex was – by general Irish standards of the day – extremely casual and often quite spontaneous. It was offered as a reward to paramilitary leaders by eager young females, but it filled the wet, grey air generally. What else was there to do in such a city, in such a dreary war? One morning at about one, I was driving home from a party when I saw a girl hitch-hiking. I stopped and asked where she was going: emerging from a party herself, disoriented, she was in fact hitching away from where she wanted to go, in south Belfast. I told her to get in: I'd turn around and drive her home.

'Where do you live?' she asked.

'North Belfast.'

'What's it like there?'

'It's like the opposite side of the city, that's what it's like.'

We studied one another in silence, thoughts filling the car. She was in her early twenties, and very good-looking. I said carefully: 'I'll take you to your home, now, and absolutely with no conditions. Or if you want, we can go to my home, in which case, we're going to have sex. What's it to be?'

She laughed lightly. 'Great minds.'

I took her home the following morning, and never saw her again.

Another girl with whom I became friendly had served four years in jail. Jackie Cassidy was a teenager when her IRA commander sent her on an officially unauthorized robbery, the proceeds from which he was going to keep personally – a 'homer' as it was called in Belfast – and she had been caught by soldiers.

The IRA wing of the women's jail Armagh was a horror, ruled at that time by some weird old self-appointed IRA crank who outlawed even solitary masturbation, never mind with another woman. 'Self-abuse' was demoralizing, unrepublican and un-Irish, and was a court-martial offence, she declared – though how evidence was to be acquired for a prosecution was not explained: perhaps anyone seen smiling at breakfast. However, so far as Jackie knew, no prisoners were court-martialled for wanking in Armagh. It was amazing how quiet you could be when you wanted, she murmured.

On her release, Jackie span right out of control, night after night getting hopelessly drunk, and having sex with any male who was present, never knowing the next day what she'd done, and with whom. She was an intelligent woman, and most of all a good one, with a very moral purpose in life: the problem was that, overall, the moral purpose was totally fucked-up. Sometimes she recognized the futility of the IRA campaign – at other times the call of the tribe was too great for her to resist. She hated the IRA for what it had done to her, but she admired its extraordinary intensity of purpose. She was, moreover, terrifyingly strong, and when her brother was arrested by soldiers it was fortunate for everyone, the arresting soldiers in particular, that he had been taken away before Jackie knew about it. She would, quite simply, have beaten them to death for harming her baby brother, or died in the attempt.

Jackie's most defining characteristic was her utter selflessness. She did nothing that served her own self-interest; she adored her family, an archetypical west Belfast Catholic gang of about ten children, chaotically adoring of one another and utterly endearing to an outsider like me. God knows what would have become of Jackie had her early terrorist career not been cut short by prison. With her focus and intelligence, she could well have gone on to do both mighty and terrible things.

The fates of these two girls were entirely different to what I had expected. The last I heard of Jackie is that, for all her intelligence she went abroad and married a member of a lunatic fringe republican organization who had drifted into drug dealing and petty crime; while Danielle married a prosperous Protestant businessman, and raised her children as good Protestants, no doubt with hardly any mention at all about her teenage feats with a wee bit of string and a letter box flap.

Nineteen

THE DEFEAT of the Peace People was, as we now know, a
catastrophe. It was not merely the fact that this mass movement
to end the Troubles was brought to its knees, but the manner in
which it was accomplished: by intimidation, mockery, violence
– and most of all, wickedness. Peace marches were attacked, the
motives of the leaders systematically impugned, and the supporters of peace were singled out for abuse and sneering, which are
the classic Belfast tools of social enforcement.

Republicans routinely spoke of the movement as the 'peace
people wankers' and McGuffin always referred to Mairead Cor-
rigan, who – remember – had lost her two nephews and a niece,
and nearly lost her sister Anne to the IRA (and in time effectively
did) and who worked so hard to raise money for peace, simply as
More Aid Wank Again.

But for all the problems of leadership, the central reason why
the Peace People failed was that they couldn't succeed: the building that was Northern Ireland was collapsing as if its foundations
had been dynamited, and it is not possible to arrest precipitating
rubble, never mind restore it to its original place in the edifice.

Meanwhile, Barney and I would spend evenings with one

another in grim little pubs, all of them potential targets for spray jobs by loyalist gunmen. Like every other customer, we would sit so that we could clearly see whoever came in.

Women came and went in my life. I was not cruel, but nor was I kind. One day I got a phone call from a woman acquaintance: her husband Erskine and her toddler son Trevor were visiting his parents with whom she didn't get on. She was sun-bathing and enjoying a bottle of wine – would I care to join her?

Bored sitting alone on my few square yards of lawn, I drove over to her. We lay in the sun while I weighed up in my mind what the chances were of a bit of action. I turned to look at her. She was classically Protestant: her name was Trudy, she was blonde, and her husband played rugby for Ulster.

'Have we got the time?' I asked.

She opened her eyes and made a face. '*Finally.* Yes, we have, but what fucking kept you?'

We kissed briefly, and then rose to seek the privacy of her bedroom, which was in the front of a ground-floor flat. She slipped the catch on the Yale lock, just to be sure, and then stepped out of her bikini. The sight of her naked body vanquished any fears about her husband. We fell on the bed and I had just entered her when we heard the front door of the house opening.

'Neighbours,' she hissed. 'Don't stop.'

I didn't, not at first – but by God I did when the key entered the door of the flat, and metal met unyielding metal as Erskine the rugby player tried to enter his home.

'Fuck!' spat Trudy. 'He must have had another row with his mother. They're always fighting.'

'Always?' I quavered. 'Then why …'

The door rattled and Erskine began to shout, 'Trudy! It's me. The lock's jammed.'

Trudy was made of sound Ulster Protestant stock. Calmly she whispered to me – 'You hide behind the bed there. I'll get Erskine into the kitchen. He can't see the garden from there. Go out in the garden, get your things, and leave by the side entrance.'

I leapt nimbly over the bed, and lay alongside it, in the small gap between it and the wall, beneath the curtained window. But it had all taken too long. Erskine had grown impatient, and had gone to the front of the house, where he was hauling the unlocked sash window open, just inches above me.

'There you go,' he said, lowering a small boy onto the floor beside my naked frame, the little sandalled feet landing beside my ribcage. I stared at them, while inches away their tiny owner was facing out over the bed and across the room, incredibly without seeing me. Erskine's well-muscled shoulder then began to follow the boy above me, and just inches away – at which point I consigned my soul to the divine mercy of what I hoped was a non-rugby playing Providence.

But I had reckoned without the splendidly resourceful Trudy. She had made herself decent and now, suddenly, was screaming from the street that people would think that terrorists were entering the property: Come back out this second! Now! Instantly! Unbelievably Erskine's shoulder paused and withdrew, and Trevor rose as he was lifted back out of the window, his little feet vanishing over the edge of the window into the open air of the small front yard.

With a presence of mind that would have done credit to Bismarck, Trudy took big Erskine into the kitchen where she scolded him for so publicly letting the family down. Nakedly, to the sound of her coruscating words, I stole into the garden, hurriedly got dressed, and tiptoed out down the hall. This was the second time a husband had nearly caught me, but on different sides of the sectarian divide. With such gallant cross-community endeavours as mine, peace was surely at hand.

One afternoon not long afterwards I was listening to the police radio when I heard of a foiled bombing at a furniture warehouse. The bombers were believed to have fled to a certain house, and the address was given over the airwaves. I instantly got into my car and drove there pell-mell before the backup from the security forces had arrived. I found the house, got out of the car, and hid under a hedge in the front garden; with my tape recorder on. I had just bought an extremely expensive microphone with an extraordinary range, containing its own batteries. I turned it on as events unfolded.

The police soon surrounded the front garden: there were gunshots, followed by shouted demands for surrender, and others of defiance. A priest arrived, and after lengthy, violently worded negotiations, a surrender was agreed. The occupants of the house emerged, to be arrested, as I dictated a running commentary into my recorder from under the bush. This was a major scoop – and even larger than I realized, because one of the arrested, Bobby Sands, was to lead the hunger strike in which he was himself to perish five years later.

But it wasn't a scoop at all. I had in the excitement of the moment accidentally hit the off-switch on my brand-new microphone. So, I recorded nothing at all of the last moments of freedom and the first moments of captivity of the most important IRA man of the entire Troubles.

Such drama was not the norm, for that was more usually provided by walls of rain sweeping from the Black Mountain and the Cave Hill, with wet soldiers looking into cars and waving them on. I kept running into my Scottish friends, Jock and Andy, and their moods were radically different. Their tour was coming to an end, and Jock was longing to get home. His wife had given birth to a little girl. He had only seen a photograph of her. He was overjoyed, but desperate for the tour to end. Andy, however, was convinced that if he stayed just a little bit longer, one of these byootiful Belfast girls would fall in love with him, and he would sweep her off her feet, back to his little Scottish town.

And maybe he did. I don't know. But I do know that two days before his friend, decent, quiet Jock Marshall from Dundee was due to return home to his wife and his two daughters, the most recent of whom was barely a fortnight old, he was shot dead by a sniper in Ardoyne.

Summer became winter, and winter spring, and the dreary pattern of life in Belfast continued. It was clear now that the Troubles would last a long time, and would certainly outlast any dwindling interest I had in them. I decided to sell the house, regardless of the loss, and get out. I contacted a few estate agents, most of whom turned me down without even seeing the property, the old adage, *location location location*, having a plangently melancholy timbre to it beneath the spell of the Cave Hill.

A couple of estate agents viewed it, said it was very nice, and they would erect a board and would put it in their books, but it would be a waste of money to advertise it in the papers: recent ads for houses in the area had attracted no enquiries whatsoever.

I ignored their advice and took out ads in the three morning newspapers; they were expensive and drew not a single reply. I could not leave the house and return to Dublin, because that would simply forfeit me whatever savings I had. I was in a prison, the door to which had been opened by a single fleeting attack of rheumatoid arthritis, and had then closed resolutely behind me.

I harboured no resentment towards Róisín over my sacrificed career in London; quite the reverse. I remained obsessed by her. I would take out photographs of us on holiday in west Cork and think, *so near so near.* This had been mine, yet I had lost it. How did I get it so wrong? What was it about me that caused her finally and so totally to shun me as she did?

I didn't always sleep alone, but the sex was as resolutely casual as the door that confined me to Belfast was resolutely shut. I sensed myself growing harder and colder, and I welcomed this, because being cold and hard must surely diminish pain, and perhaps might confer protection against my nocturnal visitors.

In this hope, I was mistaken. Nightly I would wake up and hear the silence of the city – for unlike other cities at night, Belfast was almost noiseless. It was waiting. Nobody moved. People lay in their beds, listening to thousands of other people listening. A single noise, a snapping twig, would get an entire multitude of pulses hammering like protesting prisoners with their tin mugs in a cell block.

I picked up an art student called Brenda in the Bank Bar and took her home. She was a virgin: she told me – be careful. I was, and next morning I drove her back to her flat. I kissed her goodbye, and returned to Knutsford.

A couple of days later I walked into the Bank again. She was sitting by herself. I waved at her and walked down to the end of the bar to join the usual crowd. Later, I was walking to the men's toilets, and she was sitting where I had last seen her, weeping. I went over to her.

'What's the matter?'

'What's the *matter?* You took my virginity the other night, and you walk past me today as if you'd hardly ever met me. That was my *virginity.* It'll never come back. Do you know how terrible that makes me feel – to think that I gave my virginity to a fucking bastard like you? Jesus, do you know how long I've been fancying you, and then you treat me like shite?'

Shocked, unable to speak, I told her I'd be back, and went into the men's room where I had my piss. Jesus Christ. What was happening to me? The one virtue that I was sure I had was decency. It was the one quality that I thought I had retained from my Catholic upbringing: never hurt anyone. Never.

'What is it? Am I that ugly that I'm only good for a fuck and then good night?' Brenda asked me when I got back, tears rolling down her cheeks.

'No, Jesus, you're not ugly. Look, I was being stupid: a mister cool, sex-isn't-such-a-big-deal arsehole. I'm sorry. Forgive me. But I can't undo what I've done, and I'm terribly sorry.'

She dried her eyes. 'You make me feel dirty, even though I've done nothing dirty. You're the dirty one, you prick.' She sniffed, rose and left.

A couple of days later I walked into the bar and saw Brenda sitting at the same table. I turned, walked out, went to a record shop and bought a copy of Beethoven's *Fifth Symphony* with the Berlin Philharmonic and von Karajan. Then I bought a card, and wrote a message of regret, regard and apology, and wrapping it up, returned to the bar within. She was still there, looking forlorn.

'Do you know how you've broken my heart?' she said, putting the present down without opening it. 'Do you know what you've done to me? You haven't a clue. Not a fucking clue. You play with me like I was a wee bag of sweeties.'

Soon afterwards I met another art student. Her name was Angela and she was from Tyrone. She was almost ludicrously beautiful, and very clever. Though she was not a virgin, my behaviour to her was, if possible, even worse, more cavalier, more heartless than it had been to Brenda. Having had sex with her on half a dozen occasions, I lost interest. She, however, had not lost interest in me.

I'd crashed my car and smashed the radiator. A new one was horrifically expensive, and so I was looking for a second-hand one. In the meantime I was getting around on a bicycle, when Angela arrived uninvited at the house. She stayed for a few days. We slept together, but without having sex, for I had told her that aspect of our relationship was over. One night, I said I was going out to Pat's Bar for a quick drink. I did not invite her: I was on my bike – how could I? My bike was then stolen from outside the bar, so I returned inside. There, I met a woman, Paula, who invited me to her home outside Belfast. Before I left, I rang Angela to tell I would be back late. At Paula's, I found her phone wasn't working, so I could not then ring Angela to tell her I would be staying away all night. This would be inexcusable behaviour anywhere: in Belfast it was almost satanic. Poor Angela sat through the night, convinced I was dead, and was almost in hysterics by the time I returned.

There had to be an end to this heartless gallivanting, especially with the young and vulnerable. So on Saturday nights I would go down to Pat's bar in the docklands, which was agreeable because the clientele was religiously mixed, it was safe because of a harbour police sentry post alongside it, and there was often traditional Irish music. Usually, everyone would go back to somebody or other's house with six-packs for music and dope. I swore no oath of celibacy – merely one of restraint. I genuinely thought either my capacity for love had perished for all time and that I could not handle the consequences of any further emotional involvement.

One woman wafted through the company in Pat's like Cleopatra: she was serene and beautiful and clever, and was called Anastasia McMahon. Coincidentally, her English cousin had been at Ratcliffe with me: together we had been members of the secret, briefly lived and thoroughly pretentious confection called The Committee of Thirteen, formed by him to raise intellectual standards in the school. She was sexually unapproachable because she had a rugged and thoroughly likeable boyfriend, so her companionship was very welcome – but then they split up.

One night we all went back to her place, and in time and unintentionally I found myself the last guest there. We were sitting on the sofa together, and we started kissing.

She said: 'You know everyone has been warning me about you.'

'Everyone? Who's everyone?'

'Everyone. They say you just fuck women and leave them. The way I feel tonight, that sounds all right by me.'

'You want a fuck?'

'That's exactly what I want. A straightforward fuck, with no complications.'

She had a Giaconda smile, and her eyes were glowing with assent. She was impossibly lovely.

No complications for her maybe, but I could feel complications for me. I was suddenly sure that if I had sex with this woman, there would be emotional residues, and they were precisely what I could not cope with.

246

'No,' I told her. 'It's not going to work. I'm not up to it tonight. I've had too much drink. Thanks for asking, but no thanks.'

Anastasia looked puzzled, but smiled her enigmatic smile. 'All right. This is not *quite* what I was expecting.' A dry quizzical smile was playing on her lips, her eyes were scanning my face, trying to work out what going on. Emotional cowardice was going on, but of course I didn't say that.

I kissed her goodnight and drove home, once again well over the limit, along roads where there were no police or soldiers, and where only the occasional sad drunk took his chances with the Shankill Butchers and the rain.

The drink. Drink was the demon in Belfast, the all-prevailing devil that haunted lives and drove madness galloping through estates. When pubs were not open, clubs were; and when those melancholy places closed, shebeens opened up. Barney Cahill swore there was a shebeen on the New Lodge Road that kept its stout in a zinc bath, into which glasses were scooped. One night when too much was still not enough, Sean O'Hare, a friend from Beechmount, took me to a shebeen on the Falls Road. It was called The Cracked Cup, after the shop for chipped china – all that the poor could afford – that had once been housed there. It was a tiny upstairs room in one of the tenement hovels that have all long since been demolished. The floor consisted of rotting boards, with many gaps. On the wall were pictures of the Virgin Mary and Patrick Pearse. There was a basic table, bearing bottles of Guinness, namely, the bar. Men sat in small huddles on rickety chairs, barely talking, their bottles on the floor. The men's room was just that: the room next door, where you urinated against one wall and onto the floorboards, and defecated in the corner, a strictly bring-your-own-paper affair. Both areas had been comprehensively availed of, but if anyone had used paper, they appeared to have taken it away with them.

The most legendary drinker on the Falls Road was Tom

Samways, an *Irish News* journalist whose alcoholic consumption was terrifying, and who was regularly being dried out. I walked into a bar the day I knew he had just left hospital. There he was, drinking a bottle of Carlsberg Special Thermonuclear Brew, three of which could incapacitate the entire population of Finland.

'Jesus Tom, what the fuck are you doing?' I cried.

'Just having a wee beer, Kevin, for fuck's sake. Whisht wi' your gurning.'

'How many have you had?'

'Thirty four.'

Niall Kiely, a journalist with *The Irish Times* and, next to Barney, the best friend I had, would sometimes join me to drink in Ardoyne social club, with an ex-IRA man, Eddie McClafferty. Eddie and his friend Brian Smith had been shot, both unarmed, in a cold-blooded ambush by paratroopers. Brian – whom I had known, and who rather paradoxically was engaged to an English girl – had been killed instantly. Eddie was charged with possession of a non-existent weapon, and a very existent court had sentenced him to eight years' imprisonment. Before Eddie had finished his time, one of the soldiers in the ambush party, disillusioned because he was on a military charge, contacted the press with the true story and in due course Eddie was released. This was the kind of murderous, casual injustice that entered the folklore of Ardoyne, and stuck in the communal craw, like an anvil wedged in a well.

About half a dozen of us would drink together, and when last orders came, we would each order a round of drinks for the final half-hour of drinking: say six drinks per person, never mind what was already on the table. Niall might come back to my place, each of us clutching a six-pack. Little wonder that some days began with nightfall. Each Sunday there was Richardson's club, and the usual crew, most of them from the Markets, all of them dressed up as if it was gala night – for Belfast people take their nights out very seriously indeed. None of the middle-class caper of jeans and a dirty sweater: they all wore suits and ties, but each night would nonetheless end in a multiple round: and then like good citizens we would all dutifully drive home.

I don't recall where I met Siobán and Geraldine, but they both ended up back in my place, and in my bed. My two guests had one characteristic in common. They both had colossal breasts: not big, but simply enormous. We were all in bed together, not because I was so very attractive, but because we were all so very drunk.

Now threesomes with two big-breasted women will seem very exciting to most men, and – why – not a few women, and no doubt they are, provided that firstly the place isn't Belfast, and secondly, everyone knows in advance what they intend to do. We – alas – shared no such common vision. Each woman wanted to have sex, but not with one another – a key feature, surely, of any threesome, as defined in the Sexual Deeds Act (Threesomes) of 1972. Nor did they want to have sex simultaneously with me – another legal requirement under the same liberal, far-seeing law. Each wanted sexual intercourse, but presumably only while the other lay indifferently or impatiently beside us – with no lawyers present, we didn't get that bit sorted out.

I was doing my heroic best with one, while disapproval and resentment simmered alongside me. So I made my excuses and hopped over to the other side to quell the mutiny there, only to find big-breasted insurrection smouldering in the corner of the bed I had just vacated. Finally I abandoned this futile steeple-chase and went to sleep.

At four o'clock came a huge hammering on the front door, and I leapt from my bed as if I just fallen ten feet onto a trampoline. I instinctively knew it was the police.

I clambered into my dressing gown and in a giddy panic toppled downstairs to halt the din. Outside, lights were flashing as if from a flying saucer. I opened the door, and half a dozen officers ran past and began to fan through the house. Two ran upstairs towards my bedroom, with me but-but-butting feverishly in their wake. They charged in, and there they found Siobán and Geraldine sitting upright in bed, their vast breasts hanging free, looking wide-eyed and innocent.

I think at this point the sergeant in charge of the raid – he seemed like a decent, church-going Protestant chap – nearly had a heart attack. He stood stock-still, paralysed, blinking like an owl in headlights. I steered him gently onto the landing, where he stood inhaling deeply and greyly hyperventilating. I asked: 'What is all this, please?'

He had trouble speaking, and was scratching his brow in a distracted, feverish way. Finally, as if he were talking in a trance, his voice intoned: 'We had an anonymous tip-off that there were armed men in the house.' He paused, palely. 'The caller was a woman.' His eyes slid meaningfully towards the bedroom. 'About half an hour ago.'

After a cursory and apologetic inspection of my home, the police left. I rather think house raids in Ardoyne, where they probably sleep in coarse flannel bodices, arc-welded shut in October, weren't as rewarding as that one had been. And so back to bed.

Breakfast was, shall we say, somewhat strained. Intuitively, I knew which girl had been responsible for the call. A couple of days later I ran into her in the Bank Bar and lied to her, saying that the RUC had played the tape to me. Why did she do it?

'Because you spent more time on Siobán than you did on me, you cunt,' she pouted. 'You fuckin' won't do that again.'

By God, she was right there. With that singularly successful encounter, my experience of threesomes began and ended. On a trip to Dublin I met an expansive Irish-Canadian with a bright orange wig called Peadair O'Doherty: I instantly dubbed him McGoldwig. He was editing a weekly Irish magazine in Toronto – would I write a column from Belfast at $100 a pop?

I needed this. The NBC money was drying up. Northern Ireland yielded behavioural squalor that was incomprehensible to the native mind, never mind to that of any outsider's. Moreover, other burdens upon me were steadily intensifying. At night, I was now utterly unable to bear the huge weight of solitude that bore down on me, and the sense of loss that had defined my life for the past two years. I desperately needed other people to be with. For when alone, I would play 'Paddy's Green Shamrock Shore' by Horslips almost obsessively, the anthem from west Cork nearly five years before, tears running down my cheeks as I got drunker and more and more maudlin and thought of Róisín.

Carless, bikeless and nearly penniless, I too joined that sad throng who preferred death to solitude, and thus would take the terrible risk of walking the Cliftonville Road at night, perfect targets for the Shankill Butchers. For like so many citizens living between Carlisle Circus and the Cave Hill, I craved two things, quite literally, more than life itself – company and alcohol, and I would find both in Pat's Bar in the docklands.

Actually, sometimes the company would be poor or even non-existent. But the drink was always there. I would not get drunk, just anaesthetized, and close to midnight, I would walk home towards the Cave Hill, along murder mile by North Queen Street, New Lodge Road and then Cliftonville Road, crossing the lightless road repeatedly, trotting, sprinting into new positions, dodging into tiny front gardens, making myself an inconvenient and confusing target. Just like army foot patrols did – except of course they were armed.

Then home, to Seamie and to Jimmy. Great days.

Why did I do this? To save money on taxis, I argued to myself, but there is no logic there. I wasn't so much saving money as seeking danger, the maddest, craziest danger of all, with no thrills but which promised a quite terrible end if things went wrong. This wasn't the young Kevin Myers of 1971, pushing at the door of peril, looking for the intoxicating adrenaline rush of violence. This was an older man who was toying with death as an end in itself.

Of course, I didn't consciously think like that. At least I had the promised income from Canada. So I would type out my dispatch each Monday morning and would walk down to the telex office in the centre of the city. I would then slowly and laboriously type my copy onto a telex tape, which would then be fed through a telex machine to Canada. Each transmission fee was about £25 – which was what my weekly earnings from NBC were now reduced to.

That year the Queen was visiting Northern Ireland as part of the celebrations of the twenty-fifth anniversary of acceding to the throne. Journalists had been invited to RUC headquarters to hear details of her visit. We were given copies of the royal schedule, and bound by oaths of secrecy, which – since this was an affair of life and death – were surely unnecessary.

A few days later, I was, unusually, in the bar of the Europa Hotel, a dire place where the toxic sense of solitude would make even the Osmond family feel lonely and unloved, when I was approached by a vaguely familiar man: a journalist, for sure.

'I know you,' he said. 'You were at the RUC press conference for the Queen's tour, weren't you, squire?'

I confessed I was. We introduced ourselves, and he winked at me. 'Pulled a fast one there,' he confided, 'and no mistake.'

I smiled politely and asked what he meant.

He looked around him. 'You've got to play your cards right in this game,' he said. 'The only way, sunshine, the only way. You got to stay one step ahead of the posse. I slipped Sinn Fein a copy of the Queen's itinerary. Who's going to get all the IRA scoops from now on?' He tapped himself on the chest. 'Yours truly, sunshine, yours truly.'

This was such an unspeakable act of betrayal of a central professional trust that I did not know what to say. I was tempted to go the RUC and reveal all, but informing on a fellow journalist did not come easily to me. Nor would that have necessarily been a wise move: was I being set up? In the coils and tangles of treachery that Belfast had become, who remained true to what moral code? If he was close to Sinn Fein, and some journalists were actively working as IRA agents, was I being tested in some way? However, the tour was some time away, and no imminent danger was presented by the IRA's knowledge of the royal itinerary. My dilemma was resolved when a couple of weeks later the IRA newspaper *An Phoblacht* published the full details of the royal tour. I felt great relief. The leaked information could not now be used for an attack against the Queen.

I had, of course, missed the point. When accreditation finally came for the royal tour, I was given the lowest possible security rating, while the traitor who had leaked the schedule received high access. I can only suppose that the RUC apparently thought it was me who had leaked the plans. Presumably, my friendship with Mickey Hamilton and the fabulously indiscreet McGuffin had not helped, and my revelations about UVF connections with elements of the British army had probably intensified suspicions against me. I might not always be a good person, but I do keep my word, uttered or otherwise.

NBC was surprised that their London-based correspondents – it sent a couple over – had achieved better access than I had, as indeed in their place I would have been. They grew less interested in both me and Northern Ireland, so I spent much of my time thinking about and preparing my columns for the Canadian-Irish newspaper.

Week by week I would file, and week by week would pay for the telex costs, for which I billed in each following telex. I waited for fees and expenses, until finally, three months later, and in despair, I rang Canada. However, my despair was nothing compared to that of the woman who answered the phone. Employees of the company had been encouraged to put their savings into it, which they had duly done. They had turned up for work that morning – by chance the very day I phoned – and found the editor's office had been cleaned out.

McGoldwig was gone: the newspaper was closed, and in addition to not being paid for anything I had done, I had also lost all chance of reimbursement for my telex expenses.

Twenty

AS WINTER drew to an end, and what passes for spring began to arrive in Belfast, interest in the house slowly started to pick up. Nobody made a bid for it, but the very possibility of a visitor obliged me to get out of bed in the morning and keep the place presentable.

Mary Chaplin, a journalist from Dublin rang me: an American friend of hers called Shannon was coming to Belfast – could I possibly put her up? Of course. The company would be an improvement on the emptiness of the house, which was occasionally broken by Barney's cheerful presence. Almost inevitably, his massage parlour had been burnt down – well after all, this was Belfast – and he was now back in the building trade again. He was not actually building anymore, but he had entered the social insurance and tax fraud system that was costing the British government millions. He explained it to me once: it was like listening to a description of the workings of an electron microscope. But to Barney's mind, and to the scam-literate minds of nationalist Belfast, it was as clear as Aegean daylight.

He and a few Markets men were at the game, and it was colossal: but was dangerous. The British were determined to crack the rackets, and he was in competition with both the Provisional and the Official IRAs, who had rival schemes. Frankly, I would have stuck to the massage parlours.

By this time, I'd found a suitable second-hand car-radiator, and my Triumph was working – sort of. The bodywork admitted rain in all four wings, which in the Belfast climate soon became water tanks: when the car stopped suddenly, the contents would move backwards and forwards, like bathwater in an earthquake. One night coming back from the pub, very, very drunk, I drove round and round the little roundabout that was Carlisle Circus, in the wrong direction, waiting for a police patrol that never came, the water sloshing around like four synchronized swimming-pools.

I met Shannon at Belfast railway station. She could have had a big sign saying AMERICAN on her forehead.

'Shannon,' I said, shaking her hand and leaning forward to kiss her cheek. 'Stop that right now,' she declared, pushing me sharply away. 'The first step in the degradation of women is the sexualization of platonic relationships.'

'I'm sorry. I didn't ah … Where's your bag?'

'This man was good enough to offer to carry it for me. Perhaps now you've arrived, you'd oblige.'

I took the case from the stranger, who smiled with a sudden and radiant gratitude. I immediately – but incorrectly – assumed I fully understood why: that it apparently contained a brick wall. 'I thought you were staying for the weekend,' I wheezed.

'What gave you that idea? No, I guess I'll be here a while. The men here are such *chauvinists*. Like that guy who was carrying my bag, he insisted on buying me lunch on the train. How reactionary is that?'

'And you let him?' I gasped, tottering with her bag.

'Of course. I'm a feminist. Not a fool.'

We drove back towards Knutsford Drive. 'Who were you staying with in Dublin?' I asked.

'Mary Chaplin,' she said.

'How did you get the idea to come up here?'

'Mary suggested it,' she said at a traffic light, looking round. '*God,* aren't the people here *ugly?*'

When we got home, I showed her to her room.

'A little small, but I guess it'll do. Can we get a couple of ground rules established right now, so there's no misunderstanding? Language. You Irish guys tend to call women dear, love or sweetheart. Cut it out – okay? And particularly, I will not tolerate the c-word. Ever. You hear? *Ever.* You knock on this door whenever you want to speak to me, even if the door's open. I do yoga most mornings, and I'll need more space than this. I'll do it in the sitting room. Between two and three in the afternoon, I usually masturbate, so under no circumstances am I to be interrupted at that hour. *No circumstances.* You got that?'

'Ah.'

'I've got special dietary needs, so I'd be grateful if you bear this in mind when you're making us our evening meals. I'll tell you what they are later. Now if you'll excuse me, it's already ten after two.'

I trickled downstairs and rang Mary Chaplin. She answered the phone and then instantly slammed it down when she heard my voice. I rang back. Engaged. The phone had been left off the receiver.

I was reading *A Bridge Too Far* when Shannon came down.

'Ah, military pornography,' she declared. ' You know all battle is merely a metaphor for rape? That is the real evil about war – what is says about men's attitude towards women. We are chattels to be conquered and raped.'

I shifted in my chair. 'I don't recall any stories about British and American troops raping German girls in 1945,' I said, perhaps a little testily.

'Ah, but they were doing it in their minds. Which is the same thing you know. And I'd prefer if you didn't take that patronizing tone, if you please.'

'Are you saying that my thinking about raping you is the same as doing it?'

'Not in my case, because my yoga gives me the inner strength to resist mental rape, just as being a 4th dan at karate gives me the physical strength to resist your actual rape attempts. I once overwhelmed four black men in Harlem who were trying to rape me.' She smiled sweetly at the memory. 'They were merely trying to enact on me the rape which white, capitalist society had inflicted on them. I empathized with their plight – I just wouldn't let them rape me is all.'

'That's impressive.'

'Not really. Not if you knew me. Now. What are we going to do?'

'Do? What do you mean, what are *we* going to do?'

'Mary assured me you were a real helpful kind of guy. That's why I chose you. I do hope you're not going to let me down.'

'You chose *me*?'

'Certainly. And I need to get around Belfast if I'm to check out the exploitation of the working classes by US imperialism.'

'US imperialism? I'm not sure there is any here. Anyway, I think a lot of people around here might welcome a bit of US capital coming in here and creating a few jobs.'

'I guess you're one of the neo-reactionary left who think that there are positive aspects to US imperialism. Oh yeah, I forgot. Thursday mornings, I do my blackheads, and I'll need the bathroom all to myself. No interruptions, okay? What might be a good start now is if you take me to a Protestant area.'

'And leave you there?'

'Sure. You don't think I need you holding my hand everywhere I go, do you? God, you men.'

But I was already running towards the car, with the jubilant realization that she didn't know my address, and all I had to do once I got home was to leave the phone off the receiver.

I drove her to the middle of the Shankill and told her of the loyalist club round the corner. If she met any UVF men, she was not to say she was staying with me, not to mention my name, or refer to me in any way. The evil Billy Marchant was now a powerful force in the UVF: beside him even the awesome Bunter Graham appeared quite genial.

I bade her farewell.

'Aren't you forgetting something?'

'What?'

'Your address, stupid. God. Some people. How can I find my way back to where you live without your address?'

The slender hope that was even then taking wing in my soul fell to earth, an arrow through its tiny heart. Sorrowfully, I made a note of it and gave it to her.

'God your handwriting. It's just terrible.'

I drove home filled with dread. Shannon was surely the most mesmerizingly horrible person I had ever met, yet I had been utterly incapable of resisting the onward rush of her authority – and clearly Mary Chaplin in Dublin had been as powerless as I was.

Shannon arrived back at about eight. 'It's all right, I've eaten,' she trilled. I had already taken the precaution of wolfing a hasty meal. 'Is there anything to drink in this house, or does your hospitality match your conversation? God, before I came over here I heard so much about Irish people and what fluent talkers they are, but here, I have to do all the fucking talking. It's very wearing. What have you to drink?'

'Nothing, actually. I thought maybe you'd like to help out with household expenses and buy a bottle of wine.'

'Did you now? Sorry, no can do. Didn't Mary tell you? My cheque from the States hasn't arrived, so I'm broke.'

'How did you pay for the train fare?'

'I didn't. Mary did.'

'Return?' I asked in a hollow voice.

'No, one way. God, is she tight or what? If you're going to the liquor store, could you get some gin please? And tonic. Schweppes, not that Irish C & C stuff. Can't you do anything right in this country? Sorry, you can. Whiskey. Can you get some Jameson? I like a hot Irish whiskey before going to bed. Or two.'

Clever Mary and her one-way fare, I was reflecting as I made my way out of the front door. But why only to Belfast? Why not to Cambodia, where a rare old time was being had by all?

'Hello?' came Shannon's voice from behind me. 'I'm allergic to white wine.'

'You don't have to drink it,' I called back.

'Sorry. No white wine in the *house*. I'm allergic to its vibrations. My yogi tells I have the most sensitive karma he's ever come across.'

I came back laden with booze, intending to anaesthetize myself against her unspeakable company. All I needed was an alcoholic cushion against this woman, and maybe tomorrow I could and would work out some way of expelling her from my home. I put the drink on the table, got some glasses and set to.

It was with more horror than it is now within my power to describe that I woke in the early hours of the morning and found myself coiled nakedly around a woman's body. No, no, no, this could not possibly be. Oh but it was: for entwined with me slumbered a similarly naked Shannon, and in her bed. How had such an utter catastrophe occurred? Finding myself in the arms of my nude grandmother would not have been so appalling. I lay there, paralysed in disbelief, my limbs frozen around her like those of a fossilized crab, my mind numbly trying to reassemble the scattered jigsaw pieces of the evening.

So. We had watched television, while I had drunk some beer, then some wine, and then some whiskeys, and Shannon had of course freely helped herself before she went to bed, almost formally bidding me goodnight, and after she'd gone I had a nightcap or three.

Then what happened? Think about it, carefully. Then I too

went up to bed. Slowly, shoelessly, so as not to wake her up. But the lights were on in Shannon's room as I stole past it, and the door was wide open, as indeed were her legs as she lay naked on the bed, her feet towards me. 'I hope you don't mind but I started without you. Had two already. Don't you think I've got great tits? They were voted best tits in Las Vegas last year. You want to feel them while I start on the third?'

That was where it all began. Where did it finish? Nothing could extract the dark secrets of what subsequently occurred that night from the depths of my memory, to which they had been banished as finally and conclusively as Lucifer had been cast into the hell where I had this night now joined him.

I could not stay a moment longer. I gently loosened my limbs and then slithered out of Shannon's bed like a droplet of oil trickling down a series of cogwheels, stealing with serpentine care from her room to the blessed sanctuary of my own.

Daylight provided a return to the nightmare of the early hours. Had I actually had sex with the most unspeakable woman I had ever met?

The only way of dealing with the crisis was to stay in bed until all memory of the horror had vanished. But I had an appointment that morning with some prospective buyers. So, I rose and danced hastily to my bathroom for some swift and rudimentary ablutions before fleeing back to my own bedroom. Of course, all my clothes were on the floor next door, so I had to find a fresh set of everything before I tiptoed in my socks past Shannon's bedroom, as softly as if the child Jesus were being born within, a breach birth plus complications, while the three wise men watched.

I made tea in my kitchen, and sat at the table, my back to the door, lamentation ululating in my harrowed soul, until I felt a pair of hands close suddenly over my eyes.

'Guess who?' twittered a voice, and my heart plummeted to some abyss hitherto unplumbed by any human heart.

'Shannon?' I whimpered.

'Oh you naughty, naughty boy, you must have peeked.'

The hands were removed from my eyes and she stood there with two pigtails pertly arranged around her shoulders. She was wearing quite skillfully applied make-up. The feminist of yesterday had gone. In her place stood a bobby-sox, high-school cheer-leader.

'Darling, thank you for such an unexpected visit,' she cooed. 'You took me quite by surprise, barging in like that, and my, in such a *manly* fashion. I hope I did not disappoint.'

In a grim but silent panic, I busied myself with the toaster, while Shannon tutted disapprovingly. 'Bread? Wheat? All those yeasts entering your poor system and disturbing your natural balances. You should be eating more fruit and oats, my darling. So much better for the bowels.'

Courage, propelled by despair, bade me speak. 'Please, not bowels, not at this time of day.'

In a single bound, the ardent feminist was back, quivering with an instantly summoned rage. 'Are you repressed about your bowel movements? I'm not about mine. Are you ashamed of the human, the animal you, the real you? Why, I am proud of what I am. You are the typical modern male: anally repressed, patriarchal, and proto-rapist. This is so, so disappointing – and I had such hopes for you!'

My head was aching. 'Look, if you don't mind, I've got some people coming to look at the house at eleven.'

'Oh, have we?' she said with a sudden and uxorial sweetness. 'That *is* good.'

I muttered weakly: 'I'm going to have a bath, freshen up, and so on.'

'Fine, so long as you don't expect me to wash your cup,' retorted the feminist. 'I'm not the hired help around here.'

I was listening to the radio perched on the ledge beside the bath when a voice said: 'Hi? Can I come in?'

Well, I no longer had any secrets from her, so in a low,

defeated voice I whispered yes. No doubt she wished to discuss the night before.

She walked in, lowered her jeans and sat down on the lavatory. 'Sorry!' I cried, 'I didn't know you wanted to have a piss. Otherwise, I'd have …'

Clenching her facial muscles, Shannon opened her bowels in a loud and voluptuous cataract. The rest of what might have been visible or audible or detected by any other sense organ was concealed from me because I had instantly immersed my entire face, prepared to drown rather than endure any more of whatever atrocious intimacies she might wish to inflict upon me.

Later, as I lay in the cooling bathwater I wondered if this were the nadir, or was there worse to follow? Who could say? I got out of the bath and towelled myself with all the arthritic infirmity of an old man trying to scratch dead centre between his shoulder-blades, before tottering into my bedroom.

The doorbell went while I was still dressing myself.

'I'll get it darling,' fluted a voice from below.

Jesus, Mary and Joseph, the people to view the house! I pulled on my trousers and my shirt, hunting feverishly for shoes before tumbling out of my bedroom only to meet Shannon arriving on the landing, with two strangers.

'These are the Maguires. I thought I'd show them the upstairs first while you get the kitchen tidied up. You left it in a terrible way.'

The Maguires nodded to me as if I were the home help and Shannon gestured to her bedroom.

'The first guest bedroom, as you can see, is quite small. I sleep here because I find having separate bedrooms increases sexual passion – doesn't it darling?' She made a larger gesture to her right. 'And here we come to the master bedroom. I do apologize for its condition.'

Brokenly, I made my excuses, went downstairs and sat in the kitchen, barely bothering to look up when the Maguires were shown in. 'It's not as tidy as it might be, but that's men for you,' Shannon said sweetly. 'Oh honey, you haven't cleaned the cooker. And you *promised*.'

After she had seen the Maguires out, she returned: 'Well, I think that went very well, all things considered. Could we have the house just a *little* neater when we have people viewing in future?'

Something approaching spine began to take shape just south of the nape of my skull. 'Shannon, this is my house, and I really don't want you showing it to people as if it were yours.'

'Excuse me, if I hadn't been here to open the door, they wouldn't have even seen the house while you were upstairs jerking off. God, you men.'

'Excuse me, I was not …'

'Look, I haven't got time to argue with you all day about how you spend your time. It's your body, after all. A little bit of gratitude where it's due wouldn't go amiss – that's all. And now, thanks to you, I'm running late. I've got some people to see on the Shankill. Can you drop me off there? *Excuse me?* Sort of *now*.'

The only weapon in my armoury was Barney. After I'd dropped Shannon off, I went to see him in his latest flat, and pleaded with him to rescue me. He was to come round that night, to kiss her on meeting her, and be as crude and offensive as possible – he was to call her love and sweetheart, be derogatory about women, and to say cunt at every single opportunity. If we sufficiently enraged her she would surely leave.

He duly arrived that evening, and rather artfully, I let Shannon open the door to him. And Barney – stout fellow – went into action immediately.

'Agh! What about ye love,' he said. 'My name's Barney. Kevin in?' He grasped her and kissed her warmly on the cheek.

'What a very nice man,' she said, turning to me. 'He could teach you a thing or two about how to treat a lady.'

'That's because I think the woman's place is in the home,

sweetheart, not like this stupid cunt here. For fuck's sake, he believes in equal pay and shite like that.'

'Well I'm all in favour of diversity of opinion,' she said. 'I'm not sure what this cunt here, as you so colourfully call him, really believes in. He doesn't say much. Would you like a drink? I'm afraid this cunt here has a pretty poorly stocked drinks cabinet.'

Barney was looking vaguely harpooned. This wasn't what he had prepared for. Myself, I was feeling like a weary British general in the desert, hearing the sound of Rommel's tanks coming over the supposedly safe dune behind him, *yet again.*

There was nothing to do, except for us all to get plastered, which is what we did. Hours later, I made a bed for Barney on the sofa, then I gratefully retired to my bedroom, and Shannon to hers. I only grasped the stunning magnitude of my defeat shortly afterwards when I heard her slip downstairs and bring Barney back to her bed, for – as he sheepishly told me later – the most astounding night's sex he'd ever had. But he didn't have to tell me: for I had heard every single shriek and wail throughout the eternal, livelong night that followed.

Shannon stayed five weeks, at the end of which I was a feverish, twitching wreck. Among her many lunatic infelicities, she had told the UVF she was staying with me, even giving them my address in case they wanted to come and see her. To see her? Everyone – even the UVF thugs – who had ever met her thenceforth lived in terror of her. This included Barney, who notwithstanding both his personal resilience and her sexual prowess, never returned to the house while she was there.

She was a truly remarkable woman; my kitchen became an apothecary's lab, and my saucepans an alchemist's vials as she brewed identical sticky unguents for her face, her hair and her stomach. Wherever she walked, she ruled, at one moment the dire feminist full of rage, the next the food neurotic denouncing the toxins of ordinary carbohydrates, the next the Las Vegas stripper which she had claimed once to have been – 'nudity, and the arousal of the male by the female form, is so truly *liberating.*'

Meanwhile, NBC had not entirely lost interest in Northern Ireland – I occasionally threw in the odd morsel of unspeakable terrorist filthiness to keep commuters in Muskogee and Danbury happy if baffled. But then the IRA in due course presented them and me with a real jewel: the La Mon massacre. Here terrorists attached home-made napalm bombs to the window-grilles of a hotel hosting a gathering of dog fanciers – all Protestant, the breed of dog being the Scottish collie: yes, sectarian divisions ran that deep. When the explosions occurred, an ocean of fire flash-flooded through the hotel ballroom where these poor innocents were swapping Lassie stories.

Suddenly dog fanciers became screaming human infernos. Men pulled down long curtains in vain attempts to extinguish the pyres that were their burning wives. Those that blast and flame did not kill were suffocated by lack of oxygen or poisoned by carbon monoxide. Twelve people – including three married couples – were burnt alive at La Mon: one moment they were chatting happily, and some five minutes later – a long five minutes – they were burnt beyond recognition, reduced to ashes.

Stunned at the scale of the atrocity and by its unmitigated vileness, I managed to do just one report for NBC on La Mon, and then froze in despondent, speechless horror. For each dead victim, I earned slightly over two dollars from that first report. NBC were frantic for more, and I could of course increase my income vastly by reporting more details of this abominable act, and on the aftermath of loyalist rage, fury and retaliation. But I would not because I could not. My heart was turned, my stomach sickened, my mind disordered with the ultimate horror of La Mon.

Each penny I earned in this way now depended on someone's death. No killing, no money. The relationship was immutable and unavoidable. A fireman watching television in the base earns the same as the firemen fighting an inferno. Not me. I needed bodies. After my initial report about La Mon, I told NBC to seek elsewhere.

Finally, I was finished with Northern Ireland. I had touched a dead boy's still warm face, smelt the livers and lights of strangers, and watched as life vanished from a man I could have saved. I had seen men burn alive, their bodies twitching and flailing, their skin breaking open as the boiling flesh within erupted.

Now that it was over, I felt a huge relief. I was henceforth committed to an existence with almost no income, pending the sale of my apparently unsellable house. I went to the bank and arranged a fresh loan against its value, and began to learn what it is to spend my life in bed. Unlike a woman, whose talents in such matters apparently know no limit, or as dear Audrey had assured me all those years before, a man can masturbate only so many times in a day, and I tried to find out what that number was.

When finally the sexual option was exhausted, I would lie in bed, revisiting the landscape of my life as it was now laid out in my mind, returning to the good times. Day after day, night after night, I journeyed through my past with Róisín, not sexually, but in the sunlit pastures of remembered companionship, inhaling there the giddy fragrance of an ancient happiness which now seemed gone from my life forever.

My days in Belfast were coming to an end. With an almost symphonic touch, I managed to find a buyer for the house. But while the legal niceties were being sewn up, news came through of the death of Harry McCormack, my lovely, troubled RUC friend, who haunted by the monstrous things he had seen, had got drunk for the last time and had driven into a tree.

More news came from Italy that same week. Henrietta Guinness who had married an Italian lorry driver and gone to live with him in his native village had been pursued to her new home by her demons. One day, they finally triumphed. She walked to the centre of a high bridge over a nearby gorge, paused for a moment, and then threw herself to her death.

I had a few final sessions in Richardson's. Josie McKee was getting increasingly agitated, because his namesake, a well-known IRA man, was being released from the Maze Prison. 'Nng whong nnhow whung chung crung,' he complained.

'He thinks he's going to get nutted by mistake,' explained Tealeaf, rising to buy another round. 'That there other McKee there caused a lot of trouble with loyalists inside.'

'Ngng whung bt chn crung,' Josie lamented.

'I know,' I declared with agnostic sympathy as Tealeaf departed.

'Qur lkthn mrung?'

'Mmm. Maybe.'

I began to learn other little titbits such as, that by evil coincidence, my friend Mickey Hamilton, Róisín's brother, had arranged from the safety of Long Kesh to have my landlord William Staunton shot, because of a heavy sentence he had passed on a friend of his, Martin O'Grady, for rioting. I knew O'Grady well: I had – perhaps imprudently – done him many favours. Thus was joined the entire cycle of murder: culprit, commissioner, friend, landlord, tenant and finally, and inevitably, victim. That was it. That was Belfast.

McGuffin began to show signs of going mad around this time. Though not even five foot six, he weighed about eighteen stone. One evening, he told some friends of mine up from Dublin, that he was an IRA sniper, even though once on his belly, it would have taken heavy machinery with stout chains to get him vertical again. He boasted of the men he had killed, and then played the recording of the gunbattle with which I opened this account, and in my hearing – *my hearing* – told my own story to an entranced audience as if it was his, he was Seamus, and I was not present – either in the room or at the ambush.

Belfast had triumphed over him, as it had over me, and as

it would for years to come over other journalists and an entire generation of soldiers and policemen would begin and end their careers within its malignant force field.

Time heals. The love that seems ineradicable does eventually fade. But the earth might have to go round the sun many times before that happens. For six full years a savage ache prowled within me like Cerberus, keeping any semblance of happiness at bay, from the day that Róisín left me until the darkness of my loss was slowly lifted from my soul. During that time, I permitted no one to come close to my heart: emotional vapidity was now my guard and shield, shallowness as much my enduring friend as Jimmy and Seamie were.

But it was more than the loss of Róisín that caused my enduring and open wound. The loss of human life around me exacted an emotional price that writing this memoir in part is helping me pay. I personally knew nearly forty people who were killed in the Troubles. Eight others were killed at my side.

I went to Northern Ireland bright and cheerful; I left it brooding and troubled, my hair turning grey, my nights infested with murderous strangers, and my mind regularly revisited by the scenes that I had witnessed. Of all the people from that time, I have thought most of Robert Bankier – even more so than of Róisín – for I had foreseen his death, but did not prevent it.

Once clear of the drumlins and their malignity, I began to reconstruct my life and my mind. Gradually, Seamie and Jimmy began to drop in less often than they used to, and after a couple of years living in Dublin I actually found myself able to sit in a pub with my back to the door, without fear of a spray job.

Many of the participants in this narrative are dead. Billy Marchant was murdered by republican terrorists. Tucker Lyttle – a killer whom I liked, though he had killed the wonderful Rose McCartney – and Davy Payne – a piece of scum – died of heart attacks. John McGuffin died of cirrhosis of the liver. Liam Hourican went on to become one of the most distinguished public servants in Ireland, and died in his forties of a heart attack. And poor Josie McKee did not survive as long as any of them. Shortly after I left Belfast, he was shot in his butcher's shop, just as he predicted he would be. His was the last funeral I ever attended in Belfast, and with his death and the attendant obsequies, I drew a curtain over the demented rituals of that place.

All the foregoing names are genuine. Those that follow are not. As far as I know, the breathtakingly evil Rab Brown is still alive, his place in the catalogue of human abomination curiously unrecognized. Undercover soldiers attempted to assassinate Seamus, my teenage gunman. Paradoxically, he was rescued by a foot patrol of uniformed soldiers just as his would-be killers were about to finish him off. He became a very senior member of the IRA and – like almost every IRA commander – a very prosperous businessman, in his case both in the Republic and Belfast. He now actually owns the pub where we met. Barney Cahill died of lung disease. The fair Shannon became a successful Wall Street broker. McGoldwig, my Canadian nemesis, lives in Florida, still spending other people's money. Róisín went to the very top of her profession in unprecedented time and is now extremely eminent in medical circles in London. I had been so grievously wrong about so much. Only when going back over the history of the time, talking to people, in the preparation of this memoir did I learn that I had probably been fooled by Joe McCann. As Barney had once intimated, he was no hero. The real truth about McCann was that he was not just the handsome broth of a boy that he had seemed to be, but was in fact a hardened killer. Shortly before I met him, he had captured a young Irishman serving in the British army. Private Robert Benner had gone to see the priest who was to marry him and his fiancee in Dundalk a few days later. McCann abducted him during the visit, and then took his captive into South Armagh, where, along a country lane in the shadow of the drumlins, shot him dead. I had gone down to South Armagh to report on this killing, and had seen the sodden corpse on the roadside, lying like fallen washing amid the winter grass. And only weeks later, I was to be enchanted by the killer. I have recently been told, however, that Joe McCann had nothing to do with the killing of Corporal Robert Bankier. He had made up that account, including the pious hope that the soldier didn't suffer. In other words Joe McCann was merely a brutal fantasist, a young Seamus Twomey in the making.

What about Ben Madigan, the name borne by all those streets in the course of the driving lesson with Róisín? In time, I learnt the truth about Ben Madigan. There was no person called Ben Madigan. Ben Madigan is the original name for the Cave Hill. It comes from the Irish, *Beann Uí Mhadsgáin*, which means Madigan's Peak. There are at least two versions of every tale in Northern Ireland, and a brace of names for this hill. My ignorance of this, after so often confidently and endlessly pronouncing on the nature of the problems of the province, must have confirmed Róisín in her opinion that I was no more than a noisy fool.

For, it was on the slopes of Ben Madigan – or Cave Hill, if you wish – that the United Irishmen in the 1790s had first sworn an oath to form a separate Irish republic. Beneath its shadow, that struggle, now in a mutant, barbarized and utterly bloody shape, had been waged throughout my time in the city, and was set to continue as I finally turned my back on Belfast.

For other and more celebrated journalists of roughly my generation – Bob Fisk, Max Hastings, Jeremy Paxman, Simon Winchester, Olivia O'Leary, Liam Hourican, Mary Holland, Henry Kelly, Martin Bell, John Simpson, Conor O'Clery – Northern Ireland was an upward step in their ascending and broadening careers. Others, such as David McKittrick and Ed Maloney, turned the Troubles into an object of academically distinguished studies. I, on the other hand, had used it as a way station into a dimensionless void, in which almost all energies that I expended vanished without purpose or consequence, as if floating aimlessly in outer space. My breath shed there had no value, other than as a means of survival: for me, as for so many people in the province, verbs possessed no real tense, other than the present uncertain and the past continuous.

Decades have passed since these events occurred, and I am only able to write this because I am now an extremely contented man, made so by a happy marriage to a wonderful woman, Rachel. For lives sometimes move in different cycles, so unrelated that they can seem to belong to different people. Did these events happen to me? Was that melancholy, weak, ruthless, strangely crippled, handsome young man really me?

The answer is yes, sort of: and more powerfully than I can possibly even begin to report, my present life – with me well steeped in age, my hair grey and thinning, an uninvited extra couple of stone about my person – is infinitely more rewarding than all those years of my youth in Belfast. Yet the darkness of my time there is now a vital part of my being. For in time, I learnt that despair and unhappiness are mere seasons in our span, which will sooner or later pass if we urge movement on the planet of our life – and in due course, pass they finally did. But they still form an indispensable prelude to the man that I am: to the life that I live, the wife that I love and the world that is mine.

So there it is. That is our ration, promised to all who see thirty, and which includes so few who have featured in this book: one life, one youth, one stab at being in one's twenties. Beneath the long shadow of Ben Madigan, watching the door, waiting for death, this was mine.

A chronology of the main events in Northern Ireland covered by this book

October 1968   Civil Rights march in Derry, banned by the Northern Ireland government, is broken up by truncheon-wielding police.

August 1969   Protestant marches in Derry lead to rioting by Catholics, which spread across the province. Protestants and Catholics fight pitched gunfights in Belfast. Hundreds of Catholics are driven from their homes. Police use machine guns on civilian targets in Catholic areas of west Belfast. British troops are deployed in trouble spots across the province.

August 1970   The IRA kills two policemen in the first steps of its campaign to force the British out of Northern Ireland and bring about a united Ireland.

February 1971   As rioting intensifies in Belfast, the first British soldiers are killed in the city, followed by two policemen.

March 1971   Three unarmed, off-duty Scottish soldiers are murdered by the IRA.

March–August 1971   IRA campaign intensifies.

August 1971   The British and Northern Ireland government intern hundreds of suspected IRA activists, triggering a massive upsurge of violence.

December 1971   Fifteen Catholics are killed in a loyalist bomb attack on McGurk's pub in north Belfast. The IRA bombs a Protestant shop in revenge, killing four, including two infants.

30 January 1972 Paratroopers shoot fourteen people dead during a Civil Rights' march in Derry City.

March 1972 A loyalist counter-terrorist campaign against Catholics begins.

March 1972 The British government prorogues the Northern Ireland parliament in Stormont and introduces Direct Rule.

June 1972 IRA ceasefire. British–IRA talks.

July 1972 IRA ceasefire ends, and violence sweeps across the province. Ten die and hundreds are injured in IRA bomb attacks across Belfast. Dozens die in sectarian attacks. Operation Motorman, mounted by the British, asserts military authority in nationalist areas of Belfast and Derry.

December 1972 The Dublin government sacks the RTÉ authority over broadcast with IRA man Sean Mac Stiofain.

1974 Author brokers talks between loyalist paramilitaries and the IRA. In May loyalist strike and paramilitary terrorism bring down power-sharing executive between constitutional nationalist and loyalist parties.

January 1975 IRA ceasefire. Shankill Butchers begin murder campaign in north Belfast, and sectarian killings now become a norm across Northern Ireland.

January 1976 IRA massacre ten Protestant workmen in south Armagh.

March 1976 A long-since-meaningless IRA ceasefire called off. All further attempts to broker a political settlement came to nothing for the rest of this narrative.

February 1978 Twelve Protestants burnt alive and twenty-three injured by IRA incendiary bomb at La Mon House Hotel in Castlereagh, Co. Down.